FOR WHOM THE VIRUS TOLLS

Resilience, Perseverance, Fortitude, and Survival in the Face of COVID-19

D. JOHN JACKSON

For Whom The Virus Tolls
Resilience, Perseverance, Fortitude, and Survival in the Face of COVID-19

ISBN: 9798891095120 - paperback
ISBN: 9798891095113 - hardcover
ISBN: 9798891095137 - ebook

This book is dedicated to all the lives lost and the courageous men and women who fought the virus on the front lines.

This day is a gift to you, never to be given again.
It will never occur again in your future, and its existence will be relegated to the annals of human history.
You will never be able to get it back or physically revisit in any way.
So, enjoy the day and moment; think about all your days differently and how you can make the most of each day.

—D. John Jackson

TABLE OF CONTENTS

INTRODUCTION

John Donne (1572–1631), the English writer and poet, was a huge figure in Elizabethan literature. He created his literary work "For Whom the Bell Tolls" in 1624 as a part of *Devotions upon Emergent Occasions*, a series of prose writings split into three parts: "Meditations," "Expostulations to God," and "Prayers." "The oft quoted 'no man is an island' line, as well as the 'for whom the bell tolls' one, come in the seventeenth Meditation in Donne's Devotions."[1] There, he takes a deep introspective look into life, death, and the connectedness of humankind, humanity, and the human condition. His work received great attention and achieved prominence when Ernest Hemingway used the title for one of his books. Donne explored the unseen interlocking mechanisms that bond together every individual on earth, their inextricable link to each other, and how everything that happens affects all of us, and we should be cognizant of that deep interdependence and interrelatedness.

For Whom the Bell Tolls

No man is an island, entire of itself; every man is a piece of the continent, a part of the main. If a clod be washed away by the sea, Europe is the less, as well as if a promontory were, as well as if a manor of thy friend's or of thine own were any man's death diminishes me, because I am involved in mankind, and therefore never send to know for whom the bell tolls; it tolls for thee.

—John Donne

---

1 The meaning and origin of 'for whom the bell tolls; it tolls for thee'. Interesting Literature. (2022, July 13). Retrieved March 31, 2023, from https://interestingliterature.com/2021/08/never-send-for-whom-the-bell-tolls-it-tolls-for-thee-meaning-analysis/

In Donne's essay, "For whom the bell tolls" is the imaginary question of a man who hears a funeral bell and asks about the person who has died. Donne's answer is that because none of us stands alone in the world, each human death affects all of us. Every funeral bell, therefore, "tolls for thee."

> The meaning of "never send to know for whom the bell tolls" is fairly straightforward. We should feel a sense of belonging to the whole of the human race and should feel a sense of loss at every death, because it has taken something away from mankind. The other famous phrase from this Meditation that has entered common usage is "no man is an island," because no individual can subsist alone. We need not only social company and companionship, but also an awareness of how we all have a share in the world: we are all part of the human race and the suffering and passing of another human being should affect us, not least because it is a regular reminder that one day, it will be us for whom the funeral bell is tolling.
>
> The funeral bell that tolls for another person's death, then, also tolls for us, in a sense, because it marks the death of a part of us, but also because it is a memento mori, a reminder that we ourselves will die one day.[1]

John Donne's powerful message remains remarkably relevant to our present circumstances. Global calamities vividly illustrate our vulnerability and underscore the crucial interdependence among all of us for survival. I have always passionately emphasized the significance of standing together as we confront the challenges of this world. Unfortunately, the dominant theme for far too long has been individualism—every person for themselves—pervading big business, global politics, and even daily life. This perspective has led to a devaluation and misunderstanding of the importance of each and every life in the fabric of our existence on earth.

It often takes a tragic or all-consuming event to make us pause and appreciate the value of life. Only then do we realize the devastating impact a large-scale loss of life can have, disrupting our normal equilibrium and shattering the norms we had grown accustomed to over time. Regrettably, it seems to require an apocalyptic event akin to the four horsemen sweeping across the world to capture our attention, focus, and thoughts. Such events demand collaboration and unity to work toward positive outcomes.

The recent outbreak of a new coronavirus exemplified this reality, leading to global supply chain disruptions, overwhelming health care systems, and sparking social and political unrest. The virus, much like the bell in John Donne's "For Whom the Bell Tolls," invoked an ominous multifaceted reckoning that we must confront, as it has forever changed our way of life.

In *For Whom the Virus Tolls*, I explore these themes further, emphasizing the urgent need for solidarity and collective action in the face of this transformative global event. It serves as a reminder that we must recognize the interconnectedness of humanity and work together to navigate the challenges that lie ahead.

This book endeavors to examine the pandemic's impacts from various vantage points, encompassing historical context and the diverse perspectives that collectively define humanity's experience. Through its pages, individual stories of facing the challenges of today and enduring their long-lasting consequences are woven together to create a tapestry of shared human experiences.

In essence, this work seeks to tease out the intricate interplay of personal narratives and broader societal implications, shedding light on the ways in which COVID-19 has shaped and reshaped lives across the globe. By capturing these voices and insights, my aim is to offer a comprehensive understanding of the pandemic's far-reaching consequences and the resilience of the human spirit in the face of adversity.

For Whom the Virus Tolls serves as a revealing exposé and a poignant awakening, delving into the history, factual aspects, and untold narratives of the devastating impact wrought by the COVID-19 virus on countless lives. Within its pages, this book embarks on a journey to explore the personal experiences and firsthand testimonies of individuals who confronted the harrowing effects of the pandemic.

The stories within encompass a wide range of struggles—from resilient entrepreneurs fighting to preserve their businesses amid unprecedented challenges to individuals struggling to adapt to a new and unfamiliar reality. Tragically, too many accounts recount life-and-death battles as the virus relentlessly attacked their bodies or those of their loved ones.

Through this gripping portrayal, *For Whom the Virus Tolls* sheds light on the human dimension of the pandemic, painting a vivid picture of the trials and tribulations faced by ordinary people in extraordinary times. By sharing these unheard stories, the book aims to foster empathy, understanding, and a collective resolve to confront the profound consequences of the COVID-19 virus on individuals, families, and communities worldwide.

The COVID-19 pandemic forced us into a grim reality, revealing the fragility of our world and our lack of preparedness for a global calamity of this magnitude. The virus's indiscriminate attacks, combined with isolation, quarantines, and business shutdowns, created an unprecedented crisis.

The haunting imagery of hospitalizations, where the virus ravaged patients' lungs, was unbearable. Being placed on a ventilator became a life-and-death proposition, with death still a high probability even with such interventions. Medical professionals and hospital staff worldwide displayed heroic efforts in combating this invisible villain, enduring long hours, sleep deprivation, and mental and physical fatigue. Yet the toll on their mental health was severe, as anxiety, stress, and burnout compounded while they isolated from their families to prevent spreading the disease.

The death toll overwhelmed hospitals, leading to the need for mobile freezer trucks as makeshift morgues in some places. In countries like India, bodies were cremated in large numbers, and mass graves became a heartbreaking reality. Funeral homes faced an inundation of service requests, leading to long lead times for scheduling.

Economically, the world shut down, leaving businesses struggling to stay afloat and adapt to remote work setups. While some companies managed to pivot successfully, others could not overcome the immense challenges they faced. Small business owners bore the brunt of the economic tsunami caused by COVID-19.

Schools and colleges also grappled with major challenges, transitioning from traditional brick-and-mortar setups to online education and engagement for all students. This required significant adjustments and resource allocation.

The COVID-19 pandemic exposed our vulnerabilities and tested our resilience on personal, societal, and economic levels. It demonstrated the immense courage and dedication of health care professionals while highlighting the urgent need for preparedness and cooperation in the face of global crises.

Through the lens of *For Whom the Virus Tolls*, I had the privilege of interviewing a diverse group of professionals and individuals from various backgrounds and industries to understand how they navigated life during the COVID-19 pandemic. As the pandemic thrust us into a "new norm," I found myself reflecting on its impact not only on my life but also on the lives of countless others. This introspection compelled me to delve deeper, capturing the personal and business stories of those whose lives were disrupted and transformed by the crisis.

While *For Whom the Virus Tolls* explores the far-reaching ramifications of COVID-19, it is not exclusively about death. Instead, it focuses on the resilience, perseverance, fortitude, and survival displayed by individuals in the face of the pandemic. Together with a camera crew, I ventured into the homes, workplaces, and places of worship of interviewees, uncovering previously unknown and unheard stories of this pivotal moment in history. These interviews form a crucial part of the documentary film that accompanies this book, providing a broader context for the human dramas that unfolded.

I hope this work prompts us to consider the lives of our fellow citizens and recognize our inherent interconnectedness. Understanding and respecting the humanity of others and acknowledging the hardships they endure can provide clarity on how our own existence impacts the world around us. Despite the horrors and devastation of the virus, COVID-19 sparked introspection and reflection in many individuals.

By telling these stories, I aspire to raise consciousness and compel readers to reevaluate their lives, placing priority on what truly matters. This might involve focusing on health, personal growth, stress reduction, mental well-being, pursuing meaningful activities, and cherishing time with family, loved ones, and friends. Above all, it emphasizes the universal connectedness we share with everyone we encounter, underscoring the importance of belonging, caring, purpose, and accountability in our lives.

Chapter 1

THE GREAT WAR AND THE SPANISH FLU

If we don't end war, war will end us.
—H. G. Wells

Before we venture into the destructive effects of COVID-19, let's take a walk through history and review factors leading up to the Spanish flu of 1918 and how they compare to similar experiences associated with COVID-19 one hundred years later. Numerous other historical factors upset global stability. "Both the COVID-19 and 1918 influenza pandemic similarly caused significant negative impacts on the global economy, affecting international relations and had considerable delay in its diagnosis, treatment and vaccines."[2] "The COVID-19 pandemic has become the deadliest disease event in American history, with a death toll surpassing that of the 1918 Spanish flu."[3]

PRELUDE TO WAR

The world in 1914 teetered on the brink of an all-out world war as global powers vied for dominance and control in military,

2 Liang, S. T., Liang, L. T., & Rosen, J. M. (2021, May). Covid-19: A comparison to the 1918 influenza and how we can defeat it. Postgraduate medical journal. https://www.ncbi.nlm.nih.gov/pmc/articles/PMC8108277/#:~:text=Victims%20of%20the%201918%20influenza,response%20resulting%20in%20organ%20failure.

3 Branswell, H. (2021, September 20). Covid-19 overtakes 1918 Spanish flu as deadliest disease in American history. STAT. https://www.statnews.com/2021/09/20/covid-19-set-to-overtake-1918-spanish-flu-as-deadliest-disease-in-american-history/

economic, and political realms. This precarious situation did not arise suddenly; rather, it was the culmination of long-standing, festering conditions that eventually triggered the catastrophic outcome. Several factors contributed to this volatile environment:

- Years of colonialism by major European powers, leading to territorial disputes and competition.
- Fragile alliances between nations, adding complexity and tension to international relations.
- Failures in diplomacy, which exacerbated misunderstandings and mistrust between countries.
- Increased militarism, with nations heavily investing in military buildup and preparedness.
- Imperialistic ambitions driving countries to assert dominance and expand their influence globally.
- Monarchies seeking to maintain their power and authority amid rising challenges.
- Competing ideologies and mistrust among nations, fueling ideological conflicts.
- Economic and territorial competition, intensifying rivalries and territorial claims.
- Social and civil unrest within certain nations, further destabilizing the global order.

These factors collectively created an environment in which even the smallest spark could ignite a cataclysmic conflict with far-reaching consequences for the entire world.

Prior to the outbreak of the Great War, the world had evolved into several major power centers, each driven by monarchies, empires, or powerful governments. The most formidable and influential players were the French and British, who had engaged in colonization for centuries, bolstering their economic and military strength. Other major European powers like Germany, Austria-Hungary, and the Ottoman Empire sought to protect or expand their global influence, contributing to heightened tensions on the European continent. These tensions eventually culminated in the formation of two opposing alliances: the Central Powers, comprising Germany, Austria-Hungary, and the Ottoman Empire, and the Allied Powers, including France, Britain, Italy, the Russian Empire, Canada, the United States, and Japan.

The events leading up to the First World War marked a critical turning point in history, reshaping the geopolitical landscape and forever altering the course of humanity.

ASSASSINATION OF ARCHDUKE FRANZ FERDINAND OF AUSTRIA

Franz Ferdinand was assassinated on June 28, 1914, by Gavrilo Princip, a Bosnian Serb, in Sarajevo, Yugoslavia. The Slavic Serbs wanted independence from Austria-Hungary and the Ottoman Empire. Just prior to the beginning of World War I, Serbian nationalism was in a heightened state. "Ferdinand was chosen because he was the heir to the Austro-Hungarian Empire. The archduke was in Sarajevo to inspect the imperial armed forces in Bosnia and Herzegovina." While riding down the street in an open car, the archduke and his wife, Sophie, were fired upon and killed. Austria-Hungary demanded that Austrian officials be allowed to play a role in the investigation, capture, and prosecution of the perpetrators. Also, Austria wanted Serbia to denounce the act in the strongest terms and gave Serbia a forty-eight-hour ultimatum. Serbia rejected the request—considering it a violation of Serbia's sovereign rights.[4]

The declaration of war by Austria-Hungary against Serbia, supported by Germany as part of the Central Powers alliance, sparked World War I. The preexisting imperialism had led to numerous alliances based on mutual support and protection agreements, ensuring that if any party was attacked or went to war, others would be drawn into the conflict. In this web of entanglements, Russia came to Serbia's defense, aligning itself with France and Britain in what was known as the Triple Entente. On the other side, Germany supported the Ottoman Empire, which in turn had a connection with Bulgaria, and with Austria-Hungary and Italy formed the Triple Alliance.

As the war raged on, the grim and unsanitary conditions of trench warfare created a breeding ground for the Spanish flu, which eventually transformed into a global pandemic, becoming a deadly menace worldwide.

In the course of the war, additional nations like Japan and the United States aligned with the Triple Entente, joining the conflict, and further escalating its scale and impact. The devastating combination of war and the Spanish flu pandemic had profound and far-reaching consequences on a global scale.

SPANISH FLU

In 1914 the world had a much more agrarian economy, with society relying on farming as a way of life. Many people during this time were primarily focused on producing food through agriculture. This was especially the case for various regions of Europe and in the United States, where the days were long and

---

4 Six causes of World War I. Norwich University Online. (n.d.). Retrieved March 31, 2023, from https://online.norwich.edu/academic-programs/resources/six-causes-of-world-war-i

the focus was on innovating farming processes, improving the quality of soil, bringing a profitable crop to market, and most importantly, producing food for survival. "In the 1900s, just under forty percent of the total United States population lived on farms and sixty percent in rural areas."[5]

Over one hundred years ago, the world was stunned by a deadly global influenza pandemic caused by the H1N1 virus. "This virus is a combination of viruses from pigs, birds and humans that causes disease in humans. H1N1 influenza is a subtype of influenza A virus, a communicable viral illness which causes upper, and in some cases, lower respiratory tract infections in its host. This results in symptoms such as nasal secretions, chills, fever, decreased appetite, and in some cases, lower respiratory tract disease."[6]

This virus was one of the worst contagion crises the world had ever seen. In the United States, it was first identified in military personnel in the spring of 1918. World War I ended in the fall of 1918, and it is conceivable that the soldiers coming home were mobile carriers, spreading the virus to their families and others.

---

5 Jayson Lusk. (2016, June 27). The evolution of American Agriculture. Jayson Lusk. Retrieved March 31, 2023, from http://jaysonlusk.com/blog/2016/6/26/the-evolution-of-american-agriculture

6 H1N1 influenza (nursing) - statpearls - NCBI bookshelf. (n.d.). Retrieved March 28, 2023, from https://www.ncbi.nlm.nih.gov/books/NBK568734/

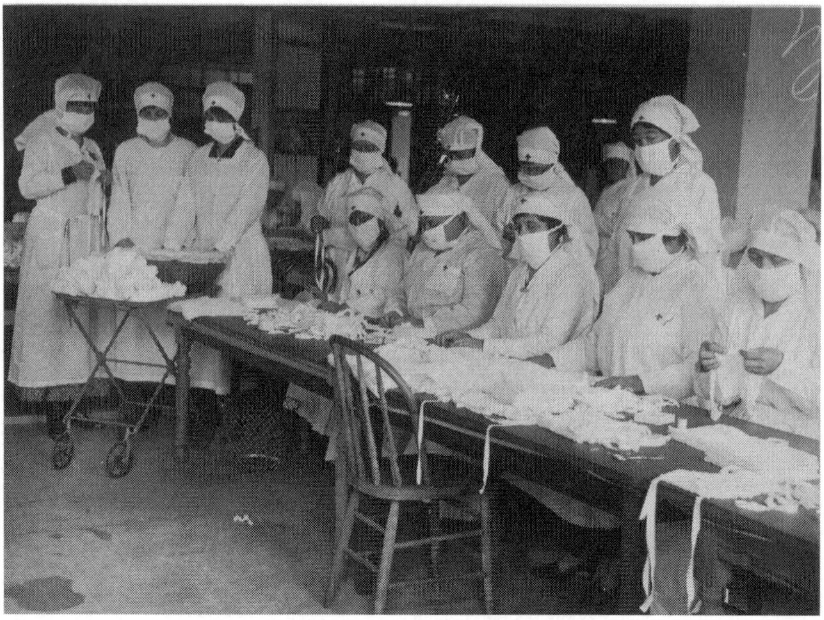

Masks for protection against influenza. States on document that, "Red Cross workers making anti-influenza masks for soldiers in camp. Boston, Massachusetts.
Source: National Archives and Records Administration

Large numbers of people were placed closely together during World War I, which created a perfect environment for the virus to spread so rapidly. And without the benefit of knowledge about the influenza virus and preventive or defensive measures, the disease had a clear path to infect as many people as possible.

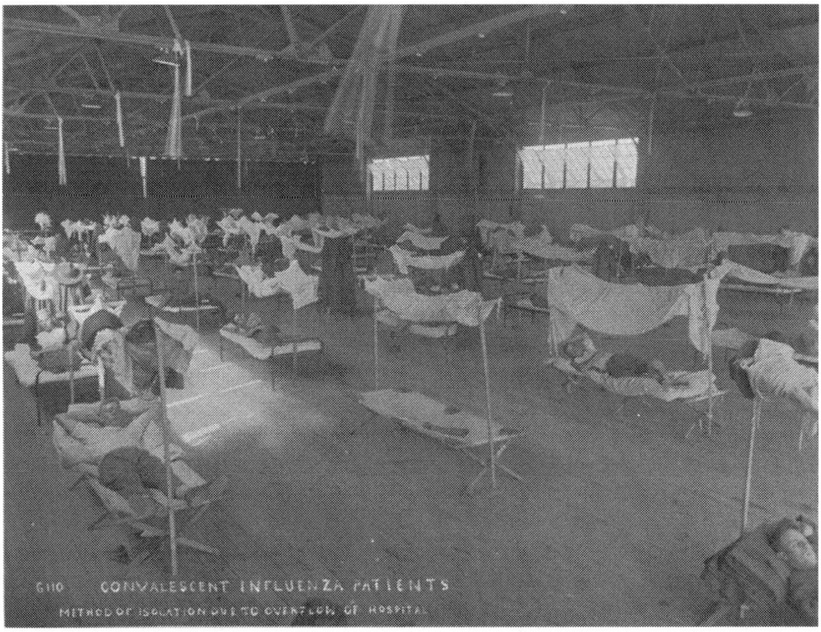

Medical Department - Influenza Epidemic 1918 - Eberts Field, Lonoke, Arkansas. Convalescent Influenza patients, method of isolation due to overflow of hospital
Source: National Archives and Records Administration

The Spanish flu affected millions.

It is estimated that about 500 million people or one-third of the world's population became infected with this virus. The number of deaths was estimated to be at least 50 million worldwide with about 675,000 Americans losing their lives to the infamous and tragic 1918–1919 influenza epidemic. Mortality was high in people younger than 5 years old, 20–40 years old, and 65 years and older. The high mortality in healthy

> people, including those in the 20–40 year age group, was a unique feature of this pandemic.[7]
>
> More people died during the 1918 pandemic than the total number of military and civilian deaths that resulted from World War I.[8]
>
> Countless numbers were left without parents, children, friends and loved ones. Communities across the country did what they could to stem the rising tide of illness and death, closing their schools, churches, theaters, shops, and saloons. Doctors, nurses, and volunteers gave their time and risked their lives to care for the ill.[9]

Per the Centers for Disease Control and Prevention (CDC), the 1918 influenza pandemic occurred in three waves and was the most severe pandemic in history.

> There were 3 different waves of illness during the pandemic, starting in March 1918 and subsiding by summer of 1919. The pandemic peaked in the U.S. during the second wave, in the fall of 1918. This highly fatal second wave was responsible for most of the U.S. deaths attributed to the pandemic.

---

7 Centers for Disease Control and Prevention. (2018, March 21). History of 1918 flu pandemic. Centers for Disease Control and Prevention. Retrieved March 31, 2023, from https://www.cdc.gov/flu/pandemic-resources/1918-commemoration/1918-pandemic-history.htm

8 Centers for Disease Control and Prevention. (2018, March 21). History of 1918 flu pandemic. Centers for Disease Control and Prevention. Retrieved March 31, 2023, from https://www.cdc.gov/flu/pandemic-resources/1918-commemoration/1918-pandemic-history.htm

9 Research: U-M Center for the history of medicine. U. (n.d.). Retrieved March 31, 2023, from http://chm.med.umich.edu/research/

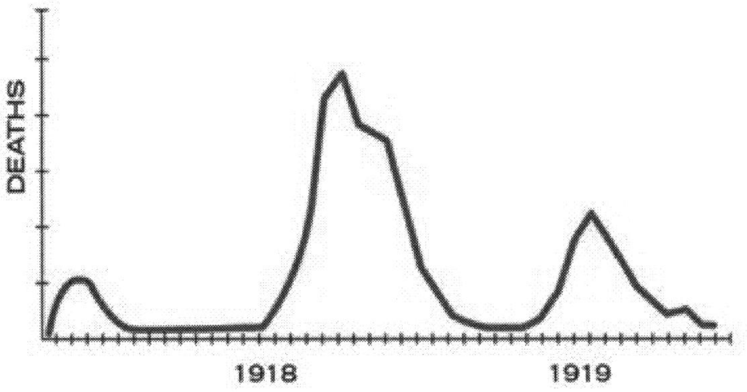

The first outbreak of flu-like illnesses was detected in the U.S. in March, with more than 100 cases reported at Camp Funston in Fort Riley, Kansas. During 1918, the U.S. was engaged in WWI. Hundreds and thousands of U.S. soldiers traveled across the Atlantic to deploy for war. The mass troop movement contributed to the global spread of the flu.

In 1918, many health professionals served in the U. S. military during WWI, resulting in shortages of medical personnel around the U.S. The economy suffered as businesses and factories were forced to close due to sickness amongst workers. A third wave of illness occurred during the winter and spring of 1919, adding to the pandemic death toll. The third wave of the pandemic subsided during the summer of 1919.[10]

10 Centers for Disease Control and Prevention. (2018, March 21). History of 1918 flu pandemic. Centers for Disease Control and Prevention. Retrieved March 31, 2023, from https://www.cdc.gov/flu/pandemic-resources/1918-commemoration/1918-pandemic-history.htm

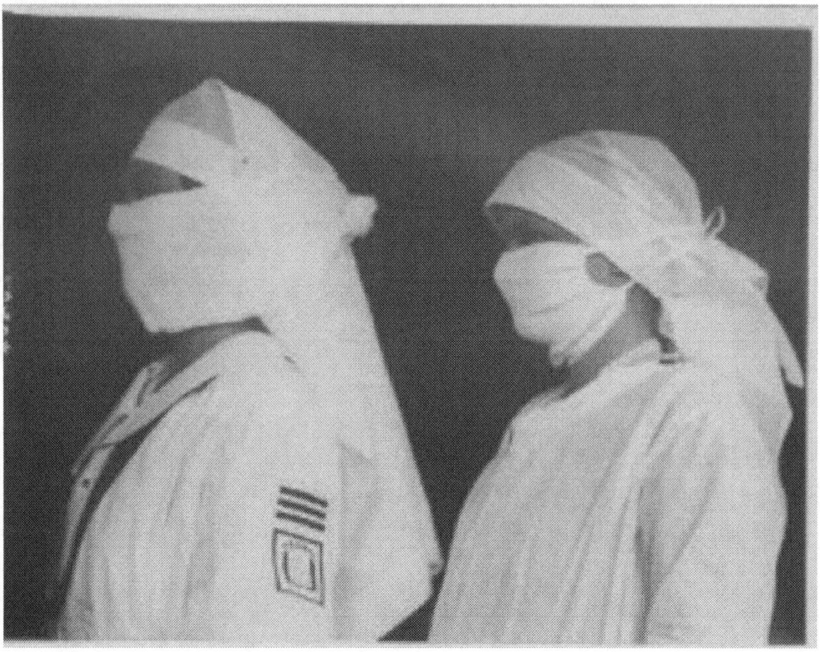

Medical Department - Influenza Epidemic 1918 - Masks for protection against influenza. Nurses in Boston hospitals equipped to fight influenza
Source: National Archives and Records Administration

The devastating impact of the Spanish flu on the world led to the implementation of strict policies aimed at curbing its spread. These measures, however necessary, posed significant challenges to the human spirit, as they involved confinement, restriction, and the suppression of normal behavior.

Policies to combat the virus encompassed a range of measures, including quarantines, mask mandates, and the shutdown of businesses, pool halls, theaters, and schools. Large events were avoided, and gatherings were moved outdoors to reduce transmission risk. Public health officials resorted to newspaper announcements, threatening jail time for those who refused to wear masks. Some cities even labeled mask-wearing dissenters as unpatriotic.

While these measures were crucial to slow the virus's spread, they also sparked discontent among many Americans. They perceived the mandates as unconstitutional and a violation of their rights. Outlawing public spitting and coughing, though necessary for public health, further fueled the frustrations of some individuals.

Despite the controversies and challenges, the implementation of these policies was driven by the need to protect public health during the Spanish flu pandemic. The situation highlights the delicate balance between safeguarding public well-being and preserving individual freedoms, a challenge that remains relevant in times of crisis even today.

Streetcar conductor in Seattle not allowing passengers aboard without a mask 1918.

Source: National Archives and Records Retention

In 1918, citizens were required to wear masks to prevent the spread of the Spanish Flu
Source: National Archives and Records Retention

During the Spanish flu pandemic, tensions arose as many individuals resisted and defied mask mandates implemented across the country. This widespread noncompliance undermined efforts to prevent the virus's spread, leading to issues where shop owners and public transportation services failed to enforce the mandates. People felt they were successfully evading the law, and some shop owners and individuals refused to provide names and addresses of mask mandate violators.

Resistance to mask mandates is not uncommon when everyday activities are curtailed for public health reasons. In such situations, some individuals believe that individual rights outweigh the collective societal good, even in the face of a challenging public health crisis. This tension between individual rights and public health measures was evident during the Spanish flu outbreak in 1918 and continues to be a dilemma today. Balancing personal liberties with the need for broader public health protection remains a complex and contentious issue in times of health emergencies.[11]

Police in Seattle wearing masks during the Spanish Flu in 1918
Source: National Archives and Records Retention

Similar to the circumstances preceding World War I, the world in 2019 was also divided and marked by growing tensions among major global powers. Just as the 1914 world was carved up by monarchies and empires seeking competitive advantage through colonialism and conflict, the geopolitical landscape in 2019 was shaped by the ambitions of the three great powers: the United States, China, and Russia.

Tensions were evident in various hot spots, including the South China Sea, Taiwan, Japan, and international waters in Asia. China was asserting its authority, claiming areas

11 Mask resistance during a pandemic isn't new – in 1918 many Americans were 'slackers'. [Home]. (n.d.). Retrieved March 31, 2023, from https://www.michiganmedicine.org/health-lab/mask-resistance-during-pandemic-isnt-new-1918-many-americans-were-slackers

considered international waters as its own and insisting that Taiwan had belonged to mainland China since the end of World War II, despite Taiwan's claim of independence and alliance with the United States. Taiwan's production of highly sophisticated computer chips, essential for industries ranging from automobiles to advanced fighter jets, made it a critical target for various democracies, including the US, to safeguard this capability against falling into Communist China's hands.

As seen in history, the conflicts preceding World War I eventually led to war, creating the conditions for the incubation and global spread of the Spanish flu as soldiers returned home at the war's end. Similarly, growing tensions among major powers in 2019 raised concerns about the potential ramifications for global stability and security.

Both in the early twentieth century and in contemporary times, the world has grappled with geopolitical rivalries and territorial disputes that have far-reaching consequences for international relations and public health. These historical parallels serve as important reminders of the complex and interconnected nature of global events and the need for diplomatic efforts to address tensions and avoid conflict.

Russia's return to Soviet-era saber-rattling has been evident through its actions, such as the invasion and annexation of Crimea from Ukraine in 2014, followed by another invasion of Ukraine in 2022. This increased aggression, coupled with its new alliance with China, has created a destabilizing atmosphere in the world. Espionage, mistrust, and cyber warfare among these nations have reached alarming levels, leading to concerns that under the right circumstances, war could become imminent. These conditions bear a striking resemblance to the events that precipitated World War I, particularly the assassination of Archduke Franz Ferdinand.

Furthermore, other state actors like Iran and North Korea are fervently pursuing the development of long-range nuclear weapons capable of reaching the United States mainland, which raises the specter of a wartime footing for the world. These scenarios cast a dark shadow on global peace and stability. It is crucial to hope for the success of diplomatic efforts while remaining prepared to defend the vital interests of the United States.

Looking back at the last century, since the end of the Spanish flu, numerous tumultuous events have impacted the United States, including the Great Depression. However, none of them have shaken the core foundation of society as profoundly as the COVID-19 virus.

The current geopolitical climate and the challenges posed by the COVID-19 pandemic serve as stark reminders of the importance of diplomacy and preparedness to safeguard global peace and stability. History has taught us the devastating consequences of unchecked aggression and the need for concerted efforts to promote dialogue, cooperation, and peace in an interconnected world.[12]

Little did the world anticipate that a scourge akin to the Spanish flu would once again afflict humanity, this time manifesting as the deadly COVID-19 virus. This unforeseen pandemic has unleashed havoc on lives, businesses, and the delicate fabric of the global order.

---

12 Matta, S., Arora, V. K., & Chopra, K. K. (2020, December). Lessons to be learnt from 100 year old 1918 influenza pandemic viz a viz 2019 Corona pandemic with an eye on NTEP. The Indian journal of tuberculosis. Retrieved March 31, 2023, from https://www.ncbi.nlm.nih.gov/pmc/articles/PMC7543972/

Chapter 2

The Unfolding Century of Turmoil and Triumph: Is History Repeating Itself?

We are all tourists in history, and irony is what we win in wars.
—Anatole Broyard

Over the past century, the world has witnessed several traumatic events that left their mark on history. From devastating wars to social movements, each era brought its challenges. However, nothing would prepare us for the overwhelming impact of COVID-19 on society, making it the most crippling event in recent history. Since the end of World War I, there have been many periods of global disruption that threatened stability, peace, the economy, and our overall way of life. Let's take a journey through the significant events that shaped our world over the last one hundred years.

1920s–1940s: A Time of Crisis and Conflict

- The stock market crash on Wall Street in 1929, which triggered the Great Depression, causing widespread economic turmoil.
- The surprise attack by the Empire of Japan on Pearl Harbor on December 7, 1941, which propelled the United States into World War II.
- The rise of fascism and Nazism in Europe, culminating in World War II (1939–1945). The Axis powers, led by Adolf

Hitler of Germany, Benito Mussolini of Italy, and Hirohito of Japan, unleashed a reign of terror and aggression, resulting in widespread suffering and devastation.

- Ultimately, the Allied powers, including the United States of America, Great Britain, France, and other nations, came together to defeat the Axis powers, ending the war in 1945.

In summary, this period witnessed the profound impact of the Great Depression, the global conflict of World War II, and the triumph of the Allied forces over the Axis powers.

1950S–1960S: THE ERA OF COLD WAR AND STRIVING FOR EQUALITY

- The Korean War (1950–1953) saw a conflict between communist Chinese-backed North Koreans and democratic South Korean forces, with the United Nations coalition led by the United States of America supporting South Korea.
- The Cold War tension between the Soviet Union and the United States resulted in several proxy wars fueled by the opposing ideologies of communism (Soviet Union) and capitalism (US). These proxy wars included conflicts in Laos, Cambodia, Congo, Angola, and the Vietnam War (1954–1975).
- The period also witnessed a fierce Space Race between the Soviet Union and the United States. It began with the Soviet Union's launch of the first satellite, Sputnik, and reached its pinnacle in 1969 when the United States became the first country to land humans on the moon—Neil Armstrong and Edwin "Buzz" Aldrin.
- The Cuban Missile Crisis of 1962 brought the world to the brink of nuclear war as the United States and the Soviet

Union faced off over the placement of medium-range nuclear ballistic missiles in Cuba, just ninety miles from Florida and capable of striking Washington, DC in minutes.

- The Civil Rights Movement of the late 1950s and 1960s exemplified civil disobedience using nonviolent strategies and tactics to fight for civil and human rights. The movement addressed issues of segregation and equal rights for African American citizens, causing deep divisions within the United States.
- Tragic assassinations also marked this period, with the killings of President John F. Kennedy in Dallas on November 22, 1963, Dr. Martin Luther King Jr. in Memphis on April 4, 1968, and Robert F. Kennedy in Los Angeles on June 6, 1968.

In summary, the years between 1950 and 1969 were characterized by geopolitical conflicts, technological advancements in space exploration, significant strides in civil rights, and the heart-wrenching loss of notable leaders through assassination.

1970S–1980S: PERIODS OF CHANGE AND CHALLENGE

- The Watergate scandal in 1972 involved the Nixon Administration attempting to cover up its involvement in the break-in at the Democratic National Headquarters in Washington, DC.
- In 1976 an Ebola outbreak occurred in Africa, believed to have originated from bats, leading to significant health concerns.

- The Iran Hostage Crisis (1979–1981) started when militant Iranian students seized 52 American diplomats and citizens, holding them hostage at the US Embassy in Iran.
- The HIV/AIDS epidemic began in the United States in 1981, leading to a global health crisis.
- The fall of the Berlin Wall in 1989 marked the end of the Iron Curtain that had divided Europe between the Communist-led East and the Western Bloc led by the US and NATO allies. President Ronald Reagan famously urged Soviet leader Mikhail Gorbachev to "tear down that wall," and Gorbachev's policies of *glasnost* (openness) and *perestroika* (restructuring/reform) eventually led to the dissolution of the Soviet Union, effectively ending the Cold War in 1989.[13]

In summary, these events from 1972 to 1989 encompassed political scandals, public health crises, international conflicts, and the transformative fall of the Berlin Wall, reshaping the global landscape.

2000S: DIVISIONS, TRAGEDIES, AND SHIFTING ALLIANCES

- In 2000 the United States witnessed one of the closest and most divisive presidential elections in history, pitting George W. Bush against Al Gore. Partisan tensions reached a peak during the mandatory recount, and the Supreme Court's decision in favor of Bush further fueled the divisions.
- On September 11, 2001, an infamous terrorist attack occurred when nineteen hijackers targeted the World Trade

13 Blunden, A. (n.d.). The collapse of Eastern Europe. Retrieved April 14, 2023, from https://www.marxists.org/subject/stalinism/origins-future/ch4-1.htm

Center in New York City and the United States Pentagon in Washington, DC, by crashing passenger airliners into these iconic landmarks. Another hijacked plane crashed in Pennsylvania as courageous passengers fought back, preventing further destruction in Washington, DC.

- In 2002 the SARS-CoV-1 outbreak originated in China. It was traced back to bats and caused significant health concerns worldwide.
- In 2009 the swine flu H1N1 pandemic spread across the globe, including the United States, affecting millions.
- In response to the September 11 attacks, the United States engaged in wars in Afghanistan and Iraq, aiming to pursue those responsible for the attacks and combat terrorism. This eventually led to the death of Osama Bin Laden in a US Navy Seal raid in Pakistan on May 2, 2011.
- In 2012 a severe viral respiratory disease called MERS (Middle East Respiratory Syndrome) was first detected in Saudi Arabia.
- The avian influenza A H7N9 virus was detected in 2013 in China, originating from birds and posing a threat to public health.
- An Ebola virus outbreak occurred from 2014 to 2016 in West Africa, resulting in thousands of deaths.
- The early 2000s were characterized by growing divisions in society, rapid cultural changes, and a seeming roller coaster of economic fluctuations.

In summary, the early 2000s were marked by a mix of political controversies, devastating terrorist attacks, and several infectious disease outbreaks that challenged societies worldwide. These events shaped the decade's narrative of division, resilience, and global health concerns.

The sweeping changes and challenges of the twentieth and early twenty-first centuries gave rise to a resilient global economy, forging novel geopolitical alignments and alliances. Amid these transformations, subtle hints from past decades foreshadowed the new problems that lay ahead, offering real-world clues of the possible future we would encounter.

In a constantly evolving world, the geopolitical landscape shifts as nations redefine their roles and global influence. These changes are shaped by economic, technological, and social developments, as well as shifting political dynamics. Key players like China, the United States, and Russia, each with distinct ideologies and ambitions, contribute to this evolving global order.

1. China has emerged as a significant global power, achieving remarkable progress in financial, economic, technological, and military domains. Its unique approach combines elements of communism with capitalist practices, allowing it to capitalize on international markets for consumer, commercial, and military goods.
2. Following the collapse of the Soviet Union, the United States assumed the position of the world's sole superpower. It upholds treaty commitments with NATO member nations, including influential countries like Great Britain, Germany, and France, to collectively defend against hostile aggression.
3. Under Vladimir Putin's leadership, Russia has pursued an agenda to reclaim imperialistic strength and assert its dominance on the global stage. Despite Russia being officially described as a federal democratic republic, there are concerns about increasing centralized control and Putin's firm grip on power. Russia maintains a formidable nuclear arsenal, contributing to its perceived might.

These three major camps each represent distinct political ideologies and wield significant power in their own ways. The United States and its allies champion democracy and capitalism, backed by nuclear capabilities. China, while also a nuclear power, employs a hybrid system of communism and pseudo capitalism to expand its economic and military influence worldwide. Russia appears to be moving toward a more centralized and authoritarian regime, emphasizing its nuclear capabilities as a symbol of strength.

The interactions and interplay between these global powers will continue to shape the future of international relations, the world economy, and global security. As the world evolves, understanding these dynamics is vital for fostering cooperation, addressing challenges, and building a more stable and harmonious global community.

The escalating tension between these three global players has far-reaching consequences across multiple domains, including politics, economics, climate control, finance, trade, and global peace. Even our response to a pandemic must be viewed through the lens of this evolving geopolitical landscape. It's important to recognize that other countries also play pivotal roles, as many have existing or potential alliances with one or more of these major players, thereby influencing their actions and decisions on the world stage. Understanding and navigating this intricate web of geopolitical dynamics is essential for addressing challenges and fostering cooperation on a global scale.

During this period, the world experienced two transformative revolutions—a technological revolution and a consumer revolution—unfolding simultaneously. The medical and scientific communities made astounding breakthroughs, continuously pushing the boundaries of human capabilities. Artificial intelligence and machine learning became commonplace terms, and computing technology advanced rapidly, reaching terabyte storage levels. The fastest supercomputers approached processing speeds of over a billion-billion operations per second, reaching the remarkable milestone known as an exaflop. This era witnessed unparalleled progress in various fields, promising a future where technology and human ingenuity would propel society to new heights.

This was the backdrop against which COVID-19 emerged on the world stage. Within this context, the response to the pandemic varied significantly among global players and their allies, shaped by their geopolitical postures and ideologies, as well as underlying divisions and competitiveness. Furthermore, at a more intricate level, disagreements arose within countries concerning the legitimacy of COVID-19, as well as the formulation of policies and procedures to curb the spread of the virus. The pandemic laid bare the complexities of global cooperation and highlighted how different worldviews influenced approaches to tackling this unprecedented global crisis.

Chapter 3

THE VIRUS BEGINS: WUHAN, CHINA

Coronavirus may well represent the biggest health crisis any of us experience in our lifetimes.

—Liz Truss

In December of 2019 in Wuhan, part of an obscure province in China, a strange disease was baffling public health professionals and causing an increasing number of deaths. Researchers and epidemiologists believe that lurking in one of the massive live animal markets was the coronavirus SARS-CoV-2. According to the World Health Organization, "Coronavirus disease (COVID-19) is an infectious disease caused by the SARS-CoV-2 virus. Most people infected with the virus will experience mild to moderate respiratory illness and recover without requiring special treatment. However, some will become seriously ill and require medical attention."[14]

There are several theories as to the origin of this virus becoming zoonotic and jumping from animals to humans or possibly an infected person spreading the virus to many other individuals. Some have even speculated the virus could have been an accidental release from a Chinese lab. Whatever the truth or final analysis may show with regard to the origin of the virus, the strange occurrences in this faraway corner of Asia would eventually hold the world hostage.

---

14 World Health Organization. (n.d.). Coronavirus. World Health Organization. Retrieved March 31, 2023, from https://www.who.int/health-topics/coronavirus

There were a few short news stories in the United States and Europe on various networks, with only minimal coverage given to the looming problem thousands of miles away. Many around the world were in the midst of the Christmas, New Year, and other holidays focused on sharing time with families and friends. Communities were gearing up to enjoy the traditional festivities, sharing and receiving gifts with family, friends, and coworkers. Little did they know the next several months would reveal a challenge no one could have expected. In January 2020 China would report its first death from the new coronavirus. Subsequently, a Diamond Princess cruise ship, with its approximately 3,700 passengers and crew, would face a COVID-19 outbreak that required quarantine while docked off Yokohama, Japan. The efforts of health care workers and the processes and protocols seemed inadequate to combat the spread of the virus. In the same month, the doctor who is considered the virus whistleblower succumbed to COVID-19 in a hospital near Wuhan. Near the end of February 2020, the first reported COVID-19 death occurred in the United States in the state of Washington.

THE WORLD IS SHOCKED AND STUNNED

I was casually watching television when breaking news blared on March 11, 2020, that Rudy Gobert, National Basketball Association (NBA) star for the Utah Jazz, had tested positive for the COVID-19 virus. I paused, and all my attention focused to hear more details about this ailment that afflicted this seemingly healthy basketball player. The strangest feeling came over me. It was a mix of uncertainty, anxiety, and nervousness because I didn't know what this meant. The NBA would suspend its season indefinitely the next day due to fears of COVID-19. The other major sports leagues, Major League Baseball, National

Hockey League, Major League Soccer, minor league teams, and tennis associations at all levels followed suit the next day. The NCAA men's basketball tournament was canceled. Ultimately, the Tokyo 2020 Olympic Games were postponed to 2021. The US government declared a national emergency as COVID-19 was detected in all fifty states and infections and deaths started to rise. Hospitals and health care workers were reporting increasing numbers of patients with respiratory difficulty and testing positive for the virus. As hospital emergency rooms and intensive care units begin to explode with activity, many medical facilities across the country started to exceed their capacity to deal with the onslaught of COVID-19 patients. Family members, neighbors, and colleagues began to ask, "What is going on and what should we do?" People were scared. Everyone was unsure how to deal with the unknown and what they were about to face. As more information was shared on the extreme contagiousness and airborne properties of the virus, individuals, families, businesses, and all types of organizations began to shelter in place and try to prevent exposure. Cities and emergency planning apparatus started to mobilize and strategize on what steps could be taken to prepare communities across the country as the virus raged. Initially, the information from the federal government, medical community, health departments, and public health policy think tanks was sketchy. They were all scrambling in a race against the virus to answer questions and synchronize courses of action for civil society.

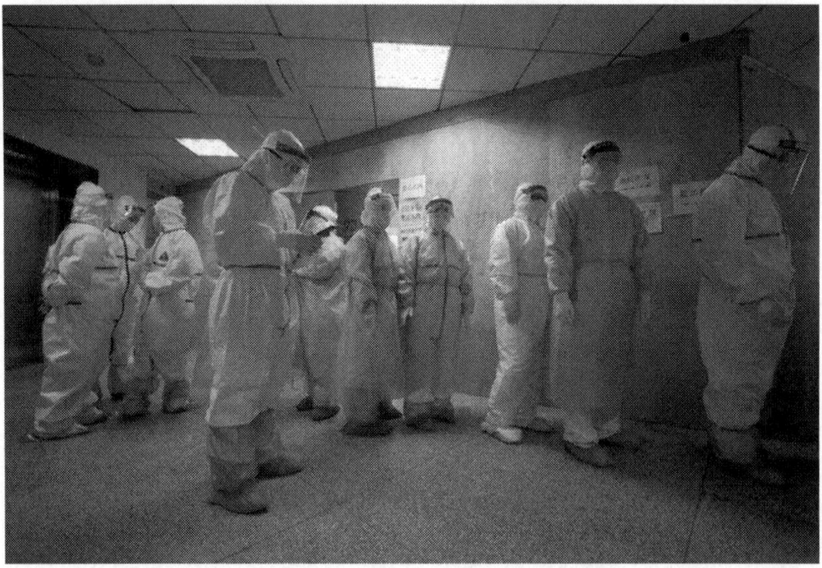

Medical personnel in China prepare to face the COVID-19 virus. Source: Hyderabad news

Chapter 4

THE DAYS THE EARTH STOOD STILL

It is not the strongest or the most intelligent who will survive but those who can best manage change.
—Leon C. Megginson

The original version of the science fiction movie *The Day the Earth Stood Still* was released in 1951 starring Michael Rennie as Klaatu, a humanoid alien visitor to earth who assumes the name Carpenter to warn the world about nuclear war. He wants to speak to all the leaders of the world together to give his message one time but is rebuffed due to political differences and conflicts among the many nations. Realizing the grave warning he must present, he resorts to the scientific community and reaches out to a Professor Jacob Barnhardt, played by Sam Jaffe, after asking Bobby, a young boy he has befriended, who is the smartest or greatest person living. He informs Barnhardt that the earth will be destroyed if it does not heed his warning and asks for help to convene scientists from around the world to meet at his spaceship in Washington, DC. Barnhardt agrees. However, he suggests that Carpenter provide a demonstration of his power to ensure the scientists will attend and take him seriously. The next day, starting at noon in Washington, DC, and lasting for thirty minutes, the entire world stands still. All cars, trains, factories, trucks, lights, elevators, and electrical equipment, except for hospitals, airplanes in flight, and other essential services, cease to operate. All electricity is neutralized. Everyone is frightened, shocked, and bewildered. Major cities around the world, such as New

York, London, Berlin, Toronto, Hong Kong, Washington, DC, Mexico City, Rio de Janeiro, Paris, Rome, Beijing, San Francisco, Los Angeles, Chicago, Tel Aviv, etc., were shut down and their streets were at a complete standstill. People hunkered down and were uncertain about what was happening. They were afraid of the unknown, and in some cases, panic became pervasive. The environment of fear fostered rumors and sensational stories that led many to jump to unfounded conclusions. A sense of helplessness pervaded their thoughts as they found themselves impotent against the unknown perpetrator of this terrifying interruption to the normal daily routine. Shops and businesses closed, and communities were devoid of activity. The earth was standing still, and there was nothing they could do about it.

Like the movie, this is how things looked during the shutdown for COVID-19. Carpenter's message was for the people of earth to put aside their differences and work in harmony to avoid placing the world in peril. Maybe we should heed this movie's message and work more collaboratively and guard against the differences or conflicts that could lead to our demise.

> Picture yourself as a small business proprietor in March 2020. Your livelihood depends on a successful small business that is not only essential for your community but also supports your household. Over the years, you've built a stable financial foundation by wisely saving and reinvesting the business income. However, with the onset of the COVID-19 pandemic and the subsequent shutdowns to curb its spread, your business's income vanishes almost overnight. Deprived of the usual revenue, you face the heartbreaking reality of being unable to sustain regular payments to your dedicated employees. In order to survive, you regrettably have to let go of some of your staff, assuring them that you'll rehire them once the crisis subsides. As time

unfolds, it becomes evident that the pandemic's impact is far more enduring than initially anticipated. To cover essential business and household costs, you dip into your hard-earned savings. Even when businesses are allowed to reopen, stringent capacity limits and reduced customer traffic persist, preventing you from rehiring your valued employees. Your once-flourishing business now barely manages to provide for your family's basic needs and shelter. The future seems uncertain, with no relief or assistance in sight. In May 2020, the Center for Financial Inclusion and Mastercard's Center for Inclusive Growth initiated a study, revealing that over a year into the pandemic, a considerable number of businesses continued to grapple with diminished profit margins. This financial strain triggered a ripple effect, affecting the livelihoods of countless individuals.[15]

The panic started to consume all segments of life. The shutdowns led to runs on supermarkets and gas stations as citizens prepared to shelter in place for an undetermined time frame. Businesses were caught completely off guard; their continuity plans never having considered an event like the COVID-19 pandemic. This was a complete disruption of economic and financial planning. Companies and employees were at risk as the world and commerce shut down. Schools were unprepared for a change in thinking that would require all instruction to be virtual. There were challenges with teacher training, school technology, technology at the homes of children, and the sheer understanding of how to engage with students

15 The precarious state of msmes: Understanding the impact of covid-19 and opportunities to support their recovery. Center for Financial Inclusion. (n.d.). Retrieved March 31, 2023, from https://www.centerforfinancialinclusion.org/the-precarious-state-of-msmes-understanding-the-impact-of-covid-19-and-opportunities-to-support-their-recovery

virtually. Universities shut down, sent their students home for spring break, and then told them not to return. Campuses were empty and instruction transitioned online. COVID-19 dealt a death blow to dining in restaurants. The entire operation and mechanisms for operating a restaurant had to be rethought. Airports were shut down, and the few flights that did occur were virtually empty due to fear of spreading the virus. All types of protocols had to be developed for mask wearing, sanitation, and proper air circulation.

FEAR AND UNCERTAINTY SPREAD

The psychological shock of the pandemic caused great unsettledness across the country. Fear of the unknown ran rampant as multiple facets of everyday life were turned upside down. Fear was prevalent in health and medical workers along with average citizens. Lack of knowledge about the disease and what threats it presented to human health were of great concern to citizens in the United States and the rest of the world. Forced lockdowns, stay-at-home orders, mask mandates, and social distancing created additional stress and uncertainty because there was no clear understanding of the course of the illness. There was a deluge of questions, but the answers lacked clarity. People wanted to know how they would be affected. What does it mean for my health and my family's health? Is it okay to leave my house? Can I go to work? Can I go to school? Those suffering with anxiety and depression disorders had their conditions exacerbated on multiple levels due to this confusion.

The outbreak changed behaviors and everyday interactions. In-home services and repairs declined as individuals feared exposure and infection. Ambiguous reports and unclear media updates added frustration because there was not a clear outline of what was happening or a solid risk communications plan.

During the initial stages, coordination between the government and public health entities was inconsistent and hampered clear direction on policy, how to control the infection, and how to protect yourself.

Shopping for groceries took on a whole new critical process for sanitation. Shoppers were masking up and donning surgical gloves and other protective gear to venture out for vital supplies. Groceries were wiped down and sanitized before being brought into the home to minimize risk of exposure. A crisis of this magnitude creates an inordinate amount of distress as individuals attempt to navigate their lives while defending against infection and illness, not knowing what the next day would hold.

Over the next thirteen chapters you will read personal stories of resilience, perseverance, fortitude, and survival in the face of COVID-19.

Chapter 5

MAN CAVE AWAY FROM HOME

We can't be brave in the big world without at least one small safe space to work through our fears and falls.

—Brené Brown

The neighborhood barbershop has been a fixture in the community for as long as I can remember. It's a culture where the rites of passage continue from generation to generation as fathers bring their little boys for their first haircut. The cycle repeats itself over the years as little boys grow into young men and do the same for their sons. They form a camaraderie with their barber, other barbers, and various patrons of the barbershop. It's a place of communication and a trusted source of discovery on many topics—from men's health to sports cars. There are discussions on sports, life, politics, pop culture, relationships, and current events. And oh, did I mention sports? Barbershops have been used to encourage men to get physical examinations and focus on their overall health and well-being. There is a certain acceptance, trust, and social connectivity that exist within the "man cave away from home." It is somewhat of a social club with rules and traditions. Men come to the barbershop to relax, let their hair down, and debate various and sundry issues. All the men know there is a sense of belonging, restoration, and an outlet for mental healing. It's like a brotherhood where one can come for a haircut but hang around afterward to weigh in on the issues of the day. It could be about who will win the Super Bowl or the NBA finals or if the Yankees will beat the Red Sox. Every person has their favorite team . . . and they don't lose any time in sharing their point of view and defending the team they have been loyal to through the years. The race for the next president or local mayor or alderman is all fair game for barbershop discussions. There are televisions on each wall showing sports, news, or some movie that everyone will tend to comment on. These conversations can last for hours, as different patrons come and go, and the conversation rekindles. Clients physically engage with handshakes, sit in proximity, gather in tight spaces, eat snacks, and consume beverages from the Coca-Cola vending machine, which adds to the ambiance of the barbershop and the lore passed down through history. However, COVID-19 changed all of these interactions. According to the Nature Public Health Emergency Collection, "COVID-19 and the resultant government-mandated shutdown had a negative impact on the livelihood of barbers working in predominantly Black barbershops and their families."[16]

I had the opportunity to sit down and chat with Mr. Al Harris, Owner/Operator of the Barbershop Lounge. As we sat in his spacious eight-chair shop, he shared his experience dealing with COVID-19 and what it meant to his business and the industry in general.

16 Taylor, N. K., Faulks, M., Brown-Johnson, C. G., Rosas, L. G., Shaw, J. G., Saliba-Gustafsson, E. A., & Asch, S. M. (2022, November 22). Pandemic through the lens of Black Barbershops: Covid-19's impact and barbers' potential role as public health extenders. Journal of immigrant and minority health. Retrieved March 31, 2023, from https://www.ncbi.nlm.nih.gov/pmc/articles/PMC9684895/

DJJ:
What were your initial thoughts when businesses started closing and COVID-19 was called a global pandemic?

Al*:*
Initial thought was more subdued. It was like one of those moments where you say, "Okay, this is really happening. This has really hit home." When it first came out, and we heard about it over in China, and then we heard about it over here in the States, it wasn't really in Memphis to the full extent like you've heard about other places. Then I was like, "Okay, so now businesses are closing. What are we going to do?" I more so was thinking about my business partners and the other barbers, and the ones I know that are the head of households and all the responsibility, financially, is on them. They've been able to come here freely, make all they want to make, and then leave. And I was like, "That's going to end." I think that was the biggest thing, like, "Okay, what do we do now? What do we do now?"

DJJ**:**
Was there any fear or uncertainty?

Al:
I wouldn't say there was fear. I was really, more, or less, shocked. When I experience things, I'm taken aback, and I just sit back and observe. I'm not really quick to have emotions. But at this moment when I finally did reflect on it, I was like, "Okay, what's the course of action?" So what I did first was, I prayed to God about it. I was like, "Hey, we've been through things before. I know You didn't bring me this far to leave me, so I'm going to trust in Your Word. I'm going to rest in the shadow of Your wings, and coach me through this." And that's what He did. So, I'm not going to say I was at peace, but I was melancholy.

DJJ:
Did you think it was going to ever get this big or global?

Al:
I didn't. That was the biggest part of it. The fact that it was global, that everybody was experiencing something from it, that everybody had been impacted. Then I also looked at the fact that over here in America, we're blessed. We had alternative measures. Where when you look at some of these other poor countries, they were hit a lot worse than we were. So I guess, maybe, I was more so concerned about other countries that were less fortunate, more so than I was us here.

DJJ:
What was your personal experience during the COVID-19 pandemic?

Al:
Personal experience was, "Okay, we're here. Have to be strong for the family. I have to be strong for the barbers and give them a sense of direction of what direction we should go." Then I was like, "Okay, so let me be okay with not going to the shop. Let me be okay with spending more time with the family and see what that side of life is about."

Because for so long, I had been all about coming to work, making the money, and this is what I'm about. Honestly, I would hate to say it, I don't want to sound harsh, but when I reflected on it, I saw that it was a lot about me. And the pandemic made me slow down and make it about them. The fruits of that were better than anything else. Me not having to come in as much and living below my means and being content with where we were, was real big. And the fact the family was okay with it too.

We all took it with grace. So, I think that's what I would have to say.
DJJ:
Do you think you thought about family more? Did you get closer to family?

Al:
Definitely got closer to family, talked to them more on the phone, told them we love them more. Even if it was just sitting around watching TV and laughing and joking and playing games. You know, the things that we take for granted when we are always working. It made me realize that there's more to life than just being behind the chair. There's more to life than just . . . It made me appreciate life more. Because I know when I'm gone, life is going to go on.
So how will my life impact others, is where I was going. I need to make it to where they miss me, where we have memories, and they can cherish what we had. So, I think that was the best part of that.

DJJ:
Do you think your family appreciated having more together time?

Al:
Most definitely. I've always thought that I was there, and I was there. I went to all the family, I don't know, not all the family events, but I didn't miss outings and kids' football games and basketball games. I was there. But I think that when the pandemic really set in, I made them a priority, as opposed to work being a priority.

DJJ:
How did your business change? In the beginning? During COVID? And now?

Al:
Hmm. Everybody was on high alert. You couldn't come in and hang around and talk like we used to. That whole family, the barbershop, use to be a safe haven where you could come, but now, the brotherhood and the connection was disjointed. We didn't want them coming in. You couldn't wait around. You had to wait in your car. You had to be sanitized. You had to be temperature checked. You couldn't blow your nose in here without us looking at you crazy. So, I think it was affected more so from that standpoint. The community bond was broken.

DJJ:
Did that become even more intense as time went along? There was a beginning of COVID, but then it really reached its height. Did that even become greater in terms of what you're describing?

Al:
Yeah. That was the new normal. That was the new normal. Even now that we're, I say we're post-pandemic, we still don't do the things we used to do. A lot of that camaraderie we once had has been definitely severed.

Somebody comes in now and they're a walk-in, we may not be able to get them. And it's across the profession. I've noticed that a lot of the barbers now aren't as open to taking new clients. They're screening the clients more. They're more selective on who they choose to be their client. Because I know when the pandemic first hit, and we were able to go back to working, if a new client came in, we're wondering, "Why aren't you going to your old barber? Does he have COVID? Did you just get over

COVID and he wouldn't cut your hair, so now you are coming here?"

So, all those questions went into play. As opposed to you just greeting them and saying, "Come on in. We're going to take care of you," we want to screen them and to see actually why. So, I think I would say our defenses were up more.

DJJ:
And now as things have subsided just a little bit, it's still different - isn't it?

Al:
Still different. I'm going to speak for myself. I still screen them pretty tough. They actually told me I need to lighten up a little bit. So, it's my harshness, my delivery. So, I thought about that, and I started doing better with that.

DJJ:
Do you agree, before COVID, there used to be a lot of talk, a lot of banter in the barbershop, a lot of people sitting around?

Al:
Right.

DJJ:
But now with COVID, tell me the difference between before and after.

Al:
Okay. You can't come in with your friends. If they're not getting serviced, they might as well stay in the car. You can't go and talk chair to chair. Matter of fact, a lot of guys do that. We're all friends in here. So, it might be Calvin's client, but he's at my

chair talking. We're not doing that anymore. Definitely want you to be a safe distance away. And we're more assembly-line now. We want to get you in and get you out. And yeah, the time that you have with us now is while you're getting your service in your chair.

DJJ:
Explain how you survived and the things you did to survive. How bad did it get?

Al:
Like I said, for me, it was a little different. I think the unemployment helped. For us, that was about $400. You know what I'm saying? So, the whole scheme of things, for some it may be a lot, for others maybe not. But it was enough to help sustain and help cushion the blow, I would say.

Yeah, it didn't get as bad as it could have gotten. It didn't get as bad for me as it may have gotten for others.

My family and I, we were in a different place. We had enough saved and enough planning. We did a lot of the things beforehand to be okay during this time, if that makes sense.

DJJ:
What did you see or hear about from others in the industry? What are some of the challenges they faced?

Al:
People losing shops. They were losing barbers. Because now, you got to think about it. If these barbers are home now and they're going house to house, that's their new normal now. They may like that situation better. They may not want to come in here and pay booth rent, because they're independent contractors. So, a lot of guys didn't come back to the shop.

Then on the other side, a lot of barbers ended up taking jobs. So now you're thinking about them in the sense that now they became an essential worker. They may have gone and started Amazon. They may have gone to the Walmart, they may have gone to the Costco's, because they had to make ends meet. Some of those people, if they were making enough money doing that, it became their new normal, so where they didn't really see the barbering industry as the viable means of income anymore.

DJJ:
What changes did you have to implement at the barbershop?

Al:
Okay. Let me walk you through that. A customer comes in, we greet them at the door. Our hours did change. We started staggering the way the barbers came in. So, if you were an early bird, you may have started your day at 7:00 a.m., when the regular hours were 9:00 a.m. And then you would cut all your early people, you would cut them first, so you wouldn't have a bunch of barbers with a bunch of clients in here at the same time.

Some barbers came in a little later. They may have come in around 10:00, and then they would cut. But now, one thing we had to do was each one of our chairs had to be six feet apart. So, we knew that we were safe in terms of the distance from chair to chair. So, when a customer came in through the door, we'd take their temperature, they would come in with a mask. Now, mind you, we want to keep the mask on the whole time. So, while they're sitting there, they would remove the mask from one side of their face and hold it in place while I shave that side. We would go to the other side and repeat the process.

And then once I lean him back for the shave, though, all games are off. He doesn't have a mask on. So now that's the critical time where I have my mask on, and sometimes we'd see barbers, they might have two masks on, just to make sure they were covered. You remember, we had a shortage of the N95 masks. It wasn't really conceivable for us that one little thin mask was full protection like an N95. You'd see guys having two masks on, or they may have the mask on and then the one you tie on around the head. So, we did little things like that to try to minimize the risk, because once COVID got in the building, it could've spread through all of us, and we're sending it out to potentially 80 different people at a time because we have eight chairs.

So that was one of the things we did, and then you've got to think about another multiple streams of income that we had in here was from selling drinks, chips, and things of that nature. We no longer used the drink machine. We no longer sold the chips. We used to sell hot dogs and things of that nature. We couldn't do any of that. Little changes like that were something that I think impacted us being able to maximize our earning potential.

DJJ:
How did your customers respond to these new business rules?

Al:
And so, a lot of the sanitary measures that we take, taken for granted in the past, we had to be on them. And a lot of clients didn't like that. A lot of clients didn't like you having to tell them that they need to be, that they need to come in with their mask. And honestly, and I'm sure some of the other shop owners and shop patrons can attest to this, even the barbers even got a little lax at times. So, across the board, it was that whole thing of trying to make sure everybody stays safe, and we couldn't get comfortable was a big thing. Especially when we ran out of

supplies and ran out of, um, Lysol. Those things were hard to get.

I saw scarcity of a lot of supplies, and I saw an increase in pricing. And that was at the beauty supply places; everyone was having a hard time getting any necessary supplies we needed. Uh, so that was the biggest thing. It was hard. Now as time went on, we started having people look out for us and bring us in those supplies we needed. We started getting that extra hand sanitizer and wipes and things of that nature that people may have had up in stock.

DJJ:
Al, how long have you been in the business?

Al:
Okay. I've been in business a little over 20 years. Things have been good. Yeah. Over those 20 years, this has been my main source of income. And so, in the barber industry itself, we have a term that we use where you're a full-fledged barber. You're a, you're a grand master barber. It means that you've cut over 10,000 heads. And with that distinction means that you're totally dedicated to the craft.

DJJ:
Obviously during COVID-19, there were lots of things going on, but what did you see across the industry? How did it affect the industry? How did it affect barbers—from your perspective?

Al:
I saw it affect in various different ways. Some of it was with the way the barbers correlated to their customers. Some of it was with the personality shifted to a little more—less personable. You know, we've got this thing where we try to speak to the

clients as they come in. And what I've noticed across the board when I visited other shops, you know, they lost a lot of that touch.

You know, it was more so, I felt like the barbers started acting like the customer needed them, as opposed to them needing their customer. And so that was different for me. That, that's been a little hard to deal with, you know, in the, this transition from the older-generation barbers to the new. And then with the social media . . . You know, COVID brought a lot of social media out, in terms of how you market your business, how you get your clients. And instead of . . . They've got these apps out now. There's Booksy and all these other apps that the client can go in and book their appointment. You don't even know who they are.

So, when they come in, they're like, "Oh . . ." They tell you, "Okay, I have an appointment with, uh, so-and-so." And he's like, "Oh, okay. Are you waiting on me?" You know, and so it's lost a lot of that one-on-one interaction and the whole sense of, you know, you getting to know that person. To me, you know, when you have a client, that's somebody that you're building a relationship with, and that's somebody you want to keep long-term. And I think since COVID, we've lost a lot of that. One of the things I noticed and one of things I saw as well was that the shops, they lost a lot of good barbers. You know, I see a lot of other genres associated with the barbershop die off, like the shoeshine. It's a dinosaur now. You know, and I said, I think that since COVID, there are going to be a lot of good barbers that get out the industry.

DJJ:

What was the impact on older barbers? And what's the basic age range of a barber? You got older barbers. You got younger barbers. So, what does the makeup look like now?

Al:
Yeah, I think, I think the older barbers now are starting to transition out.

I think the newer barbers, the younger generation, period, just have a, a different makeup. They're just a little different. I think the older barbers are having a hard time adjusting to the new way things are changing. We try to instill some things in them from the old craft. And you know, of course, just like children, they want to do it their way.

And a lot of clashes happen, you know, as a result of that. I think a lot of new barbers now feel like they don't have to pay their dues. Or they can do it their way and it's going to be successful. And some of them are successful and some aren't. But I think as a whole, you know, our industry is suffering as a result of that disconnect.

Older barbers. I might fit in that category. For me, the family dynamic, like, and it may be for a lot of barbers, when you have older family members that live with you, you know, uh, their immune systems may be somewhat compromised. And for me going home, or for a lot of barbers who are older, you have to worry about you coming in, you're making a living, you're dealing with multiple clients a day, day in, day out basis. And then you get to the house, you don't know what you may be bringing home to your elderly loved ones. And that was one of the biggest concerns, although we're out here trying to make a living, you know, we have to be conscious of the fact that we have loved ones that we may be putting in harm's way.

I saw a lot of older barbers retire. I saw a lot of older barbers decide that they were going to work from home and change, get out of this industry and do something altogether. A lot of that I talk to saying that it was just too risky. It wasn't worth risking their lives for the money that they make here. And like I said before, a lot of new clients started coming in, and that was just too much. That was too dangerous; that was too risky.

And when you think about the barbershop, you have some clients, some barbers who are willing to take that in, but as the owner, you have to be conscious of making sure that they stay focused on being safe, that they follow the guidelines, that they continue to keep their mask up over their face, that they continue to make sure that they are sanitizing their hands and that they're spraying down their capes and that they're spraying down their utensils.

DJJ:
Tell me about the economic impact of COVID-19 on barbers.

Al:
That was tough. A lot of barbers have multiple streams of incomes. They may be a barber, but they also detail cars. They may be a barber, but they may also flip houses, or be a contractor, or may work another job. You know, so, I think that . . . I saw a lot of ingenuity come out of it, but at the same time, the barbers who were living for the days, as I like to say, that weren't really saving and weren't prioritizing how they budget their money, they struggled the most.

A lot of them I've seen actually have to get out of the business altogether. Because when you're an independent contractor, and I try . . . What we try to convey to a lot of them is that you have to put up for a rainy day. You have to start your own 401(k), you know, things of that nature. And that's the business side of it that a lot of the younger generation, they're not ready to fully grasp. They want to come in. They want to make their money. They want to leave when they're done. And there's no thought for the future.

DJJ:
Did governmental aid play a role in your survival, and barbering in general?

Al:
That's a great question. From my own personal experience, those funds were hard to get.

From the government, there was a lot of red tape. You had to know somebody who knew how to actually do that paperwork for you in order to get it done. We felt like, or I felt like, and I know a lot of people that I talked to felt like, they put it out there, but they really didn't expect us or want us to have access to it. So that was challenging. And now, normally, what we started doing, though, was once we found somebody or heard about somebody who would do it, then everybody would go to that person.

And I think that was the saving grace for a lot of us. And then the fact that the landlords had to prorate the rent and reduce it. I think that helped. But what they did, much like the mortgage industry, is that they backdated all those things. They put it at the end of your lease. So, you're still responsible for that money. And if you're one of those unfortunate groups of barbers that weren't able to get the PPP loan. I think they had the EIDL, some people. They had the grants. I think the grant was like, you get $1,000 per barber. But for this industry, that was hard to prove. You know, you had so much corruption going on. You had so many people saying that they had these businesses and getting access to this money.

It seems like when it came to the barber industry and the beauty industry, they scrutinized us even more. Because a lot of people tried to say they had barbershops and beauty shops and nail shops and all that. And they were getting the money. But then the ones who really needed it, we didn't experience that trickle-down effect.

DJJ:
What is the new normal for your business industry? Or have things relaxed and gone back to pre-COVID-19?

Al:
Okay. Yeah, it's funny that you asked that. I had a client in here the other day, and he was laughing, and we were talking about that. Because he was like, "Man, when you going to start letting us hang out and, you know, talk trash and this, that, and the other? You know, and while we're waiting on our haircut, we're in here talking with the rest of the fellas, fraternizing." I said, "It's not going to happen." He said, "Man, COVID is over." You know what I'm saying? He said, "We're not even wearing masks anymore." I said, "But we still have to be cautious. COVID is not over, and I don't think we'll ever get back to being that comfortable where you're in here, and five, ten, eight guys are in here all just shooting the breeze." I said, "I don't think that's going to be something we'll ever do."

Because you asked if COVID is over and have we gotten comfortable enough to go back, and as long as they're having different strains of the virus coming out, ah, I don't think that we'll ever have a normal situation with that.

I'm not going to say back to pre-COVID-19, but things have relaxed. We no longer take temperatures. The mask is optional. Sometimes I wear mine, sometimes I don't. So, it's one of those things where if we may not have our mask on, but if you cough, your mask is going on. It might be too late [*laughs*], but you know. And I have a lot of clients that still wear their masks. So, although I may not have mine on, they'll have theirs on, and that's been working out pretty good. A lot of clients come up to the door, and we still have the signs up that's saying wait in your car, so I prefer for them to wait in their car. A lot of us still prefer to not have a full waiting area. Like, our normal waiting area for us had 15 chairs. We got maybe six now. And so, and then we've got spread-out spaces, so we have ones in the front and then we also have areas in the back where clients can sit. So, we kind of keep them still at a safe distance.

DJJ:
How did all the changes affect you psychologically?

Al:
I don't think it affected me psychologically as it may have others. When it comes to certain situations and things, some people are more, shall I say "detached" than others. So, for me, psychologically being that I was already kind of rooted in my faith and believing that everything was going to be okay and that we would get through this, I didn't worry about that as much. I kind of rolled with the punches and took things as they came.

Now, earlier I mentioned that my value or . . . not my value. My concern wasn't so much about making money, and enjoying life became more of a priority, then I adjusted to where I didn't stay late. You know, whereas we used to take clients that were called, and I'd make sure I stay here and get them all taken care of, now I made it more about me and my family and the quality time that we started to enjoy and share. So, I would get home at decent hours.

Now, a typical day for some barbers are those hours, say, open at 9:00 and close at 7:00. They may get there at 7:00 a.m. and close at 10:00. And a lot of us in the industry, depending on how your clientele was and depending on how dedicated you were to your craft, you would stay here to accommodate your people. So, I think the biggest thing about COVID was that family should be first.

DJJ:
Did you lose close friends or family members due to COVID-19?

Al:
I didn't lose any close friends and family. I did lose some associates that had a similar work ethic as mine, and that hit me different. That jarred me and woke me up and made me realize that I needed to get vaccinated. Because I was one of the people initially that said, "Oh, okay. Well, you know, we ain't got to get the shot. You know, I'm healthy. I, I don't get sick often, and out of all these years I may've missed, you know, five days of work.

So even the common cold is something that I just don't normally get. So, I had this false sense of security in thinking that it wouldn't happen to me. So once a young lady ended up passing from COVID, and I said, "Okay, well, I'm going to go ahead and get vaccinated. Enough of the games. You know, I don't want to take this home to my family, and I definitely don't want to end up dying as a result of me having this false notion that this vaccine is not good." So, I've taken other shots. I might as well add this to the list and be safe.

DJJ:
How do you think COVID-19 changed cosmetology or barbering?

Al:
I see a future where, if the barber is dedicated and he's true to the craft, I see this industry thriving. Although we have different variations of it, you're going to have your mobile barbers. You're going to have the ones who cutting at the home. You're going to have the ones who still want to be in the shop.

Now I go back to the days before I was licensed, when I was what we called the bootleg barber. It was in the house, in the kitchen, on the back porch, in the patio, wherever you were . . . wherever you could find to cut someone's hair. And you would even go mobile then. I think once I got licensed and once, I knew my worth, it was easier for me to be in a brick-and-mortar place because the clients were coming to me, as opposed to me going to the client. For me, and for a lot of the gentlemen that I know that have been doing this a long time, that's still the best scenario. You know, you take a lot of risks when you have clients coming to your house.

You know, you take a lot of risks when you're in a mobile spot. And anybody can just run up on you. You know, that's the thing. So, the brick-and-mortar is still the most viable situation for a barber. And you still have that sense of respect as a professional, you know. You're not just barbering being reduced to just a side hustle. You know, it legitimizes you as an individual and as a businessman. And I think that's the way it was, has been in the past. Your barbershops have always been admired in the community. And that's been a place where a Black man . . . I shouldn't say a Black man, but that's been a place where a man can come in and still be someone special to his peers.

He can let his hair down and be himself and not have to put up the facade that he may have at work. You know what I'm saying? Or if he did, he doesn't have to be that strong man at the house in this moment. He can just be one of the fellas and relax. So, I think that's one of the most important aspects of the barbershop that'll never die.

DJJ:

For the most part, we're looking at COVID-19 through the rearview mirror. Reflecting on all that has happened, how has your life been impacted or changed by the COVID-19 pandemic?

Al:

I think my life has been altered and changed for the most part in realizing just how short life is, just how precious life is, and just how soon it can be taken away from us. We've heard about a lot of people who were one day healthy and the next day on a ventilator and the next day gone, never came back from that. And one of my biggest fears, or one of my biggest concerns with that, we spend so much time behind the chair, ministering to our clients, helping other people, that we give of ourselves so much and we don't take time for ourselves.

And a lot of the guys that I talk to in the industry, we started saying that, hey, we don't want that to be the thing that defines us. "Oh, that Al, he sure was a great barber. He sure was always there when you needed him. He sure was dependable," and all those things sound good. But then when you look back and then your family says, "Well, we didn't see him because he was always at work," you know, what quality of life was that? And so, I don't want to get caught up in that. I don't want the barbers that I know to get caught up in that.

Because a lot of us have such a great work ethic that we have to tell each other, "Hey, man, go ahead and take that trip with your family." You know, "Go ahead and get off early and take your wife out." You know, "Go ahead and spend some quality time with friends and loved ones and do more of those things that really matter other than money."

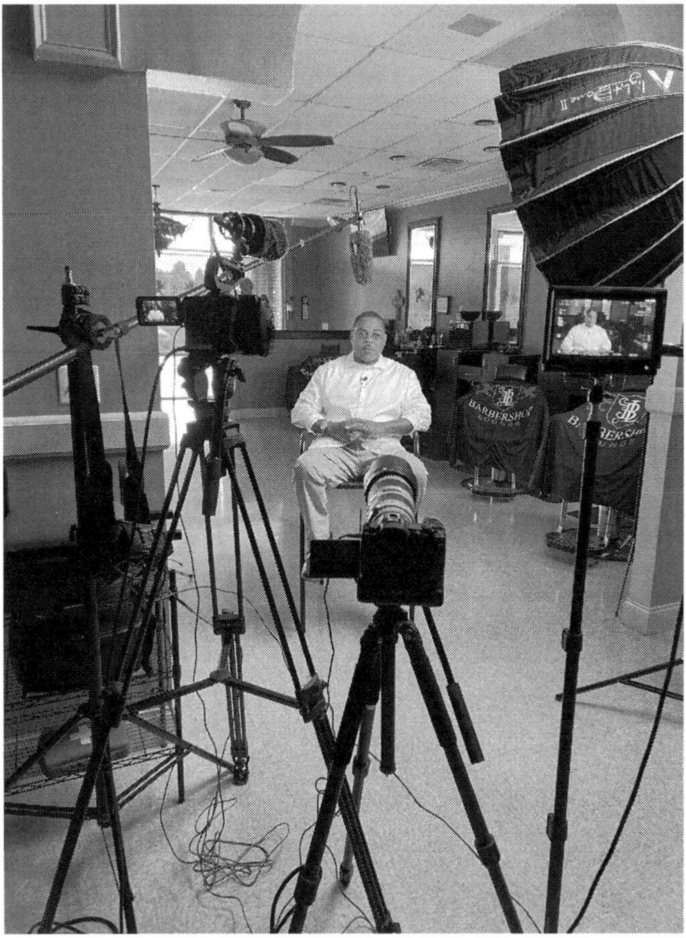

Al Harris – Owner/Operator, The Barbershop Lounge

As you can see from my interview with Al, those in the barber industry faced extreme challenges and changes to how they ran their businesses and provided services. Medical spas experienced similar challenges related to COVID-19. Yet some in the health and beauty industry, specifically medical spas, realized an increase in business. COVID-19 and the constant exposure on Zoom meetings brought a new focus on skincare.

CHAPTER 6

BEAUTY, IN THE EYE OF THE BEHOLDER

Beauty is no quality in things themselves: It exists merely in the mind which contemplates them; and each mind perceives a different beauty.

—DAVID HUME

During the pandemic, Zoom and Webex meetings brought stark reality to many people about how they really looked, as they stared at their images for hours every day. It was like looking in a mirror magnified daily. They realized the blemishes and the state of their looks and where their skin, hair, and other body parts had changed for the worse. Along with associated skin issues from masks and years of sun damage, these images on the ubiquitous 2 x 2 Zoom across the world raised alarms as many didn't like how they looked. Seeing ourselves on Zoom during the pandemic was a shock that triggered many visceral reactions. When Americans were forced to sit for hours looking at themselves during work meetings, social events, conferences, family gatherings, church meetings, and even dating, many were inclined to seek solutions to improve their skin and move away from heavy makeup and products that were not great for the skin. Organizations like SkinBody were sought after to improve looks and skin health while trends leaned toward a more natural appearance, which revitalized overall looks. Dr. Michelle De Souza, a plastic surgeon for the University of Kansas Health System, noted, "It's a Zoom thing. The camera is not flattering, and with mask wearing all the attention goes to the forehead and the eyes." Potential patients inquire about plastic surgery, but some opt for other, minimally invasive treatments — "Botox, soft tissue fillers, chemical peels, laser hair removal, and intense pulsed light treatment, a skin treatment that works similarly to laser therapy."[17]

Award-winning nurse Era Mae Ferron of The Writing Era notes that as time goes by, the face ages. Therefore, the cosmetic industry is booming. "In 2020, $16.7 billion was spent on cosmetic procedures in the United States."[18]

The modern-looking, open, and airy interior design of SkinBody creates a very inviting environment. It was a perfect place to sit down with Ms. Tomi Beckemeyer, Owner of SkinBody Clinic, and discuss COVID-19 and the health and beauty industry.

DJJ:
What were your initial thoughts when businesses started closing and COVID-19 was called a global pandemic?

Tomi:
To be honest, I thought it was a lot of hype and it wasn't real. I thought there was no way we were going to be in a pandemic in this day and time.

We pretty much all felt the same way. There was only one here that was getting a little scared about it, but I . . . most of us thought, "Oh, this'll be over in a few weeks. This is crazy. It's just a lot of hype. They're not going to close businesses. This is America." So, we did not believe that this was going to turn

17 Don't like how you look on zoom? more people are asking plastic ... (n.d.). Retrieved March 31, 2023, from https://www.gmtoday.com/health/don-t-like-how-you-look-on-zoom-more-people-are-asking-plastic-surgeons-to/article_9162f4b2-ee34-11ea-8364-7f4306673587.html

18 Era Mae Ferron, P. D. (2021, December 13). The top 5 minimally-invasive cosmetic procedures. The Writing Era Inc. Retrieved March 31, 2023, from https://www.thewritingera.com/blog/the-top-5-minimally-invasive-cosmetic-procedures

into what it turned into. That's for sure. We did not have a magic ball.

DJJ:
What was the uncertainty or fear experienced when COVID-19 first began, and when you were required to close your business?

Tomi:
My biggest fear was I had 18 girls working for me, and I worried about all of them. My business was fast-growing, and I was in an upward swing, and I certainly didn't want to stop that. I did not believe that they would actually close our businesses. And when they did, I did get scared. I still had to pay rent. I had laser payments. Nothing stopped for me, except the supplies and some of the payroll.

DJJ:
Wow! And I'm sure their fear started to grow as things became worse.
Tomi:
Yes, I helped them get unemployment, each and every one of them. And one . . . I had hired a new manager and she wanted to continue working, so I let her.

DJJ:
For spas, massage therapists, and other wellness professionals, the coronavirus outbreak impacted their business in several ways, but how did you protect and deal with a) reduced business, b) disruption in the supply chain, and c) health risks?

Tomi:
For the reduced business, as I said, I had one manager, a new manager that wanted to continue working. So, I let her work. She was by herself, and she took phone calls for skincare, and we were doing little Facebook Live things on some of the skincare, so that they knew we were open and had them. And she would do curbside delivery, or she would ship it to them. So, we had some income coming in, doing that. The supply chain, I was lucky. One of my client's husband was an importer, and I bought cases of gloves and anesthetic wipes because those were so hard to get. So, I bought cases and cases of those. I just finished going through them about six months ago. So, if you weren't a hospital, you couldn't get gloves for a little while. And with what we do, we have to wear gloves.

As far as the health risk. Well, of course when we reopened, we did the temperature checks. We had the six-foot spacing on the floors. We required that our clients wear masks; we wore masks. Because our business relies heavily on sanitation anyway, we didn't have to add any extra sanitation. We were already doing that.

DJJ:
That's really good. So, you were kind of ahead of the game.

Tomi:
That's actually what I told the mayor when we were trying to get reopened. They were trying to make us stage three, which would've kept us closed about three months. And they were opening for hairdressers, because they banded together, on stage two. So, a bunch of us medical spas got together, and we talked to the mayor and explained to him how really clean and healthy our environment was and talked him into letting us open in stage two. So, we got an extra four weeks.

DJJ:
Tell me the day-to-day processes, the heightened PPE, and everything that went on.

Tomi:
Some days were comical. We actually had code enforcement called on us a couple of times. They came in and said we were fine. I think that was either competition or angry clients or whatever. There were clients that didn't want to wear their masks and they would take them off, and we'd have to go over and tell them, "You have to put your mask back on" to make everybody else feel safe.

We had people walk out because of it. They did not want to wear their masks. And one time one of my girls lifted her mask to answer the phone, and a client took a picture of it and posted it on Instagram that we weren't wearing masks inside. I had to go beg her to take it off of Instagram, because she was just talking on the phone. She just lifted it to talk on the phone. So, there were people who were, yes, they were heightened in sensitivity. There was heightened sensitivity over all of the requirements.

DJJ:
What extra things did you have to do within the shop, other than masks, to really meet the standards or requirements for just keeping people safe?

Tomi:
We were trying to monitor how many people we had in at a time. A building the size of ours, I think we were limited to 30 by code enforcement. And that's one of the times code enforcement came in because they were counting the people that were in there. And we were within the rules, and that's all I can really think of.

DJJ:
Did the mask mandate change what makeup was worn and or how much was worn?

Tomi:
Absolutely. No lipstick anymore. Nobody was wearing lipstick. They definitely weren't wearing makeup because it would rub off on the masks. And so that, I'm sure, led to, and I didn't even think about that until we started talking this out. I'm sure that led to a lot of people got tired of wearing makeup, and so they just didn't want to go back. They want to get their skin looking good, so they didn't have to go back to wearing makeup.

I mean, it was just, for everybody, it's uncomfortable with those masks all day long, and I forgot talking about the masks and makeup. People were not wearing makeup when they were wearing those masks. You really couldn't because it was all going to rub off onto your mask. I think that's another reason why the makeup just started going down after the whole COVID thing, and good skin started going up.

DJJ:
Do you think people will ever return to wearing a lot of makeup, or has that ship sailed?

Tomi:
I think it's going to trend toward no makeup. I think that's the trend that it keeps going.

DJJ:
So, Tomi, tell me about the demographics of who you serve and how that was impacted during COVID-19. I know you see baby boomers, Gen Z, Gen X, etc. Tell me about that.

Tomi:
Prior to 2019, probably the major, our major client base was 40 and above. But now people start coming in their 20s. They want fuller lips; they want better skin. They want to preserve what they've got. They're even doing Botox in their 20s. And these are people that, this is a generation that's grown up not caring if they spend money on themselves, a more self-absorbed, I want to say. They do what they want to do. And if that means maybe they can't pay rent, they don't care; they're going to get their beauty treatments.

DJJ:
And do you think that relates to just a different health perspective overall—healthy being—healthy body?

Tomi:
Yes, I think so. I do think this generation is trying to save our planet too. They're more concerned, and health is a concern for them.

DJJ:
Tomi, I know the vaccine has a lot of political undertones and overtones. So, what did you experience, and what made you change your mind about it?

Tomi:
Well, I did actually think it might be political for a while. I hate to admit that, but it just didn't seem possible that this was really happening. Then an uncle of mine died, my favorite uncle, and most of the family didn't go to the funeral. He was a very popular man, and his funeral was very small, so I felt like I had to go to the cousin's house to pay my respects after the funeral, and three of us ended up with COVID. That's how I got it the first time.

Well, I grew up during the polio vaccination period, so I was ready to get vaxxed. I'm fine with vaccinations, but there are a lot of people that are not. At least half of my staff did want to get vaccinated, and a few did not. They would come to me and say, "Well, I don't want to work around her if she's not getting vaccinated," or something like that, and I'd just say, "That's her business. We can't require her to get vaccinated. It's against the law." So even though I believed in it, I didn't require it for my employees.

DJJ:
Do you think the politics around the vaccine made people hesitant and question the science behind the vaccine?

Tomi:
I think so. I think that a lot of people wanted to blame Trump, and a lot of people wanted to not blame Trump. I mean, it became political, whether it was supposed to or not. You couldn't help but start wondering until it hit you close, I believe, that it just didn't seem possible that this could happen in America. Business runs America.

DJJ:
Do you think we're better prepared for the next pandemic or have taken the right measures to prevent the next pandemic?

Tomi:
I certainly hope so. I do keep a stronger checking account now, if anything were to happen, because I did come close to running out of money during that closing time, and thank God, we came back strong because it all settled out before the end of the year. But I know many people who lost their businesses, restaurants. I know people in the entertainment industry that had to go get jobs, menial jobs that they didn't want to have to get, because

they had no income coming in. It affected a lot of people very badly. When you see that, that's when you realize how real it is.

DJJ:
COVID-19 forced business to adapt quickly. How did you leverage e–commerce technology, digital customer acquisition, online ordering, and delivery/logistics infrastructure in order to remain competitive?

Tomi:
We had someone here taking skincare orders, so we continued to order skincare. We did Zoom webinars. I'm not comfortable doing this and it wasn't great, but my clients were so engaged, I did "30 Tips and Tricks in 30 Days" on Instagram. So, I went on Instagram every day and talked about what they could do at home. And it kept our clients engaged, so that when we reopened after being closed for eight weeks, that first week we had two record-breaking days. So, people were clamoring to get back in.

DJJ:
During the Zoom experience, did clients stay engaged through Zoom?

Tomi:
Yes. The Zoom meetings weren't as heavily attended as we would've liked to, but they stayed recorded, and so people could go to them later. And we were mostly talking about things that they could do at home if they purchased these few products. So, it kept us alive.

DJJ:
During this time, you had to pivot from standard processes and make a number of adjustments. Tell me about how you were able to keep the business running and meet payroll.

Tomi:
Well, I had three people that were salaried: a nurse practitioner, my CFO, and my office manager, so I continued to pay them. The front desk people had no problem at all getting unemployment. Excuse me. The 1099 people did, and so we helped them get their unemployment. And I let it be known if anybody needed it for their home life, that I would loan them the money to get through. And nobody ever came to me for a loan.

It was starting to get scary. It was starting to get scary. As I mentioned, I still had to pay rent. I had a lot of laser equipment payments that had to be paid. Nobody gave me a break on any of that. It was just lucky that we had enough in the bank to cover all that. And then once again, as soon as we opened, they were beating the doors down, so we started production right up and got caught up before the end of the year.

DJJ:
With the government loans that were out there, was any of that able to come to your assistance?

Tomi:
I did. I took a small loan, and the PPP helped with the people that I was continuing to pay. I did get that covered. I took out, I think, $150,000 on the Disaster Relief Fund, wasn't it called? And that was a 30-year loan, so I'm not really worried about it. It did help.

DJJ:
How did COVID-19 affect your health and that of your staff?

Tomi:
We all got it. It came in three different waves, but all except one of the 18 employees had COVID that first year. And it came in three different waves. So, like a third of my staff was out one month, a third of my staff was out another month, and a third of my staff was out another month. So, we managed, but we all got it. Nobody had any serious aftereffects or anything like that, but we all got COVID.

DJJ:
Did the severity of it vary?

Tomi:
It did, but my girls are mostly healthy. There were no underlying illnesses that caused any long-term effects, except the brain fog, but we all experienced that.

DJJ:
So, tell me about that brain fog. What was that like?

Tomi:
It lasted about six months after COVID, and I just had COVID two months ago, so I'm back in that, and it's just . . . You'll be talking and words will not come to you that you were about to say. It's kind of funny, but we just all forgave each other and worked a little harder to try to communicate.

DJJ:
Did you experience a lot of fatigue or anything like that?

Tomi:
Definitely fatigue, especially the first time.

DJJ:
Do you think COVID-19 affected families—positively or negatively? Or did it bring families together and create some linkages that weren't there before?

Tomi:
Well, absolutely. I think it made whatever you were going through more extreme. If you had a happy home, it became an even closer, happier home because you were together all the time. If you didn't have a happy home, I think it heightened that. I know there were a lot of divorces during that time. I was one of them. I got a COVID divorce.

DJJ:
Did you ever think this would happen in these modern times or even in the US?

Tomi:
Absolutely not. Absolutely not. And even while it was going on, I was sure it was going to be over very soon.

DJJ:
Most of your clients are probably on a regular schedule, so were clients shocked when things shut down and closed the way they did?

Tomi:
Absolutely. And people like doing . . . Laser hair removal is a good example. If you stop your laser hair removal before you're completed, or if you go off schedule by more than a week or two, you have to start over. So, we had to do a lot of free laser hair removals when we started back to get people back on track. And yes, people were missing their regular monthly appointments. Just like they were missing their nail appointments and their

hair appointments. So yeah, everybody was a little uglier sitting at home.

DJJ:
Did any of your people work remotely in terms of their location in the city? Are all your staff located in the city?

Tomi:
My CFO still works remotely and giving her an office was taking up space that I could have another treatment room, so having her work remotely was really good, and she's continued to work remotely even now. Works for her, it works for us. I think that happened in a lot of businesses. A lot of people came home, and they realized they could do just as good a job from their home.

DJJ:
Is there a "new normal" for this business industry? Or have things relaxed and we're back to pre-COVID-19?

Tomi:
I think the new normal is that people are never going to give this up. I think our industry got stronger because of this, and people are not going to give this up now.

DJJ:
So, people are really more so focused on self-care?

Tomi:
They really are. They really are.

DJJ:
Self-care isn't a new topic or trend, but for most, it fell to the bottom of the priority list. Do you think there has been

a shift in priority and people are realizing the importance of focusing on health and wellness?

Tomi:
Absolutely, and it's called Zoom dysmorphia. People are watching themselves on Zoom—and Zoom meetings are still going on—and they're picking themselves apart. I saw something on TV the other day where they said, "Even if you try to focus on other people in those Zoom meetings, your focus is going to go right back on yourself." So, they were taking little things about themselves and picking them apart and coming in and wanting us to fix it. And because they weren't going into the office as regularly, they were able to have downtime. So, we were doing more serious things that have downtime. And that has continued, that hasn't stopped—it's still that way. We're still selling way more energy-based treatments or get a skin peel for four or five days now than we did before, which is good for us.

DJJ:
So that whole Zoom virtual environment was almost kind of a wake-up call for people looking at themselves?

Tomi:
Absolutely.

DJJ:
The beauty industry suffered a modest decline in the 2008 great recession crisis. Do you think "Beauty" is a recession-resilient category?

Tomi:
I think it is now. And this is my opinion. In 2008 I wasn't a business owner, but I was a 1099 service provider, so my production was what I lived off of. And I lost 60 percent of

my business in 2008 because people lost their jobs; they were moving away to get better jobs. I suffered more of a downturn in 2008 than we did in 2020.

Because I think that was pre-Kardashian. And as crazy as those Kardashians are, they're good for our business.

DJJ:
Do you think there's a mindset shift now between 2008 and where we are today?

Tomi:
There definitely is. I've been in this business since 1999, and it's grown every year since then, as in priority and what people are willing to do. They're willing to do just about anything now to look better. They really are. And they are spending a lot more money.

DJJ:
Makeup and fragrances are likely to suffer worse today due to limited social interactions, but do you think skincare is better positioned due to alignment with health and overall wellness?

Tomi:
Absolutely. Our makeup business completely dried up because we couldn't use testers on people. And they still are uneasy about it. I don't even have testers out anymore. But what has happened in the last few years is people come in and the first thing they say is, "I want my skin to look good without makeup." So, they're more concerned with the way their skin looks now than cover it with makeup, and that's awesome for everybody.

DJJ:
Many say we're looking at COVID-19 through the rearview mirror. Reflecting on all that has happened, how has your life been impacted or changed by the COVID-19 pandemic?

Tomi:
Well, personally it was changed by having it three times. But business-wise, I think COVID was a boost for us. And that may sound a little crazy, but we ended up with a very good year. 2020 turned out to be a very good year, even though we were closed for eight weeks. And it just keeps getting better. There's been a slight decline in the past few months because of the perceived recession, whether there's one going on or not, in Memphis. But I think Nashville is a recession-proof market. I'm really looking forward to opening there.

DJJ:
On a positive note—SkinBody was able to weather the storm and come out on the other side very well. You have been able to relocate and expand the footprint of your business and even have a presence in Nashville, TN now. How does the future look for SkinBody, and are you optimistic about the future?

Tomi:
I am. People tell me I'm crazy to be doing this much expansion at this time, but I'm not afraid. I think the beauty industry is still going to continue to grow. Technology is huge in our industry right now, and we keep up with the technology. I don't even want to get into how much I spend on lasers and energy devices just to keep up, but it's worth it. That's what keeps us very competitive.

My Nashville rep, almost every rep that I have is based out of Nashville, and my Nashville reps have been asking me to open a spot in Nashville for years now. And now that I finally have, I'm getting so much help from all of them. Training for my staff up there, just deals on equipment. They're all reaching out and helping me. And with all of that and just the way Nashville is growing, I just think I'm crazy not to do it.

Tomi Beckemeyer, Owner/SkinBody Memphis/Nashville

In one sense dealing with skincare and improving one's outward experience can be very important and a top priority. These things are contributing factors to self-assurance, confidence, and overall well-being. But some in our society are invisible, and as you will see in my next interview, their life experiences provide a drastically different perspective.

Chapter 7

THE INVISIBLE VICTIMS

I am an invisible man. I am a man of substance, of flesh and bone, fiber, and liquids—and I might even be said to possess a mind. I am invisible, understand, simply because people refuse to see me.

—Ralph Ellison

For whatever reason, there are those in our society who have fallen on hard times resulting in homelessness. This state of homelessness is one of the most foreboding and horrible existences a citizen can face. Whether it was substance abuse, loss of a job, spousal abuse, mental illness, or some other type of illness, something rendered the individual financially impaired to the point that they were unable to afford housing. The homeless tend to drift into a form of "sub-existence" where they become invisible to everyday society. Many might attribute the conditions of these individuals to bad decisions. But a fatal change in anyone's circumstances could potentially render them homeless—despite the best pedigree, connections, financial status, or prominence. So, it is wise not to be too critical of the condition of these, our fellow citizens, who might not have the safety net or support structure that could protect them from this predicament.

Despite the extraordinarily detailed statistics that examine the ages, races, and comorbidities of the nation's more than one million COVID deaths, no one seems to have any idea how many homeless people died due to the pandemic. For the most part, homeless individuals are not included in these numbers.

And the accounting of these deaths, like homeless people themselves, seems to have slipped through the cracks.[19]

Moreover, many children find themselves in this condition through no fault of their own. I have watched them brave the perils of life with their parents, usually a mother, who is trying to care for them while being homeless.

One cold evening while touring a homeless shelter, I witnessed a homeless mother walking down the street with her young son and daughter in tow while dressed in minimal clothing. The temperature was approaching 38 degrees Fahrenheit. I don't know where they were going, but they seemed to be on a mission as they walked away from the shelter.

I spoke with Mr. Kelcey Johnson, Executive Director at the Hospitality Hub in Memphis, Tennessee. The Hospitality Hub has been a trusted adviser and friend to thousands of unhoused people since 2007. He shared how COVID-19 affected homelessness in Memphis and the role Hospitality Hub played during the pandemic.

DJJ:
Tell us a little about the Hospitality Hub and services offered.

Kelcey:
All right. Well, my name is Kelcey Johnson. I'm Executive Director here at the Hospitality Hub, the premier resource agency serving homeless people in Memphis and Shelby County. And we just do everything we can to help people to exit homelessness. We have lots of services, but the end goal is always to see a person permanently exit homelessness, get into permanent supportive housing, get into a place that's safe

19 McFarling, U. L. (2021, March 10). The uncounted: People who are homeless are invisible victims of covid-19. STAT. Retrieved March 31, 2023, from https://www.statnews.com/2021/03/11/the-uncounted-people-who-are-homeless-are-invisible-victims-of-covid-19/

and something of their choosing. We preach to each other and everybody who will listen that every person has the right to self-determination. And so as we help a person look for somewhere to live, get a job, get income, it's never the approach where we are lords and masters, but we are students of this thing that we're going through, and we're trying to learn who you are, what got you homeless, what's keeping you homeless, wrap you up in the supports you need to help you exit homelessness.

DJJ:
Explain the differences in homelessness (i.e., sheltered, non-sheltered, encampments, etc.) and the demographics of each (if any), and which community does the Hospitality Hub serve?

Kelcey:
Well, the Hospitality Hub serves every one of those groups because we have programs that are designed to touch those people. For instance, people who are living in tent encampments and under bridges and underpasses, overpasses, we have an outreach team that goes out in Jeeps and seeks those people out. If a person calls and says, "Hey, I've got somebody sleeping in my storage shed," we have a team of people that'll go and meet with that person and take them an Egg McMuffin and some coffee and try to build rapport with that person and see if they're willing to come in and get some help. And then of course, you have those people who become homeless and the first thing they do is go try to find a shelter. Those people will ultimately get directed to us because we are the agency that's going to help them get out of homelessness, get some income, get IDs, birth certificates, all those things. They help you get your citizenship back.

Behind me, I have a mail room where over 700 people use this as their mailing address because without an address, you can't apply for food stamps, you can't apply for a job, you can't apply for disability. It's all these important things that we provide. And so, all of those agencies, all of those types of people who are experiencing the various types of homelessness, ultimately end up here. People who are getting out of the military, people who are getting out of prison and jail, this is the place that those exit counselors are going to direct them.

DJJ:
I'm certain there are several personal life events that cause homelessness, but are there any "common thread" incidents that contribute to homelessness?

Kelcey:
One of the things I've learned to believe is that a common thread is a person who wasn't paid attention to when they were younger. And sometimes a parent doesn't have time to give you the attention that my parents gave me, to give me the correction that my parents gave me, to give me the training to make me a capable, productive person. And so, one of the fastest-growing groups of homeless people right now is those people who are aging out of foster care, that 18 to 24 group. And as I'm sure y'all know, there's a pipeline between foster care and the prison system. And we have just recently started a program to combat that because we're seeing more and more young people become homeless. When a woman is experiencing domestic violence and makes that decision or musters up the courage to get out of that situation, we are a place that they can land.

And we have partners that have those places for them to land and get the resources, get the income, get the things they need to exit homelessness. The Volunteer State has a lot of people getting out of the military with PTSD and other types of traumas they experience while they were in the military. And so, we are a place that veterans can come. And I've been a veteran's advocate here now for about 12 years. And I've been a veteran myself, my son, my brothers, and so I've spent a lot of years learning what veterans are going to qualify for, what benefits they do, how to help them get their disability payments going, that kind of thing. And so, we're a place for that.

While researching the impact of COVID-19 on the homeless, getting consistent information was very challenging for homeless service partners. There was "expressed frustration over a lack of federal guidance, especially in the early days of the pandemic. In the beginning, there appear to not have been clear guidelines or protocols. So, organizations were constantly watching their local government web pages, trying to reach out to those resources—using the information from the CDC, different webinars, and seminars".[20]

DJJ:

How did you manage communication and information to stay informed?

Kelcey:

Well, one of the things we did was we initiated communication with the city. There's a doctor here in town who's also a city councilperson; we were on the phone with him every day. He came to our pop-up shelter because what happened with us is we opened a shelter the day the city and the county shut down. I sent all my volunteers home, I sent 29 interns back to their hometowns, 14 of my employees went home, and myself and five people opened a pop-up shelter and ran the Hospitality Hub with masks and fear. And I raised their salaries and paid

---

20 Rodriguez, N. M., Lahey, A. M., MacNeill, J. J., Martinez, R. G., Teo, N. E., & Ruiz, Y. (2021, September 10). Homelessness during COVID-19: Challenges, responses, and lessons learned from homeless service providers in Tippecanoe County, Indiana. BMC public health. Retrieved March 31, 2023, from https://www.ncbi.nlm.nih.gov/pmc/articles/PMC8432956/

them an extra $250 cash every Friday because they agreed to stay and work with us. And we were scared. We didn't know what was going to happen. And there were so many people dying in New York City and other bigger cities, and we figured it would happen to us in this city.

And of course, I lost two of my volunteers—died from COVID on the same day. And so, it was just a tough time for us. But we initiated communication, and we found a hotelier who agreed to allow us to move these 26 women into his hotel. We took over the whole third floor of a hotel, and we asked the city if they would pay for it and they agreed. And after about two weeks of us doing that, they asked us if we would help manage a bigger property where they could thin out the men's shelters. Because the men's shelter next door at that time could hold 325 people, and he was trying to space people out. Because before the pandemic, they were sleeping 18 inches apart, and so when they needed to go to six feet apart, and so we said we can do nine congregate shelters in hotels.

And the city worked with us to get money to fund it. And we moved 187 people, I think, into the Travelodge in Whitehaven. And I sent two of my case managers down. One of the things I had to do was I got on the phone and called some of my former interns and some bartenders and my son and my daughter and hired them on staff to staff these different places that we were working. And that's how we responded, and we were communicating with those agencies that had not shut down. The reason we had to open a pop-up shelter was because the best women's shelter in town had shut its doors and left 26 women on the street. And that next night, we had them in the basement of a church with 26 beds and meals being delivered three times a day, all of that.

DJJ:
How did COVID-19 affect the homeless population and its service providers? In general, and then your organization specifically.

Kelcey:
One of the first things that was noticeable was more people were hungry because volunteers typically run the feeding programs, and who has time to volunteer? Senior citizens and retired folks. And they were the most vulnerable to COVID. So, a lot of the feeding programs completely shut down. So, people on the street didn't have anything to eat. And if you leave the shelter in the morning, typically you could depend on somebody to pull up in the park, to pull up somewhere and serve food. That wasn't going on at all. There was nowhere to eat. And so, us and our partners were able to respond to that need. And then of course, as I said, our favorite women's shelter had shut down. And we had a program at that time called Work Local Women. And my daughter started that program, and it's a program where every Saturday morning, every Sunday morning, they would empty all the trash cans on Main Street.

And so, they were able to make $50 on a Saturday, $50 on a Sunday; it takes them about an hour and a half to two hours to do the job. Well, those women were mostly all sleeping at that shelter. And when that shelter shut down, these are women we had a relationship with. We knew them. We saw them all the time. And they came to us and said, "We don't have anywhere to go because there's no women's shelter." And so that was the main thing that happened to us. And then we went to that hotel, and then from there we were able to buy a building in midtown that we called the Original Hub Hotel. And to date, that program has had about 198 women to come to pass through its door.

Research also indicates that "pandemic-related lockdown measures caused a sudden disruption in access to public spaces, restrooms, and other resources that people experiencing homelessness typically rely on to meet basic needs. There were existing ordinances or policies that restricted the time shelters could be open that would have enabled people to rest in place and potentially limit exposure and transmission."[21]

DJJ:
Do you think federal and state policy-level changes and responses such as stay-at-home orders were not appropriately aligned with the context and realities faced by homeless populations?

Kelcey:
Well, with my experience, I think we were uniquely poised to be able to receive funds and to ask for funds. And much of the money that came into our municipality, we were able to grab ahold of it because we started programs not knowing if we were going to be able to pay for them. We had donors who would give us sizable checks to get started, and then as the city saw the success of those things, that federal money got funneled toward us. And so, I can't criticize how it went down because, once again, there was a lot of fear and a lot of mystery surrounding this disease that was killing so many people. But I'm really proud and I'm happy about the way that money came into this town, and I think it saved a lot of lives.

---

21 Rodriguez, N. M., Lahey, A. M., MacNeill, J. J., Martinez, R. G., Teo, N. E., & Ruiz, Y. (2021, September 10). Homelessness during COVID-19: Challenges, responses, and lessons learned from homeless service providers in Tippecanoe County, Indiana. BMC public health. Retrieved March 31, 2023, from https://www.ncbi.nlm.nih.gov/pmc/articles/PMC8432956/

DJJ:
What was a typical day like at Hospitality Hub? How did your day-to-day operations change, and how did similar ordinances affect your service?

Kelcey:
Well, we went from being a resource agency that was open from about eight in the morning to two in the afternoon to being a 24-hour operation with a third of the staff. No interns, no volunteers, and some of my employees working 120 hours a week, myself working a hundred to 115 hours a week, taking five or six hours off on Sunday because we just didn't have enough people and the work was 24 hours a day. And in addition to that, we also kept at the resource agency—which we shuttered those doors because it wasn't safe to be there—we had people who were using that building for their lockers. They had their clothes and work boots and stuff like that, so we'd open the doors for them to come, and the mail was still running, so people were still coming to get food stamps and just all the different types of mail that you need. So, we'd open the doors every day for that. So, we were working day and night with just a handful of people.

DJJ:
How might physical distancing and isolation interventions negatively affect individuals experiencing homelessness?

Kelcey:
It [*laughs*] looks like herding cats. The thing is that, if you are a person who has been experiencing homelessness for any given amount of time, you never eat alone, you're always standing in line, you share what you have. If I've got a sandwich, you've got a sandwich because I'm going to give you a bite of my sandwich. The other thing that we wrestled with, wrestled with, wrestled

with was trying to get people to stop sharing their cigarettes with each other. And people wouldn't listen to that. And the other thing is, if someone's smoking and thumps the butt on the ground, somebody's going to pick it up and smoke it. And just trying to get people to social distance who are so used to always being in a congregation-style setting, it just never really worked. And so, we had a bunch of positive cases.

DJJ:
So that was very aggravating to them and probably caused some mental anxiety.

Kelcey:
Of course.

DJJ:
Because they're kind of communal.

Kelcey:
Right.

DJJ:
There are a number of overlapping factors, such as mental illness, substance use, and the simple distrust of service providers, that may have contributed substantially to challenges encountered by individuals in engaging with pandemic-specific protocols. What special challenges did your organization experience in the management of people who were suspected of having or confirmed to have COVID-19?

Kelcey:
That was a tough one, especially having so many people staying in the hotels. People who had tested positive for COVID, we

wanted them to stay in their rooms and, "Let us bring your food to you. When you're through, put your plate outside the door." And some people just refused to do that. And then, in this community there are a lot of people who smoke cigarettes. And so you got somebody who's COVID positive and they're in a room, a no smoking room, one of two things is going to happen. "I'm going to smoke in this room, or you going to let me out of this room." So that was one of the big, big, big, big challenges for us is trying to get people to shelter in place. And so, one of the things that happened a little later, still in the heat of the pandemic, was we had a relationship with the health department in Shelby County, and they opened a hotel just for homeless people who had tested positive for COVID.

And each homeless person who tested positive for COVID, we could just fill out a piece of paper, scan it, email it in, and within a couple of hours an ambulance or a van would come and pick that person up from our location and drive them to the hotel. They would be in a hotel room by themselves. It was out in Lakeland. And they had a Cracker Barrel menu in the room, and they could order one entrée off the Cracker Barrel menu three times a day, and someone would deliver it to their room. And even with that, some people after a couple of days in that hotel said, "I'm not staying here. It's too far out. These aren't my people. I don't even believe I got it." That kind of thing.

And one of the things we did was, we got a contract with UT Health Science Center, and we became a testing location. And so, we were doing COVID testing every day. My staff, to stay on my staff, you had to be vaccinated, number one. And if you worked for us, you had to be tested every week. I think we were doing it every Wednesday. And if you came in contact with somebody who tested positive for COVID, you need to get tested again. If your husband or wife tested positive for COVID, you stay home for four days, and then the four days you come and get tested. So, we were really careful about that kind of thing. It didn't stop us from getting COVID. I've had it three times. Hospitalized twice. Double pneumonia twice.

DJJ:
Are you still suffering with long-term effects, and what are they?

Kelcey:
Absolutely long-term effects. I'm a piece of junk now. I used to be great [*laughs*]. My lung capacity is not what it should be. I used to be able to ride my bike 16 miles, and I live a mile from here. It's hard for me to ride my bike over here. Climbing stairs, I get winded. My breathing is much louder now.

DJJ:
How long were you hospitalized?

Kelcey:
The first time, just overnight. The second time, four days. They were giving me breathing treatments six, seven times a day.

DJJ:
Are you doing anything now for breathing treatment?

Kelcey:
No.

DJJ:
Is there nothing you're able to do now to increase your lung capacity?

Kelcey:
I probably could start working out. I don't know. It's just hard to get going, really.

DJJ:
I'm guessing people experiencing homelessness typically find it difficult to follow health directives such as physical distancing, isolation, and quarantine because of shelter conditions and other challenges. What are some things you did during the height of the pandemic to bridge the gap in trying to make your facility safe and assist those experiencing homelessness?

Kelcey:
Really just mask mandates, daily testing. We're still a testing facility. We do rapids and lab tests here now. So, if we're putting you on a bus somewhere out of town, we're going to give you a COVID test. If you are going to a treatment facility or going to a couple of different shelters, they want a negative COVID test less than three days old from us. And we are the agency that does that. We are the agency that does that for the city of Memphis. We're a vaccination site. We had big vaccination events; we had several of them. And one of the things, our Work Local Program, it's a program where, like I said, they are combating blight, and so they get in vans, ride out, and touch different places that have been called into the city that are problematic with trash, blight, tires, couches, these types of things. And everybody wants to get on Work Local.

You can make 50 bucks, and you don't have to work but a short period of time. Really, it's easy work. And so, what I did was I said, "Nobody can go and Work Local if they're not vaccinated." And so that very first vaccination event, after I made that a rule, I think we had 90 people get vaccinated that one event. And so, as time went on, everybody who wanted to do Work Local got vaccinated. We had a few people who were staunch anti-vaxxers and just said, "Well, I guess I won't be going to work because I'm not getting vaccinated." But those people were in the vast minority.

DJJ:
What approach or strategies did the Hospitality Hub implement to gain the confidence of people seeking service?

Kelcey:
We've been around a while, and we're famous for being a place that homeless people are going to get treated with respect. We know your name, I know your mama, where you're from, and all that type of thing. And so, in the midst of this, our agency is a place that homeless people came expecting to hear the truth about what was going on and "How can you help me? What's going to happen next?" I remember telling clients, "Look, it's going to be two weeks max. It's going to be over." And here we are. Here we are.

DJJ:

> Several cities and regions took measures to provide spaces for people experiencing homelessness (i.e., partnerships with motels/hotels especially since vacancies were high), to ensure physical distancing, isolation, or quarantine. Some of the larger cities with a high population of homelessness were able to create additional capacity to safely house people at risk while supporting the local motel/hotel and service industries.[22]

---

22 Perri, M., Dosani, N., & Hwang, S. W. (2020, June 29). Covid-19 and people experiencing homelessness: Challenges and mitigation strategies. CMAJ. Retrieved April 14, 2023, from https://www.cmaj.ca/content/192/26/E716

Were there any efforts on this scale required in the Mid-South area?

Kelcey:
Right, absolutely. Well, we were the agency that spearheaded that effort here in this city. And we started really with our own money by first, the pop-up shelter in the church and moving them to a hotel here—downtown. Luxury hotel, really. And the city decided to cosign with us and pick up the tab for that. And as they saw the success of it, they asked us if we could do it on a bigger scale, not just for women but for men, women, and children. And so, we got another hotel down in Whitehaven Travelodge. And I think we sent 187 people into that hotel. And that thinned out space in shelters so that they could do at least four feet of spacing, from the 18 inches that they did have with their beds.

The top 10 cities that experienced the most evictions due to COVID-19 were Phoenix, AZ; Houston, TX; Memphis, TN; Forth Wort, TX; Columbus, OH; Indianapolis, IN; Tampa, FL; Milwaukee, WI; Greenville, SC; and Richmond, VA. Memphis was ranked third. The large volume of evictions left many people unhoused as shelters were forced to reduce capacity. Interestingly, this surging number of evictions led to a federal order to temporarily halt residential evictions to prevent the spread of COVID-19.[23]

DJJ:
For many families, the economy has not rebounded, and the federal order to temporarily halt residential evictions has been lifted. What are families in this situation doing now?

---

23 The effect of covid-19 on homelessness in the US: United way. United Way NCA. (2023, March 22). Retrieved April 10, 2023, from https://unitedwaynca.org/blog/the-impact-of-the-covid-19-pandemic-on-homelessness-in-the-united-states/

Kelcey:
Well, some became homeless during that situation, or they did what we call couch surfing. You move in with a relative until you can save up some money. One of the things that we were able to do was partner with Catholic Charities in their eviction relief program, which was part of the CARES Act federal money that would help a person who, if the case had not been closed, adjudicated, then we were able to save those people if the landlord was willing to take the money. But so many times the landlord and tenant had gotten into contentious type of relationships while the moratorium was in place. And so, in those cases, the landlord would refuse to take the money, and that family or that person would end up homeless and then come here. And then we may have to put them into family shelter or individual shelter until we can find a more permanent solution for them.

DJJ:
Do you think the homeless were invisible victims of COVID-19—people who were marginalized not just in life, but also in death?

Kelcey:
That's a tough one, because in so many ways, homeless people are invisible. They don't get spoken to, nobody sings them "Happy Birthday," nobody buys them a cake. Many times, as a homeless person approaches you, you put your head up and you speed up your pace a little bit. If I'm downtown and not dressed properly, somebody might do it to me if I'm asking for directions or whatever. And so, as it relates to COVID-19, I don't know if they were thought of as invisible, because there was such a spotlight, I think, in this city, put on "What's going to happen next with this group, with that group, with this group?"

And at that time, our noses were really to the grindstone, as I told you, working over one hundred hours a week each, just to serve this community. And it seemed that some of our partners shut down and went home. Even though these are people who are serving people every day, they shut down and went home. And many of them still are not 100 percent back in the office. They're still working from home a lot and that kind of thing. And so, there were those homeless people who were left behind by those agencies. But then we had other agencies like ours who really ramped up our efforts and picked up our pace to do the best work we could do.

The thing that I can't testify to is how many homeless people I saw who died from homeless, from COVID-19. I definitely can testify to many of them testing positive for COVID. Because we were the place they got tested; we were the place that gave them somewhere to go after they tested positive. I know that we had some of our clients to die during that time. But like you said that number, it wasn't given to us that they died of COVID. I had two of my volunteers to die, and I know they died of COVID, but as far as homeless guests, I know that I had three that froze to death during the time that shelters were closing down. And so, I really don't have the answer for that question. It's a mystery to me.

DJJ:

With regard to the efforts to capture statistics about the homeless and their contracting of COVID-19, do you see efforts to carve out the numbers to determine the percentage of homeless that were affected by COVID-19? Have you seen any efforts to dive into the homeless death related to COVID-19?

Kelcey:
I have not seen anybody try to dive into that. And it's almost like anything else. If you have a parent in a nursing home and that your parent has a neighbor inside the nursing home too, if you are checking on your mom a lot and bringing personal items and that kind of thing, your mother's going to get better care than that person who's not having any visitors, no personal items, no flowers, cable not being paid for. And I think it's the same with people who are homeless. Not having people who are paying attention to them, caring about them, their number tends to not be counted. In many things, not just the COVID.

DJJ:
Homeless populations have not been part of the large conversation surrounding COVID-19 because they were never even included before the pandemic began. It was forgotten that they are members of the community who have and will continue to be affected by the virus.
Have you observed a shift in conversation (or more awareness) post-pandemic where homelessness and the inequities have become part of the larger discussion?

Kelcey:
No. No, I have not seen that. I do think that the way that we're building shelters and building facilities that are going to serve people who are poor or homeless, we're paying a lot more attention to air handling. We changed our plans in this building because of COVID, our hub studios. That non-congregate shelter was supposed to be just 10 of those, and now it's going to end up being about 40 of them in different parts of town so that people can shelter alone and don't have to share their air with someone else. I think that's a direct result of this pandemic.

DJJ:
Would you agree that people experiencing homelessness were not worrying about coronavirus? Rightfully so, they are worried about food, drinkable water, and perhaps a dry place where their children can sleep tonight.

Kelcey:
Absolutely. I would think that they were worrying about survival. And the other thing is, there's so many urban myths and our people, the communities we serve are . . . It seems like they're the first ones to latch on to these urban myths and conspiracies about, I don't know if y'all remember, but the first rumor I heard about COVID was, Black people can get it, but they won't die from it.

And so, I actually had so many homeless people tell me [*laughs*] I'm not worried about that vaccine because ain't nobody dying but White folks and them Chinese. And so, we had to say, hey man, we're the human race. If one human can die from a thing, any human can die from that same thing. And so yeah, there was a lot of those types of things. And then the vaccine has a chip in it so they can follow you around. Well, the government is giving you free food stamp, phones, and so they don't need a chip to follow you around—you got that free phone with unlimited minutes on it. And so, I spent a lot of time on this porch talking and socializing with the people who are here getting coffee and that kind of thing. So, I hear a lot of these things, and I get to debunk some of it, debate it. It's like a barbershop out there sometimes.

You have to serve it up in such a way, though, that you don't seem like the egghead specialist that knows everything. And just because a homeless person says it doesn't make it a lie or make it false. So that's what we deal with.

DJJ:
People experiencing homelessness may face a multitude of barriers to getting vaccinated. Challenges can range from inability to stay in one place for a long time to medical stigma against homelessness.

Would you also agree that people living in extreme poverty are not rushing to get vaccinated?

Kelcey:
And so, we had work incentives, cash incentives, all types of things to get people vaccinated. We had one group that came here and gave out $100 Visa gift cards to any person who got the Johnson & Johnson one-shot vaccine. And we had a line that did that. Then another time $150 Kroger gift cards if you got the vaccine. And so, all of those things were effective here. But for some people still, $100? You ain't killing me for $100.

DJJ:
Do you think COVID-19 is here to stay and a part of our lives (especially the lives of people experiencing homelessness)?

Kelcey:
Well, as I said earlier, I thought it was only going to last two weeks, and here we are. But I'm going to remain an optimist and say that I'm hoping that this is not here to stay, that it's not going to be like the flu vaccine, but people are saying that it may be a thing that maybe every couple of years you need to get revaccinated. And I'm hoping and believing that that's not true.

DJJ:

> Amid overwhelming challenges of the COVID-19 public health crisis, participants servicing people

experiencing homelessness shared important lessons learned and resilience in the process of quickly adapting their service delivery. In fact, many of the emergency measures put in place by homeless service providers created opportunities for innovative solutions to long-standing challenges faced by homeless populations that can inform better service delivery moving forward.[24]

What were the lessons learned for Hospitality Hub and the silver linings?

Kelcey:
One of the things that, I think the most valuable thing was that we strengthened our reputation in this community as people who were not going to fold up our tent and go home when things got rough. But we leaned into this horrible pandemic to continue to serve the people who needed our services the most.

And with that, we have been able to really expand our operations and fill in more gaps. One of the things we don't ever want to do is duplicate services. We don't want to do what somebody else is doing. We want to always be in communication with people who are going through this homeless situation and find out what is it that you need that you're not getting. And many times, we look to the West and see what's happening out West; places like Seattle and Portland, San Francisco, they're innovators when it comes to serving really poor people. And so, we try to bring those things here. And our Work Local program came from Albuquerque, New Mexico, and ours now is bigger than the one that we looked at when we went and looked at it.

---

24 Rodriguez, N. M., Lahey, A. M., MacNeill, J. J., Martinez, R. G., Teo, N. E., & Ruiz, Y. (2021, September 10). Homelessness during COVID-19: Challenges, responses, and lessons learned from homeless service providers in Tippecanoe County, Indiana - BMC Public Health. BioMed Central. Retrieved April 14, 2023, from https://bmcpublichealth.biomedcentral.com/articles/10.1186/s12889-021-11687-8

Yeah. Yeah. It's really been a success. And so, I think that's the silver lining in this cloud is that we got smarter, more dynamic, more innovative in our ways of serving people.

DJJ:
Is there a "new normal" because there are still concerns about personal safety, or have providers serving the homeless returned to pre-COVID-19 practices?

Kelcey:
I think that in some ways it's a new normal in that some things are going to, have gone away. We don't hug strangers as quickly. We fist-bump instead of handshake. A lot of times, if I go into a place without a mask on and everybody else has a mask on, I feel really embarrassed. And so, some of these things are going to stick with us. I think we're going to be more careful as a society and as a city.

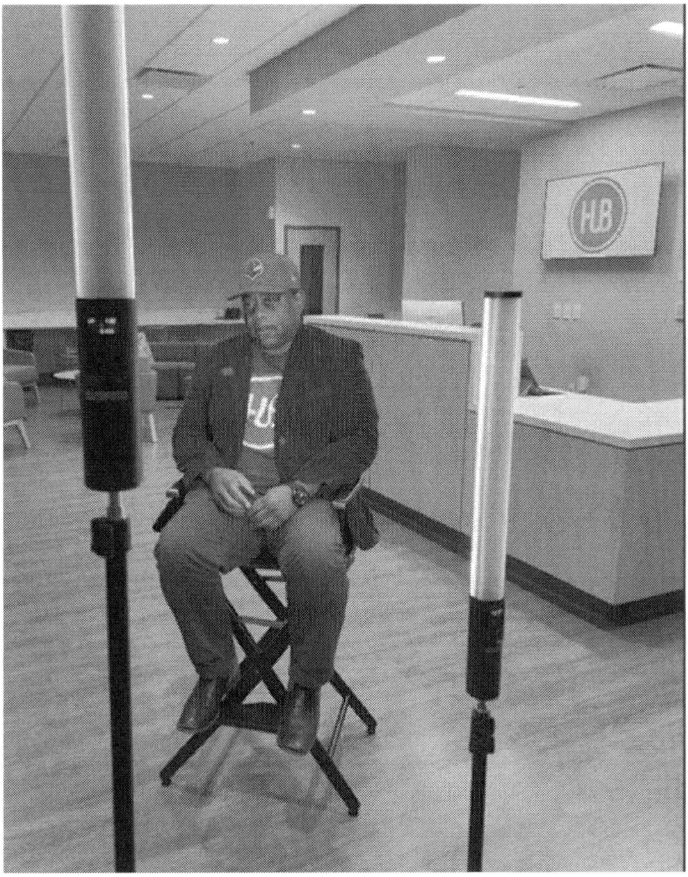

Kelcey Johnson, Executive Director, Hospitality Hub

Approximately 550,000 people are homeless each night in the USA with Black and Native Americans are overrepresented. Adults experiencing homelessness, particularly those living in congregate shelters, are at high risk of acquiring COVID infection due to environmental conditions (i.e., crowded spaces, poor ventilation). And conditions common in homeless populations (e.g., trauma, mental health disorders, cognitive impairment, intoxication) can interfere with preventive behaviors (e.g., mask wearing, social distancing) that reduce the risk of COVID transmission.[25]

The Hospitality Hub is playing a huge role in servicing those citizens among us who are experiencing homelessness. Whatever the various factors may be, the Hospitality Hub is tirelessly working to fulfill those needs. At the same time, the houses of prayer across the country are also houses of refuge for the homeless, the hungry, those in search of spiritual guidance, the abused, and those dealing with the toughest of life's circumstances. Whether churches, synagogues, mosques, or temples, they were all impacted by COVID-19, as their parishioners experienced an unprecedented disconnect when in-person worship was curtailed. My next interview examines how one church dealt with the new obstacles.

---

25 Knight, K. R., Duke, M. R., Carey, C. A., Pruss, G., Garcia, C. M., Lightfoot, M., Imbert, E., & Kushel, M. (2022, March). Covid-19 testing and vaccine acceptability among homeless-experienced adults: Qualitative data from two samples. Journal of general internal medicine. Retrieved April 10, 2023, from https://www.ncbi.nlm.nih.gov/pmc/articles/PMC8547296/

Chapter 8

EMPTY PEWS

Just as you must eat, drink, and breathe to live, you must read the Bible, pray, and be involved in a church to stay spiritually alive and vital. You never will outgrow these things.

— Greg Laurie

Many churches were shaken to their core as the reality of COVID-19 began to take hold of the world. All the government health organizations dictated churches close their doors to prevent the spread of the virus. These closures would represent an unprecedented challenge to church norms, practices, and parishioner giving. Churches changed during the pandemic. Will members and parishioners come back at pre-pandemic levels? Will a post-pandemic church resemble the pre-pandemic church? These are questions many clergy will grapple with as they look to continue spreading the gospel, albeit maybe in different forms and on a variety of platforms. A number of parishioners have changed their worship pattern and become accustomed to online services. Prior to the pandemic, the church was experiencing a decline in attendance, but this decline was exacerbated by COVID-19 closures. Recent Pew Research Center data shows Christianity in America has been declining over the last decade: "63% of Americans consider themselves Christians versus 75% a decade ago."[26] "Church

26 Smith, G. A. (2021, December 14). About three-in-ten U.S. adults are now religiously unaffiliated. Pew Research Center's Religion & Public Life Project. https://www.pewresearch.org/religion/2021/12/14/about-three-in-ten-u-s-adults-are-now-religiously-unaffiliated/

membership dropped below 50% in America during 2020 for the first time since it has been keeping data starting in 1940."[27] However, this was during the height of the pandemic, and trends show marginal improvement as many houses of worship struggle to survive. Research also shows "a steady decline in church service attendance between 2019 and 2021."[28]

Again, this raises the question, will individuals return to in-person church attendance with the rollout of vaccines and other therapies? Furthermore, we know that despite increases in online church attendance, the social connection and worship bonding are different from in-person worship. While writing and reflecting on this phenomenon, I am reminded of the following Scripture in today's pandemic context—Matthew 18:20: "For where two or three gather in my name, there am I with them" (New International Version—NIV). Clergy and their staffs are working around the clock to stem the tide of decreases, while also introducing innovative ideas to retain current members and attract a younger demographic. This younger demographic is the church of today and the church of tomorrow.

Recently I spent time with Dr. Bartholomew Orr, Pastor of the 13,000 member Brown Missionary Baptist Church located in Southaven, Mississippi. Dr. Orr talked about his insights on COVID-19 and the ongoing creative measures his church implemented to persevere.

DJJ:
Tell us about Brown Baptist and the size of your congregation.

---

27 Jones, J. M. (2023, May 31). U.S. church membership falls below majority for first time. Gallup.com. https://news.gallup.com/poll/341963/church-membership-falls-below-majority-first-time.aspx

28 Number 2 in 2022: The decline in church attendance in Covid America. Institute for Family Studies. (n.d.). Retrieved March 31, 2023, from https://ifstudies.org/blog/number-2-in-2022-the-decline-in-church-attendance-in-covid-america

Pastor Orr:
My goodness, Brown Baptist, first of all, 140-year history, church history, founded by former slaves in 1882. And currently we have over 13,000 members. Pre-COVID, there was about four or five thousand that were coming into the worship every weekend. And so Brown, I like to think of it as we're changing lives, making a difference in the community. We're that bridge builder—we're that church that says, how do you bring everyone together? How do you bring all of the issues together and not look at things from Black and White, Republican, Democrat, but how do we really use the lens of the Word of God and use the love of Jesus Christ to make our community better?

DJJ:
What were your initial thoughts when businesses started closing and COVID-19 was called a global pandemic?

Pastor Orr:
I'll be honest, John, here at Brown, they already know I don't close the church for any reason. Rain, sleet, shine, snow—we're open. And just a mere fact that they started talking about things shutting down, at first, I was one of those ones, "Well, we won't shut the doors of the church. We won't close it for any reason." And even as it started coming down and doctors started saying it, and I was like, well, we can get through it. And then it hit me that third Sunday in March, my doctor said, "Pastor, we can't do this." And that was the last Sunday that we met, literally, because he was like, "No, it's too many. It is serious, and we need to stop."

DJJ:
So, the medical professionals weighed in and gave their professional opinion?

Pastor Orr:
Oh, my goodness. And we had said on the front end that we really wanted to make sure that we are looking at this in a balanced approach. So, what are scientists saying, and how do we balance science even with our faith, even with the government, to make sure that, you know what, it's a win-win for our people and their safety is our number one priority.

DJJ:
Did you ever think this would happen in these modern times or even in the US?

Pastor Orr:
Had no idea. This was one of those things that caught everyone by surprise. And in all of my years, nothing like this has ever happened. So, this was just a total new phenomenon for everyone.

DJJ:
How did worship change during COVID-19, and what were some of the challenges?

Pastor Orr:
Well, here at Brown, we worship three times on the weekends, or a Saturday service, Sunday, and two on Sunday mornings, 8:00 and 11:00. And the first thing that I noticed people doing was consolidating their worship. I mean, the doors are closed, people are not coming in. Let's video, and let's play that video back on Sunday morning at a particular time or through all the times. And hey, it's a win-win for everyone. Well, crazy me, John, I said, Brown is used to three worship experiences that are totally different, and how do we stay engaged? And so, what we did, we said, although the church doors are closed, we're going to keep coming and doing live worship each and every worship.

So, in those early days, it was me, a camera person, a musician, we were keeping it below that number 10. But I said, as long as we have somebody to push a button, we wanted to stay live so that we can engage the people in the time frames that they were used to.

We tried to make sure that we stayed in compliance with all of the government regulations in order to make that happen.

DJJ:
How did you engage with your congregation?

Pastor Orr:
So here it is, third Sunday, March 2020, literally when I gave that last benediction, that was it. I went home, and the Lord literally just kind of spoke to me from the book of Daniel on how do we go forward engaging the people, making sure that we're compliant with the government, keeping the people as safe as possible. And so, we rolled out that plan that Monday after the third Sunday to try to make that happen. And part of that included a member engagement team. We wanted to make sure that first of all, none of our employees were laid off. So how do we repurpose them in order to keep them employed and at the same time minister to the people? And one of the things here at Brown I'm known for is calling all of our members on their birthday. So, I said, well, hey, if I can call members on their birthday, we can create a member engagement team that can call families once a month to make sure that we're staying connected with them.

DJJ:
What messages did you use to connect and keep your congregation encouraged?

Pastor Orr:
One of the things that we did, social media, I mean everybody was ramping for social media. How do we continue to get that message out? And so, I'm so appreciative that creative services literally became their own production team and keeping the message going on a daily basis, a weekly basis—how do we continue to preach and teach the Word of God? Because at the end of the day, we believe the Word of God was what was going to get us through these times.

DJJ:
How did you connect with parishioners who questioned God and their faith?

Pastor Orr:
A series of Bible studies that we did, tried to do just that, to answer some of those tough questions, to answer some of the medical questions. And so, it was nothing to see Bible studies that, first of all, relationships, of course, all of those different topics, but also Bible studies about vaccines, Bible studies about how do we weigh medicine with science? What does our faith say about what we ought to be doing at a time like this? Bringing experts in—what does the Bible say about depression? Because we discovered that mental health was so important during this time, especially as the stress and the strain was really weighing on the individual. So, we tried to really speak to the issues that were affecting the people.

DJJ:
Do you think COVID-19 has strengthened religious faith?

Pastor Orr:
Well, I do believe that we had that bump. I call it a COVID bump because as churches closed down and people start

scrambling, they didn't have anything else since everything was shut down. What's happening? Well, you know what? Everyone was watching church services. A matter of fact, my members would say, Pastor, I just didn't go to one service today. I went to four different services today because I watched you. I watched this one, I watched that one. And so, there was that bump. But as it is oftentimes in religion, as things kind of just leveled out, as things began to return back to normal, if you will, I also saw another shift downward, in terms of participation, in terms of just support. And so, in terms of just numbers, so I do believe that if someone was not grounded and that if churches did not make sure, how do we continue to grow them in their faith, that bump was short-lived.

DJJ:
Churches transitioned from a brick-and-mortar platform to conference calls, social media, or a virtual platform. How has church attendance changed post-COVID-19? What steps did you take to preserve worship?

Pastor Orr:
It is a struggle, John. It is a struggle. I mean, we were closed for eight months, and some of our counterparts went back sooner. Some of our counterparts stayed closed longer. And so, it was a big deal for us even after eight months to say, "We're opening the doors back up." But one of the things that we discovered was, attendance-wise was very slow coming back. We're still at about 50 percent to where we were pre-COVID. So, the numbers have not registered, have not come back as we would like for them to.

DJJ:
What do you think are some new tactics or things to do to preserve the worship service? I know you do a lot; what are some other things you're thinking about?

Pastor Orr:
I think we just have to do things different. We have to realize that the new norm is what many are calling a hybrid worship, and that is in person and online. Some people are not coming back in, and they're not coming back in for a number of reasons. First of all, we cannot demonize those who do not come back in because some people literally do not come back in because of the fear. COVID is still here. We're still, I just preached a funeral of a COVID patient just a couple of weeks ago. So, it is still here; it is still real. We're still having deaths associated with COVID. And so, fear and just health reasons are going to probably keep some from coming back into the worship. So, we cannot say something is wrong with a person that does not come back in, and yet how do we make sure that their spiritual experience is the same as those that are in person as well? So online campus is something that we started in the midst of this pandemic.

DJJ:
Okay. I wanted to ask you about that. I've seen some of the presentations online, and they're very well done. Do you think because you did such a good job at it that it made people comfortable?

Pastor Orr:
Well, and I like to alliterate, and so fear, I think, is keeping some folks back home. But then I think people have become familiar with . . . And a matter of fact, when I'm calling people daily on their birthdays, I'm getting members to say, Pastor, getting up

on Sunday morning, being able to watch you and still enjoy breakfast at home with the family, it works for us right now. And so, we're not coming back, and we're still supporting and we're still doing this and that, but we're just haven't come back yet. So, I do believe that the ease of it all is another reason why people are not coming back, and that's the reason why we have to make sure that we're staying engaged with them. So how do we check on them? Here at Brown, we call it "digital discipleship." Everyone is doing everything right from this phone, so how do we continue to engage with people where they can do everything right from the phone?

DJJ:
How did the pandemic affect the day-to-day operation of the church?
Pastor Orr:
It's interesting. Again, everyone went home, and so literally it was just a skeleton crew here at the church, and yet church had to go on. I mean, in the pandemic, we did not do less in the pandemic. We did more in the pandemic. And so, whereas some people probably said this was a great vacation, a great time, Brown was constantly thinking about how do we expand, how do we continue to serve the people? How do we continue to do more? Funerals alone, I was averaging preaching 70 to 80 funerals in the midst of the pandemic, and that's 70 to 80 a year. And those are just the ones that I was preaching. That's not the number, that's not including the numbers where we opened the doors up.

Because at that particular time, Brown literally became one of those community churches that said, "Hey, if you have a loved one and you need a funeral, and your church doors are closed or you need the space, call on us." And so, our members, although the staff was at home, we still had volunteers. And that skeleton crew that was here, the doors opened, ministry going forth literally around the clock.

DJJ:
There was a lot of sickness and death potentially within the church and in the church community; how did these occurrences affect Brown Baptist?

Pastor Orr:
It affected in so many different ways. I mean, it affected, first of all, just the emotional, during this time, I was literally preaching multiple family members' death. Sometimes within weeks apart. I would preach maybe a grandmother one month, and then maybe that their grandfather a couple of months later. Now, everyone was not passing away with COVID, so there was a lot of other sickness, a lot of other diseases going on. And even with health care, people are not able to get into the doctor to see the doctor. And yet, in one six-weeks period, I preached the father, his daughter, and then the son-in-law, all within a six-week period.

DJJ:
Pastor Orr, we know COVID-19 had an impact on attendance, but how did it impact giving?

Pastor Orr:
First of all, the experts said that giving was going to go down 20 to 25 percent. That was what the expert said. And again, keeping in mind all of this is new to everybody. And so sure enough, that first couple of weeks we did see a 50 percent drop in our income, because many people were having to switch over to digital giving and so forth. One of the things that really helped us, this whole digital discipleship, digital giving was something we were already doing. We just weren't doing it as well as we

should have been in terms of having more people engaged. So, after that first couple of weeks where giving went way down, against all of the odds of the experts, giving started going up. And again, I think that is part of what I call that religious bump that many churches saw in the midst of COVID, that giving was going up.

Expenses were down because what we did, we said if there's going to be a 20 to 25 percent decrease, we need to go in and see what we can trim to make sure that we're staying in line. And that trimming actually helped us at the end of the year in terms of just our bottom line. There were a lot of government programs that were going on. And again, COVID is one of those things. No one has ever done this before. And my first reaction was as a faith-based organization, we're not going to accept any governmental funds. And then I'm grateful that the Bible says, "In a multitude of counselors there is safety." And one of our bankers actually called me personally to say, "Pastor, look, this is something that would be a great help to the church. Our bank is doing it, and the whole purpose is to make sure that you all can keep your employees."

Well, that fit right into that original plan that I had in terms of making sure that no employees are laid off. So, we were able to take advantage of that. Interesting, couple of days after that meeting, that bank official passed away suddenly. And so even before in the early days of COVID, so much was going on that there was just unknown in terms of just the loss and the impact of the loss that was taking place. And so, we're grateful members, we started partnering with other churches as well as with government officials and other private sectors to make sure that food drives and things of that nature were being conducted as well. And you would be surprised, look in those food drive lines, there was everybody in those food drive lines. COVID was something that wasn't a Black, wasn't a White, it wasn't a Republican, a Democrat. This was something that affected everybody. Everybody felt the pain of it. And it was just wonderful to see everyone coming together to help support each other.

DJJ:
An article in the *Wall Street Journal* stated that "Churches Changed during the Pandemic and Many Aren't Going Back." What are your thoughts?

Pastor Orr:
Well, there are some things that did change because of COVID. And there are some things that, you know what? You ought not go back to. The future is ahead of us. We have to look at how do we do church in these new times, but then there are some traditional things that, hey, we shouldn't go back to. And so, I think that is the wisdom in terms of just weighing what is best for your particular congregation. COVID, give you a case in point.

We were already trying to limit church to the timing. Guess what COVID did? COVID knocked everybody church service times from two hours down to one hour or less, especially when you couldn't even gather for an extended period of time. And so that is something that even going forth, I do believe we still have to keep in mind of, okay, hey, how long are we going? Only because of the fact that you have people watching, and their attention span may be totally different from those that are actually in the place and experiencing worship. So, there is that give-and-take balance as to how we go forth in a positive way for everyone.

DJJ:
Many say we're looking at COVID-19 through the rearview mirror. Reflecting on all that has happened, how has your life been impacted or changed by the COVID-19 pandemic?

Pastor Orr:
Well, 2020, believe it or not, it was the "Year of Wisdom" for us at Brown. And so, I told the staff, and this was before COVID, "Hey, this is a year I'm going to slow down. I want to smell the roses." We were operating in the wisdom. I didn't have any idea that the slowdown would be a shutdown. And so, it really gave me an opportunity to see the value of time and of spending that time with family, just being home, being able to connect with my wife, and just being able to do things together.

So those are times that I don't regret at all, but it has taught me even going forth, how do we be wise with our time? How do we make sure that we're taking advantage of just spending that time? This year was the first year that I actually did a sabbatical in 33 years of pastoring, getting away. And this was the first time, keeping in mind, in the midst of the COVID, every week I'm still doing three services, still preaching on average, two to three funerals. Some weekends I was doing six funerals within just one week. So, it was just a lot on me. And then just to get away on this sabbatical, it really taught me, if there's going to be longevity for Bartholomew, or I really need to put that time in in terms of rest and just emotionally, mentally, spiritually getting refreshed. So, along those lines, COVID helped out a lot.

DJJ:
Do you think we are at the end of the pandemic?

Pastor Orr:
Unfortunately, I believe COVID is something that we're going to have to live with. And so that means how do we adjust, how do we strengthen ourselves in going forth? One of the big debates in this whole COVID thing was even when it came to vaccine, do I take the vaccine? Do I not take the vaccine? Is it a Democrat thing? Is it a Republican thing? Is it a faith

thing? Is my faith wavering and so forth? I actually wrote letters for individuals who said, "Pastor, I do not want to take this vaccine." Some felt that the vaccine was going to be putting the mark of the beast on them. And so how do you just manage all of that? I was on the fence. I was one of those that said, "Hey, I eat right. I'm vegan. I'm going to eat even better, strengthen my immune system. And if I do all of that, then I won't have to take it."

And what really touched my life and changed my heart was Proverbs 18:21. "The horse is prepared for battle, but victory belongs to the Lord." In other words, "Bart," and the Lord calls me Bart, "Bart, look, you do everything that you can do to prepare, but ultimately, I'm going to be the one to give the victory." And when I thought about that, the Lord says, "Vaccine is one of those things you do to prepare. Eating right, exercising, strengthening your immune system. Those are things that you do, but ultimately, I'm going to give you the victory." And our family went through the entire pandemic seemingly unscathed. It didn't hit our home until December of 2021. And lo and behold, everyone in our house but my wife came down with COVID, yes.

By this time, we had been vaccinated and it was very mild symptoms, but it was a reality that you know what? It really can hit anybody, even if they have done everything right now. Until this date, Valerie is the holdout in our family for never testing positive for COVID. Yes. And I thought I was going to be invincible like that because I was like, all of these COVID funerals that I was doing and I never caught it, and wouldn't you know it, right around Christmas, and I think my grandson brought it into our house.

DJJ:
Do you think we (or the church) are better prepared for the next pandemic?

Pastor Orr:
I pray so. One of the things that we did here at Brown, we actually came up with a task, I think we were calling it reopening task team, where we pulled together the professionals, the medical folks, the security, all of the pastoral team, and we met on a monthly basis to really look at all of those aspects to it. Just that strategy alone has helped us to say going forth, these are things, and these are ways that we can, if something else come up, now we know how to galvanize, come together, work as a team, let all of the experts bring their expertise to the table to work out something for the benefit of the church.

Dr. Bartholomew Orr, Senior Pastor, Brown Missionary Baptist Church

The houses of prayer searched for ways to minister to their parishioners during the outbreak and satisfy spiritual needs while actively providing support to their respective communities. As these clergy worked on matters of the soul, courageous health care professionals were in the eye of the storm working on physical bodies savagely attacked by COVID-19.

Chapter 9

IN THE EYE OF THE STORM

When you are in the middle of a storm cloud it's hard to think outside of it, but the only way out of the storm is to ride through it, and things will be a lot clearer on the other side.
— Jodi Ann Bickley

The infectious disease professionals around the world are essential to the fight against COVID-19. They have been on the front lines developing solutions and effective responses to the pandemic. During the pandemic, their expertise was called upon by patients, other doctors, government officials, and public health policy entities. These doctors became participants and collaborators on different task forces, as communities attempted to create and execute plans to defend against COVID-19. At the same time, they worked with patients and hospitals to save lives, innovate on treatments, and leverage their vast expertise and knowledge to manage the disastrous effects on society. Every day on the job was a battle with unforeseen pitfalls, and health workers were at the epicenter. The highly contagious virus attacks the respiratory system and seeks to achieve a tighter grip on bodies already compromised. At the same time, the virus lies in wait to attack healthy bodies with a vengeance. The back-and-forth combat was exhausting, as health care professionals treated patients, conducted research, and recommended vaccines and therapies while carefully taking precautions to guard their health and prevent exposure of loved ones. In some cities, health care professionals worked in over-capacity facilities with unimaginable workloads and stressful conditions. They were confused and exhausted. Death was everywhere. But these heroes were resolute and looked death in the face as they showed dedication and commitment to serve their patients under the toughest of circumstances. Perhaps they were responding to a higher calling to stand in the gap between this monstrous virus and the helpless victims under their care.

> As of March 21, 2023, the World Health Organization (WHO) confirmed 761 million cases of COVID-19 globally with 6.9 million deaths. The United States has experienced approximately 1.1 million deaths due to COVID-19.[29]

I spent an evening at Baptist Memorial Hospital with Dr. Stephen C. Threlkeld, MD, Infectious Disease Expert, Medical Director of Infectious Disease, Baptist Memorial Health Care, in one of the treatment rooms. He shared strategies used and his experiences on the front lines fighting this disease.

DJJ:
Dr. Threlkeld, tell us a little bit about yourself. What is it you do? What makes your medical role unique?

Dr. Threlkeld:
Well, I'm a native Memphian, so I love this city and always have. And so, I'm, I think, a fourth-generation Memphian, third-generation physician in Memphis. My grandfather was the original tenant in the Peabody Hotel when they built it in 1925 and wanted a doctor on the mezzanine. So, I grew up here, went to college here at Rhodes, went away for all of my medical training, and came back in 1994 to join my brother,

---

29 World Health Organization. (n.d.). Who coronavirus (COVID-19) dashboard. World Health Organization. Retrieved April 10, 2023, from https://covid19.who.int/

my biological brother, Mike. And then we added our adopted brother, Imad Omer, in our practice about 20 years ago. I'm married to a wonderful lady, Ginger, and I have two great kids, Colin and Blair, who were in New York and Dallas, respectively. So, I've been back here since '97, and we do kind of a full-time infectious disease practice. We do some clinical research, a lot of teaching, but mainly it's taking care of patients. And so, we're lucky to have a great group of people with us. I've been a nearly lifelong member of Second Presbyterian Church, and so basically, I think we all love this town, and it's been a tough time these last couple of years.

But I think most of us who are from Memphis, who really know this city, know what a charitable town it is. We are yearly, just about yearly voted as the most philanthropic city in America. And I think you always will find Memphis people to step up and do the job when they're needed. So, it's just a great place to be.

DJJ:
Communities started hearing about COVID-19 in late January or February of 2020, but the seriousness of it was unknown, and people continued their day-to-day activities not realizing what was ahead. When did the medical community realize COVID-19 wasn't just seasonal influenza but something far more serious and impactful?

Dr. Threlkeld:
Well, it was a real problem, I think, for the US. We all thought that, to coin someone else's phrase, we thought we would science this thing to death. We thought that nothing, even what we thought we might be seeing in China, would really spread here, that we would be able to knock this out. We had a little bit of the same feeling back in the Ebola problem some years ago. Turns out that wasn't contagious enough to overcome us.

But this we saw; I think what really hit us here in Memphis and the Mid-South was watching New York City. They had health care workers, younger, healthier people dying. They had people dying in large numbers. They had had freezer compartments for the bodies that were building up. It was a sort of nightmarish thing that really hit us in the face. We realized that maybe we weren't quite as good as we thought, and maybe this disease was more serious than we thought.

We learned a lot. We were wrong in the beginning. We thought it would be like a common cold, and handwashing and not scratching your nose after shaking hands with somebody would be the way to do it. But it turns out that it really was more respiratory transmitted, and that masks were helpful at preventing you from giving it to somebody else, probably as a prime mover in all this. At the same time that we saw that, and really, I think became depressed as a health care system, as a nation, when we saw that this thing was going to get the better of us. We didn't even at that point know how much. But I think locally in the Mid-South, we were fortunate because as we watched that happen, we prepared. And we prepared pretty well. We're lucky enough to have one of the largest bed bases, hospital bed bases per capita in the country, in the world for that matter. And so, we took advantage of that. We didn't have the sort of situation where the hospitals ever had to shut down because they were overcome with too many people.

We prepared in a lot of ways. We built wards in the hospital with negative pressure to keep the disease from spreading among patients, protect family members. So, we got that opportunity. Even as we watched the tragedy unfold in New York, we realized what was going on, and I think we prepared fairly well as local hospitals and as a city.

DJJ:
What was it like when the lockdown occurred, and everyone had to stay home, and cities were like ghost towns?

Dr. Threlkeld:
Well, it's interesting because I mean, as a full-time health care worker in a hospital setting predominantly, I'm not sure that we fully got an appreciation for that except what we saw through our families and what was going on with them. The biggest part of that, I think, was dealing with patients who were sick and dying in larger numbers than we had ever experienced in our professional lives, and they couldn't so much as get visitors from their families to come with them. I think that was part of the real psychological problem that hit so many people so hard. Nurses were having to deal with people hour in and hour out, day in and day out as they died from this disease, particularly the elderly. And they would try to connect those folks with family members via their own cell phones and some sort of video chat, just so families could be with their elderly relatives as they died. And it was the sort of thing that no one has ever imagined going through before, and that's why I think the nurses really took the worst of the blow of all of this problem. So, it was surreal that people couldn't come to visit their sick and dying patients. I think that was the thing that we noticed in the hospital building day-to-day. But there's no question, it's just the sort of thing that we just didn't have any reference for this sort of thing before.

DJJ:
Why was COVID-19 so contagious?

Dr. Threlkeld:
Well, there are a lot of reasons why that's the case. Diseases that are the most contagious frequently are ones that can be transmitted by a respiratory pathway. And things can be

contagious either by touch or by cough and sneezing and spread by the respiratory pathway. There was a lot of this virus in our noses and mouths, and we were able to portray that through air vents and air flows in restaurants. It was made more contagious when people sang in church choirs and spread it among them. And then there's this sort of situation called the R-naught, how many people does a given person who's infected give it to other people? How many other people get it from them? And the number was pretty large. And so, it's a disease that not many particles of that virus were necessary to initiate the infection in somebody else. And there were just a lot of people around them, and that virus hit them in the airway, the nose, the mouth, and it was off to the races.

DJJ:
How has COVID-19, or how does COVID-19 differ from the Spanish flu, that occurred during the 1918 World War I time frame?

Dr. Threlkeld:
Yeah, and let me actually make one point—let me add to that last question too. And I was thinking about, the other thing is it has a short incubation period. It makes people sick pretty quickly, and you can also transmit that infection a little bit before you even become symptomatic yourself. And so, you can transmit the infection to people before you realize you're contagious. Translate that to sort of monkeypox, for example, something we've experienced since then. It's usually the people who have sores and so forth that are the most contagious. But COVID was particularly effective at transmitting to people even as they became, in fact, symptomatic and a little bit beforehand.

So, with respect to the 1918 flu, I sort of got into science at St. Jude Hospital here studying pandemic influenza, bird, or avian flu. And so, they're very different viruses. So, it's difficult to make a significant comparison in the specifics of it, but it's also a disease that came around the world in several waves, killed millions of people, even more probably with influenza. I think what's interesting about it in some ways is the differences that we saw between the two viruses. With the flu, it really concentrated on younger people. Whereas with COVID, it was more the elderly population. Certainly, people with immune suppression and other kinds of heart-lung problems that would be predisposed to either. But the reason for that was that the older people had experienced a similar influenza year before and actually had some preexisting immunity. So, it's an interesting distinction. We didn't have that with COVID-19. There were no related viruses that an older population may have seen before and had some preparedness against it just immunologically.

So, it would take young, healthy people and kill them in 48 hours. It was an extraordinarily awful sort of illness at that time, but it went around the world in several ways. There were mass controversies; there were controversies over shutting down cities. Some of the cities that did shut down aggressively did much better with much less loss of life than some of the cities that sort of ignored it. So, there are a lot of things about it. As much as you might think politics differ in 2020 from what it did in 1918, there are a lot of things that really were very similar.

DJJ:
Did you ever think we would see the level of deaths experienced with COVID-19?

Dr. Threlkeld:
No. I don't think anybody was prepared for that, and I don't think anybody expected it, even as it happened. It just seemed to be unreal that those numbers would pile up like they did. There are a lot of reasons, I think, why it happened. Some could have been somewhat avoidable, some not. I've probably said,

"I don't know" and "I was wrong about that" more times over the last two and a half years than I've ever in my life collectively done before. But there aren't many people here who can claim a lot of knowledge about what's going to happen. I think we all underestimated this virus. And so oftentimes not even at just one turn, sometimes at several turns.

DJJ:
How did you and the staff at Threlkeld Infectious Disease align with the hospitals and the Shelby County Health Department?

Dr. Threlkeld:
I think we can all be proud as a city of how hospitals, physicians, nurses, all members of the health care team really worked together. People worked hard. I think first and foremost, they did what was necessary. And you always find people that will do the job, and we just had a lot of people in this town that did it. We did, in fact, prepare well once we were seeing the tragic events in New York City. So, I think a lot of physicians, both in our group and others, really entered into an effective partnership with hospitals to build facilities that would help control the thing. Having the proper air pressure to keep this disease from spreading in the hospitals. We built operating rooms with negative pressure that would protect the operating room personnel, which allowed us to take care of sick people and not just say, "Hey, we can't do that surgery." We were able to do it safely and not spread to other people.

We utilized, for example, in our infusion center here, we built two negative pressure rooms for which we had prepared. We figured that might be necessary someday. And sure enough, when the very first monoclonal antibodies became available, we spent the weekend building out these rooms into full negative pressures, and we were probably the first in the country to give the monoclonal antibody in this room we're sitting in. And gave thousands of those doses, even as many large academic hospitals on the coast were struggling to give any because of the way the buildings were set up, getting people in and out safely. We very simply had the opportunity to plan ahead. I think that we did plan ahead, and I think there was a lot of cooperation among physicians, other members of the health care team, hospitals in the city, and I think that saved a lot of lives in the aftermath of that.

DJJ:

> No part of the US has been fully spared, but the burdens are unequally distributed. At every point, from initial infection to intensive care, COVID-19 exposed disparities by race/ethnicity and immigration status, by income and wealth. The pandemic exposed disparities in preexisting disease vulnerability, in the effectiveness of public health efforts, and in the availability and intensity of medical care. [30]

Did you see the same disparities here in Shelby County or the Mid-South area?

Dr. Threlkeld:
I think when we take a step back and look at it, of course we did. I think you can see that anywhere in the country. I'm almost just tempted to say, I'm glad to say that those of us taking care of patients at the bedside didn't notice that as much because we were much too focused on taking care of the very next patient in front of us. And I think when you look at people who are

30 Covid-19 and health disparities: Insights from key informant interviews. (n.d.). https://www.healthaffairs.org/content/forefront/covid-19-and-health-disparities-insights-key-informant-interviews

working in intensive care units and that sort of high-intensity medical environment, that's not the environment where you tend to see anything except the person in front of you. That's the way it should be. They should be treated equally and as well as you can do it. And I think that's what happened. Now, when you look at the situation, there's no question there are so many other factors. There are people who were in underserved populations who had more chronic disease. Turns out those chronic diseases, many turned out to be risk factors for severe COVID. People in underserved populations tended to live with more people in one household, which led to more efficient spread of the virus.

Many people in underserved populations were essential workers who had to go to work and be exposed to this virus, where some people with more wherewithal were able to do their job from home via Zoom and the like. So, there's no question that those things existed. But those I think at the time were for people who were looking more at the epidemiology of it; those of us taking care of patients, honest to goodness, never really had as much thought about that. It was really about saving the people because you're talking about a time when many more, multiple people a day were dying in front of us in the ICUs. And you have to deal with the next patient and take care of them specifically and individually. And I'm proud to say I think that's what really happened in our city.

DJJ:
US closures appear to have been modest in comparison to some countries. Should the US have done more closures and increased enforcement?

Dr. Threlkeld:
Yeah, really difficult to say. As I mentioned, we saw this same sort of problem in 1918. I mean, it was highly controversial

at the time, and it's controversial now. I have people to this moment ask that, in just casual conversations, should we have closed the schools? Well, these tend to be sort of loaded questions when you hear them on the street, and somebody has an idea about it. I think it's important not to remove the context. At the time, people were dying in large numbers all around us. It's hard to know whether we did enough or too much at the time. Yes, we can look back now and see some of the costs of closing schools—they are not minimal. But how many lives did that save? Not spreading that to grandparents and other immunologically suppressed folks. I think it may be a long time before we'll be able to answer the question of exactly how we could have closed more or done less. Could we have taken some of the Wisconsin-style data, where younger school kids who were masked and spaced appropriately, there was very little transmission of the virus?

Well, it took us a long time to get those data well into the pandemic. Had we known that, of course in the beginning, I think there would've been a lot fewer school closures. They would've just been open in certain sorts of ways and mechanisms to avoid the spread of the disease. But it's a really hard question, I think, to know if we did enough, if we did too much. And I think it may be a long time before we'll be able to really answer that question very well.

DJJ:
With regard to testing, how much did testing delays, organizational infrastructure, political polarization, and the mistrust of the government contribute to the US not being able to slow the virus?

Dr. Threlkeld:
Yeah. Well, I think testing is one of the things that a lot of us did get right. I think a lot of the people who were taking

care of these patients said over and over, in the final analysis years from now, people will criticize us for not testing enough. We didn't test enough symptomatic people, and we didn't test enough asymptomatic people. That said, we did better in this town than happened in a lot of others. I think there was a fair amount of cooperation ramping up to get testing available but getting it to people in a way that they could get the test and the reality of long lines. There were a lot of logistics difficulties in having that happen. But yeah, I think testing is something that was going to be a very important way that, and of course, vaccine distribution later, it was kind of a window on what would happen, I think later. But testing was a very crucial point that I think we probably didn't do as well as we should have done. That said, we may have done here a better job than some cities.

Again, looking at what happened in the pandemic and other places, we learned from that. And there was a pretty good cooperation between government and commercial laboratories at making those tests available. We saw that echoed during the monkeypox problem later. It really didn't take off until there was a cooperation allowing commercial labs. When you're relying on purely the CDC and the public health services to do testing, you're not going to get the job done. There're just not enough tests, there're not enough people to accomplish it, and you've got to spread that out over various commercial entities to accomplish it. And I think we did, as I say, reasonably well, but we didn't test enough. We should have tested more formally. I think as a nation we didn't do well enough to get the antigen testing out. The antigen test was really a latecomer to our arsenal of weapons really against this virus.

The plain home rapid test was a great test to show whether or not you were contagious to others. It had limitations, but it was a lot better than no testing. We could have avoided a lot of infections had we really had the antigen test out to people sooner and more widespread.

Initially, there was hope that contact tracing would contain or slow the US COVID-19 pandemic, but the virus's ability to mutate and the speed and efficiency with which COVID-19 spread squashed those expectations. Other nations faced and contained the same biological-epidemiological process.

DJJ:
What was a typical day like for you during the height of the pandemic?

Dr. Threlkeld:
I think already we have sort of cleansed some of that from our memories. In the typical day for somebody that worked in critical care, pulmonary infectious disease, other sorts of docs who worked in the intensive care units and the like. Probably sort of a 7:00 a.m. to midnight sort of day. And it was that for, I think, 12 to 15 months, every single day, Monday through Sunday. And it was the sort of thing where you just got the job done as best you could, and then you laced it up and did it again the next day. And I really had very little semblance of time. It was just a job to do, and it became life. I mean, it really did. But you overlay that with the fears that we had. I mean, I slept in a different room from my wife for weeks for fear of giving other members of my family the virus. So, there were a lot of issues that made life pretty rough.

As I say, you almost forget some of it now, thankfully. I think the human body is good at that. But it was a sort of thing that I hope we never have to see again, that's for sure.

DJJ:
COVID-19 was new for many in the medical community. What type of questions were you receiving from doctors, nurses, labs, etc.?

Dr. Threlkeld:
Mostly the questions to which we didn't have answers. The questions we would get from other doctors and nurses were a lot of times very practical questions. What do I do with my waiting room? Who should wear a mask? Who should not? How should we and where should we supply our efforts? And I think a lot of the practical questions, let's just look at masks for example. That was along with an incredible success as we had with the vaccine venues and the like. The mask question and topic were probably one of our abject failures, I think. It became a political volleyball; different members of different political groups had different opinions about it depending on who was in the White House. Things that you just can't imagine. But we never really, at least in this country, got to the business of doing some controlled clinical trials to tell what mask behaviors worked and what did not.

It took a trial in Bangladesh, well into the pandemic, before we really had any practical examples of what masks did for us, which masks worked and applied to whom. There's really not a very good excuse for not being able to do some of those trials early on. So, a lot of the questions that we got were practical ones. And make no mistake, we had to take what we knew and then extrapolate to things that we didn't really know for sure but that made sense. So, there was a lot of that sort of thing. And I used to point out that a huge portion of our day was phone calls from people saying, "My mother-in-law has COVID, and these are her problems, and this is what she's had in the way of vaccine, and this is what she takes for medicines, so what do we do?" And these were pretty complicated issues of what to do. Everybody's different. Everybody has a different immune system quality; they're taking different medications. So that's kind of what made this disease particularly difficult, I think.

DJJ:
What was the physical and psychological demand on health care workers during this time?

Dr. Threlkeld:
Yeah, it's interesting. I think probably what was most poignant to me was to see moments when people had it break through and hit them. I think of an example of a very tough young nurse, who does a great job. And she was just day in and day out taking care of people who were dying and very sick in the ICU. This is an ICU-stationed nurse. And one day that nurse's patient, an elderly gentleman, died, and she had to call this man's wife of probably 50-plus years and let her know. And I'll never forget the look on her face as I realized that this older lady was sort of comforting this nurse on the phone saying, "It's going to be okay. You did everything you could." And it was just too much for this young lady. She broke down in tears as she hung up the phone at the thought of this wife of so many years, comforting her on what she was going through, taking care of these patients. It just hit her like a freight train.

And I remember she broke down in tears and said, "I'm just tired of everyone dying every day." And it was awful. I think of something else that took a toll, particularly on the nurses but some doctors too. I remember just as an example, I remember taking my family to Yosemite years ago, and there was a terrible accident at Nevada Falls where a young girl fell in. She shouldn't have been over the rail, but she fell in, and two men tried to save her, both of whom fell in too, all of them plunging to their deaths. And there was a lady behind the rail who said she will never be able to rid the memory of that man spinning around and catching her eye as he was about to fall over the waterfall. She said she's tortured by that to this day. And what I think it's helpful for people to understand is that we had that happen every single day.

Have someone look at you as you were about to put down a breathing tube and they were probably not going to survive. And they just had this look like, "I didn't know this was going to be that bad. I didn't really believe in this." And there are no words to say to that person, but the damage, I mean the wear and tear that takes on the poor nurses, respiratory therapists, critical care doctors who have to experience that all day, every day was a toll that I think was unaccounted for. People don't really think about that until long after the fact.

DJJ:
In respect to the burnout that occurred, did you see any innovative coping techniques that emerged for medical professionals to make it through?

Dr. Threlkeld:
You know what's interesting? I won't say that I could see a lot of innovative stuff pop up so much as I saw old-fashioned stuff that works pop up. People talked about it more with each other over time. At first it was very hard to process this, and you just were moving on to the next serious problem to try to avert death. I mean early on, my Sunday school teacher died. He was a tremendous man, did great work in the community. That was really the first person that I knew well who died of COVID. And it was a tragic, sort of an abrupt jolt to all of us. And that was kind of where it really hit me personally first. My roommate from a residency training in Birmingham died in Detroit, an ophthalmologist. Young, healthy, fit guy. Well, maybe not young, but he was in his fifties, and he died. This is an active guy.

So, I think all these things you need to talk to other people about. And I think over time we became more effective at talking to each other about it. And I think most therapists—my wife is a therapist. And most therapists will tell you that talking about it to people who can understand is one of the best therapies that you can do. And I do think I saw more of that over time, which was helpful.

DJJ:
Based on the multiple strands of the virus, how did patient experience differ?

Dr. Threlkeld:
Yeah. Well, it's complicated because there's several layers to that problem. There is the difference in the different viral strains and the different viral variants. There is the immunity that was kind of adding up to a previous variant that was variably effective to the next one that was coming along. I think a lot of it was very similar until we hit omicron. The previous earlier versions of the virus, first, of course, we had no immunity. And so, there were a lot of people, even in younger, healthier age groups, that were getting very sick and dying. Of course, the biggest hit would be the group of the elderly and people with immune problems, people with severe heart and lung situations. So that's always been the biggest problem group with this disease. There have been subtle differences. For example, we saw much more in the way of taste and smell problems early on. Probably earlier, probably more than we saw in some of the later variants, though people can certainly still get them. Occasionally, you would have a time where there was more diarrhea illness.

There were subtle differences in how the disease behaved, but it's very difficult to sort that out by variant, particularly with the earlier ones. Because as immunity wax and waned, and then the vaccines became available, it really was a lot of factors that were involved in that. Omicron was the big departure because it was kind of the first one that became more resistant to some of our previous immunity and was yet even more contagious. So even though it wasn't that much more severe per patient, it was so contagious and so many people got it that we had a lot more deaths in that way, and we weren't prepared for that. I think everybody thought, "Hey, we're getting better here." We were a little relaxed, kind of like we are now. And then omicron hit, and people just weren't prepared. They weren't prepared to go back to being more careful. And so, a lot weren't, and people still didn't get the vaccine who kind of didn't want it at that time. And a lot of people died unnecessarily with that omicron surge.

And it made us realize at that point, that once again, as we realized in the beginning, we're not all that good. I mean we're good in a lot of ways, but we're still, relatively speaking, at the mercy of what variant comes down the pike and how it behaves. Is it more virulent, more deadly, intrinsically? Is it more able to avoid our previous immunity from prior versions and variants from prior vaccines? And it's in that sense, it's its own natural disaster form. We can only do so much against that, and we're more powerless than we'd like to think a lot of times against those sorts of things.

DJJ:
Can you tell us what was it like in the COVID-19 wards?

Dr. Threlkeld:
Yeah, it was very strange. And even with our really incredible bed base here in Memphis, yeah, it was tight. I mean, we had to think about who to move out of the ICUs. We never really reached the breaking point, but I think I said once upon a time, we were a bit creaky at a few moments along the way. But everybody in their sort of elaborate protective equipment, I mean, it was

walking onto a moon base in some ways. Everybody was dressed out in fairly elaborate clothing, and you may change to another one and go into the next room. But entire units, every door you would go down the line were COVID patients. So, there was a businesslike, I think, character to the way people were doing their job. It had to be like that. You had to be relatively regimented in what you did so that you didn't make mistakes.

It's easy to forget and walk into a room without some of that stuff if you're not being careful. And I think people helped each other, and people made sure that each other were behaving in the right ways. But there was a focus during that time that I've certainly never seen before, and I hope I never have to see since. People were locked in to taking care of those patients, and so many died, there wasn't the casual joking around that you see sometimes in hospitals to relieve stress. There was too much for that. It was a very businesslike environment, and it was a foreign feeling. Everybody in fairly elaborate garb and going about their business, I think in a really businesslike fashion.

DJJ:
I'm guessing the scale and global impact of COVID-19 was an anomaly to you as well. What were some of your concerns and fears during this time?

Dr. Threlkeld:
Well, people used to ask me, was I going to get the Pfizer or the Moderna vaccine? And I remember saying, "Hey, you need to understand something. I've been walking around for two weeks with my arm held out and my sleeve rolled up. I'll take whatever one they bring to me first." So, we were all, I mean, you would be silly and foolish not to be afraid of dying. And I had close colleagues and friends who were quite ill in the hospital. And as I said, I had important people in my lives who actually died of this disease. So, you would be silly if you weren't in fear of your

own safety. And of course, there was the safety for your family and friends. You really didn't want to give it to them because you didn't have to be terribly sick. A lot of people weren't very ill from this virus too. That was one of the things, I think, that made us all too casual about this.

Many people got it and said, "No big deal. I didn't get very sick." But what they didn't realize is that it may have given it to a parent, a grandparent, or a friend that might die of it. And that's one thing that we kept preaching to people all along. So, I think we were certainly fearful for ourselves, for our families. And as I say, you were just afraid that it was going to get worse, and it did just keep getting worse for quite some time. But I'm mentioning it all too many times, but I'm very grateful for the time we had to prepare. Because if you compare what we went through to what some of the New York health care workers with inadequate personal protective equipment, a lot of those health care workers died unnecessarily because they just didn't have that degree of preparation. So, I'm very thankful for that. We were prepared, I think, physically if not emotionally for all that. We were prepared to protect ourselves and therefore, by extension, our families, I think.

DJJ:
What are the lessons learned, and is the medical community better prepared for the next pandemic?

Dr. Threlkeld:
Yes and no. I think we are. We're prepared for that degree of illness in folks. This followed up after all with the monkeypox situation. We learned a couple of lessons all over again that was that we didn't have adequate testing in the beginning. You had to get your testing from the CDC via the health department, and very frankly, in the beginning it was inadequate. There were people that I wanted to test; I couldn't test them. They didn't

fit all of the checkboxes that we subsequently then predictably learn don't all really need to be checked for someone to have the illness. We also learned that there needs to be, I think, a very important cooperation between public health authorities and structures and commercial businesses. We found that testing became available very quickly once the governmental agencies were able to share testing with commercial companies. All of a sudden testing became adequate and available.

So that's the sort of thing we got to do. We got control eventually, but at the beginning I think we were sort of standing there flat-footed saying, "Here we go again. We have a real problem here." But we did learn that, of course, with the Operation Warp Speed, that was what got arguably the most impressive scientific accomplishment in history with the initial COVID vaccines. It was the cooperation between the government and various companies that could get the job done. And it just goes to show you that that's really the way to accomplish things.

DJJ:
What does being prepared really mean, and what does "preparedness" look like?

Dr. Threlkeld:
Everybody working together, and I think we need better surveillance tools. There are a lot of people in public health who threw up their hands and retired or said, "This is too much." They took a lot of grief. There was a lot of criticism of those folks. Occasionally founded, but a lot of it, they were in difficult situations. So, we are understaffed, I think, nationally with public health agencies and people who do that work. We have to have adequate surveillance to know what's going on out there. That's how you know what to do. So, we have to make sure that our surveillance capabilities are adequate, both locally

and of course internationally. But then we have to be able to coordinate our system with commercial operations as well. I'll give an example. We sort of, in contrast to the incredible success we had with the vaccine, again, unprecedented throughout the history of science. We weren't very good at doing those, and I alluded to this a bit earlier. We weren't very good at doing those trials that could answer basic questions about what was effective, what medications worked.

It really took things like the recovery trial in Europe and some tests that we just weren't quite able to coordinate. Part of that was that we have a more fragmented health care system, and some of the European systems, Great Britain and the like that really spearheaded the recovery trial. They have a national health care system, and so they were more easily able to get cases, coordinate data, and do these trials. There's no reason that we can't do that too. We just didn't seem to be set up to do it. So, I hope that'll happen next time. We hope there's not a next time, but if there is, we hope that we can set up the ability to do some of these tests and trials to answer the question of what medicines work, what behaviors like masking work and where and how. We should be able to do that better and more seamlessly than we did in the COVID pandemic. And that's what I hope preparedness will be if we ever have to face something like this again.

DJJ:
Is COVID-19 here to stay or is it part of our lives like the seasonal flu, which requires an annual vaccination, or is it too early to tell?

Dr. Threlkeld:
Yeah, I think it's likely to be with us for a long time. I mean, this virus is . . . Its ability to change, to modify its surface proteins and thus its behavior, and its ability to interact with our

immune system to favor itself not us, seems to be getting larger, not smaller. So, it's very likely that the virus will be around in some form or another. We are in very little control over what those mutations and changes do in the way of behavior. Is there a limit to which this virus can change and become more adept at getting around our immunity? We don't know. Up to now, that hasn't seemed to be the case. There are variants, even as we sit here, that a lot of people haven't heard of that are out there that are more resistant to our immunity, whether they achieve it with their contagious nature, whether they can outperform the B4s and B5s of the world. We've yet to see that's what happened every time. This is population genetics.

A new virus comes along that's contagious and spreads more efficiently. It replaces the old one. It replaces it by being more efficient at infecting us. And so, we hope that there's a limited capacity for that. The difference, of course, with this and the flu is that the flu changes very rapidly. Now COVID has changed much more rapidly than we thought it might be able to. But last year's flu vaccine does essentially no good. And that's why you have to have a new vaccine prepared every year. So far, thankfully, that has not been the case with COVID. The original vaccine directed against Wuhan I, the original COVID isolate, not even the one that escaped China to the US but the original one that was the source of the vaccine, that still is very good at preventing hospitalization and death if you got the full vaccine, particularly if you have been boosted.

And that's probably because there are two types of immunity. There're more than that, but the main ones are the antibody, is the neutralizing antibody, is that zap the virus very early on and prevent any infection, even a mild one. Those things dwindled down over six months after even a very good vaccine. But these T cells have been charged by the vaccine, and they are ready to attack the virus. They keep us from getting sick after it's gotten a chance to set up. And thankfully, we have seen these

T cells maintain their effectiveness. They keep hitting hard targets in this virus that are very effective. And thankfully, when they do that, that's what keeps us from getting sicker later and hospitalized and dying from this infection.

DJJ:
Well, this term has kicked around a lot, "the new normal." Is the new normal because there are still concerns about personal safety, or have we simply learned new personal and business practices that are more effective, productive, and offer work–life balances that weren't there before? Have we just adapted?

Dr. Threlkeld:
Yeah. There are a lot of layers to that, that issue. I remember a great-aunt to whom I was very close, who nearly died of influenza in 1918. They called her family home to be with her or brother from the war. And she, to them miraculously, recovered. And she recalled very clearly that life was very different for the next two or three years after the pandemic of 1918 and '19. People didn't get together in large groups, large weddings were sort of off, and people behaved very differently. But I've always been fond of saying we have very short epidemiologic memories. And so, I think that we're already not really too worried about COVID right now. I hope that there won't be a new COVID variant that will throw us backward into having to worry about it. But it's clear that it's had an impact on our society, like nothing that we've seen in our lifetime. I mean, there's been the advent of telemedicine, for example. People don't want to go to the doctor's office anymore. They want to do this on-screen because it is more convenient.

I think there are things about it that are great. There are also things about it that are not as good. You can't examine someone—you might miss something. But there are aspects of it that are really good. Some types of health care are very efficiently and conveniently delivered via telehealth. Simple business meetings, Zoom meetings. Some of the meetings that I attend among several different branches of the hospital, for example. We have 30 people at the meeting, whereas we'd be lucky to get eight before. So, there are things about it that really accelerated some of the technology because we had to use it. Some of those things are really good that they'll make life easier. But I think we'll forget about COVID unless something replaces it that really jolts us back into worrying about epidemiology and transmission of disease. I mean, flu has killed on average 30,000 people a year in the United States for decades, some years much more than that. And people don't get too excited about the flu or getting their flu shot.

So, I think we'll sink into that sort of feeling about COVID. I hope we have the luxury of sinking into that sort of thing, and it doesn't come back at us with any larger numbers.

DJJ:
How do you think COVID-19 impacts palliative care?

Dr. Threlkeld:
Yeah, palliative care was significantly impacted by COVID for a while because palliative care is all about getting the patient cared for, sometimes in their final days, keeping them comfortable, making sure their goals were met for the latter portions of their lives. Not only just physical comfort but psychological well-being. Not having family able to visit in hospitals is a big problem when you're talking about doing that. So, I think it had a big impact on palliative care temporarily. Did it make palliative care better? Maybe, I mean, we had to adapt and look at other ways to accomplish that. If we can incorporate that into what we already did with palliative care, it may make bad matters better. But I think it had a big impact on palliative care

temporarily, because let's face it, when you have a month to live, you're not . . . I mean, you want to be around family and friends and communicate things.

And COVID made that desperately difficult to accomplish and sometimes impossible. And I think this goes back to some of the most difficult aspects of the psychological stressors on everybody, but certainly the health care people whose job it was and whose mission it was to accomplish that, and they were not able to do that. And stress in a job, I think for a health care worker, the biggest stress is looking at the end of the day and realizing you weren't able to accomplish for your patients what you needed to and wanted to that day. That's the biggest source of stress and burnout among health care workers. And I think that's the very place that health care workers were hit, both in palliative situation and even in the intensive care situation.

DJJ:
In October 2021, Johns Hopkins Center for Communication Programs reported that "More Than 8 in 10 Unvaccinated Americans Don't Want a COVID Vaccine."[31]
Do you know what that number might be today and what additional effort is needed to drive that number down?

Dr. Threlkeld**:**
I don't know the number right now. I can tell you this, though. I was lucky enough to be around a lot of elderly relatives growing up. These are people who regularly lost siblings due to childhood illnesses when they were growing up. It was nothing for that to happen. That was a commonplace of reality that they

31 Desmon, S. (2022, January 12). More than 8 in 10 unvaccinated Americans don't want a COVID vaccine - Johns Hopkins Center for Communication Programs. Johns Hopkins Center for Communication Programs - Inspiring Healthy Behavior Worldwide. Retrieved April 14, 2023, from https://ccp.jhu.edu/2021/10/25/vaccines-covid-behaviors-dashboard-united-states-data/

just faced. It was part of life. And they would turn over in their graves if they saw us not taking advantage of things like that. And of course, it spilled over not just to not wanting a COVID vaccine. Some people are not vaccinating their kids against polio and measles. And be assured, they—we will pay a price for that moving forward if that sort of thing takes hold. So, I think in that sense, yeah, it's, we paid a cost in how we do that. And I think it goes back, too, to what we were talking about earlier, and that science that is something that changes, and it advances over time. And what worries me almost more than any phrase that I've heard throughout this pandemic is that we should "Follow the science."

Generally, people by that mean that you should follow the person that they think does the science the way they think it should be and come to the conclusion that they agree with. Science is not a person. It's not even a body of knowledge that it was accomplished by science. Science is a methodology. It's a method of testing things, changing your thoughts and hypotheses, and coming up with better knowledge. The very body of knowledge that one person might swear by and another might disagree with is the thing that science is going to attack next year to come up with a better body of knowledge. And so, I think in that, we have to be sure that we're taking advantage of what the scientific method has given us—but never taking it religiously but moving forward. It's a way to improve the knowledge that we have, and we hope by that, improve our safety and our lifestyles. And you hope that that's going to be the result when we look back at this pandemic, and we will look forward to preventing the next one and to improving other parts of our life and society.

DJJ:
Looking in the rearview mirror, what could the medical community have done differently to slow the virus down or better educate the community?

Dr. Threlkeld:
Well, I mean, I'm a teacher at heart that's kind of in medical education and the like. And I think that's the one thing on which you can always improve. You can never do too good a job educating the public. I think that we did a not-so-great job at educating the public. There are things from the CDC on down that confused people. And so, I found myself forever trying to explain things that well —the rule is this, but here's why we need to deviate slightly from that rule. I always said in the beginning, in the vaccination time frame when it first came out, that if you gave me five minutes with someone who had an open mind at all, that I could convince them to get the vaccine just based on the facts. Now, if someone didn't have an open mind, that wasn't going to happen. But I think that we probably, the education and the facts and the simple data that could be brought to bear of explaining this to people, all too many times got shrouded among people's preconceptions and their political beliefs and to whom they were talking.

And it was just all too common for me to be confronted with people who said, "Well, I've done my research." And I would politely say, "No, you haven't done research. You have read other people's research and come to your own conclusions." Research is when you do trials, and you study it and you come to conclusions, and you adjust those conclusions. So, I think it was important to really know what facts were and to try to convey them in ways that were meaningful to people. People can understand things if you give it to them in a relevant kind of way. And I think that was a hard thing to do because there was just so much baggage attached to the facts of RNA vaccines.

I'll give an example. I was hit a lot of times with the criticism of, "Huh, these vaccines. Tell me what the five-year and 10-year toxicity rate and mortality is of these vaccines. How many people are going to die 10 years from now?"

And it was a meaningful question, an appropriate question, but one without the proper context. My answer was always, "Give me one example of a vaccine that caused some unforeseen problem or death 10 years after that vaccine that didn't cause a problem up front. Give me an example of that." And there aren't any, really. So, I think you have to have the right context and the right background of information to really put some of this new stuff into that context. And I think we didn't do that so well, I think nationally, and that's something we need to work on next time for sure.

DJJ:
Finally, what are some of the things about COVID-19 we don't know today and should be concerned about?

Dr. Threlkeld:
Yeah, I mean, I think that what we see in COVID-19 is the social reality that has come home to roost as it relates to diseases. The world is a small place. International travel is commonplace. It is extraordinarily more common. It has exploded geometrically over the last couple of decades in terms of things that happen in South America or the African subcontinent. Any of those places can get to Memphis, Tennessee, or Las Vegas or New York in a couple of weeks. And we saw this happen. So, I think that's a reality that we have to face. And so, we have to be very careful of international health. And so, the World Health Organization, the CDC, and its equivalents have to have proper surveillance and work together. We don't know where the next variant of this virus might come from. We don't know whether or not it

might be more resistant to our current immunity, to our current vaccine-associated immunity. It may be more contagious.

We are a lot closer than we probably thought to have had the clock turned back to March of 2020. I mean, it would've taken just another little variation and have a variant that really walled off our immunity, didn't respect the immunity that we have from previous variants of the vaccine, and to be very contagious. And all of a sudden, you're back to ground zero, to square one, and that's not a fantastic, sort of really unlikely scenario. So, I think we have to maintain our vigilance about that. Does that mean we don't relax as the incidence of this disease and the severity of it cuts down in our communities? Of course not. But we need to be careful and be watchful about that. And then one other thing about COVID that makes me nervous is that even as people worry about long-term vaccine problems, something that's never really happened before, they've forgotten about the long COVID reality.

And that is that we've seen very clearly in large studies that people who have COVID, for at least a year or two, have a significantly increased chance of strokes, blood clots, atrial fibrillation, myocarditis, all these things that can change your life for the worst and do it very quickly. They're clearly increased after COVID. Mortality around heart surgery is such that we delay heart surgeries for seven weeks or so after a COVID case to make sure it's safe enough to proceed. We don't know what that means five or 10 years from now. We may see sort of an epidemic, if you will, of cardiovascular problems that we haven't anticipated, and it really can't be measured for a while yet. The irony, of course, is that that's what people were worried about the vaccine. When it turns out, as you might expect, taking a million times what's in that vaccine, which is what you get with the real thing, plus 10 other proteins that weren't in that vaccine, you would expect that to be more damaging and to give you more potential problems downstream.

And so far, that's what we've seen. And unfortunately, I think that message is one of those things that we didn't really communicate that well to people along the way. We didn't put that in the correct terms for folks.

Dr. Stephen C. Threlkeld, MD, Infectious Disease Expert, Medical Director of Infectious Disease, Baptist Memorial Health Care

During the fight for life in many hospitals across the country, another fundamental process was going on behind the scenes—

maintaining access to a healthy blood supply. The blood supply is vitally important to all of us and especially the hospitals. However, most don't realize how fragile the process is to maintain blood on demand for use by our medical professionals. The mechanics behind lifesaving blood are discussed in the next chapter.

Chapter 10

LIFESAVING BLOOD BEHIND THE SCENES DURING THE PANDEMIC

Life is about rhythm. We vibrate, our hearts are pumping blood, we are a rhythm machine, that's what we are.

—Mickey Hart

The COVID-19 pandemic caused an unprecedented change to many sectors of the US, and blood centers who rely heavily on collections from schools, businesses, and churches were no exception. Shelter-in-place orders issued in 2020 due to COVID-19 closed these facilities.[32]

> Individuals typically demonstrate prosocial behavior during a crisis, and their willingness to help increases. However, a pandemic like COVID-19 is crucially different from other crises:
>
> a) First, it has the potential to affect every individual. The sense of personal moral obligation to help others might decrease when they themselves are affected by the crisis.
> b) Second, COVID-19 is highly transmissible and a threat to one's own and others' health, which poses unprecedented challenges.

---

32 Raghuwanshi, B., Behera, P., Singh, P., Khan, R., Munshi, R., Patil, A., & Chouhan, S. (2022, June). Blood Supply Management amid COVID 19 pandemic: Challenges and strategies. Journal of family medicine and primary care. Retrieved April 14, 2023, from https://www.ncbi.nlm.nih.gov/pmc/articles/PMC9480642/

c) Third, a pandemic is typically a long-term issue, and as such requires continuous willingness to help.[33]

As the balance between blood supply and demand is fragile, blood banks around the world were required to search for more efficient ways to recruit new blood donors. When the COVID-19 outbreak was declared a global pandemic, funding organizations had to react swiftly by directing emergency funds to organizations on the ground. They had to commit to changes in their grantmaking practices to help nonprofits face challenges brought on by the pandemic.

My conversation with Mr. David Williams, Blood Bank Regional Director, was quite illuminating as we discussed the mechanics and inner workings required to maintain the blood supply in this region and across the country. During the height of the pandemic, there was an unprecedented national blood shortage. Efforts were significantly ramped up to find creative ways to increase blood donations. COVID-19 created an astonishing demand for blood under unique circumstances. There were significant challenges with dwindling blood donations, and at the same time, trying to ensure the sustainability of the US blood supply.

DJJ:
What were your initial thoughts when collection sites you heavily depended on started closing?

---

33 Hellmann, D. M., Dorrough, A. R., & Glöckner, A. (2021, September 21). Prosocial behavior during the COVID-19 pandemic in Germany. the role of responsibility and vulnerability. Heliyon. Retrieved April 14, 2023, from https://www.ncbi.nlm.nih.gov/pmc/articles/PMC8482435/

David:
Well, one, most of them didn't close, but we have to also remember that I came into the blood service blood banking once the pandemic was about six months in, so I walked in in the middle of the pandemic. So, it was definitely a strange situation to go from Leadership Memphis, CEO of Leadership Memphis, to all of a sudden regional director of a blood bank. And so fortunately, I had a lot of great people around me with 20, 30-plus years' experience. And so, it was my job just not to mess anything up. But yeah, it was a very, very strange time. And there were members of my staff, my new staff that I didn't actually see their face for months because everybody was masked up. So, I've got a drawer full of masks downstairs. I'm happy to show you.

DJJ:
What was the uncertainty or fear experienced when COVID-19 first began?

David:
I don't know what they call it. There are the cycles of grief, right? So there had to be some sort of a cycle that we all went through. And I wish I knew, I wish I had the knowledge to know what that was, but I can just say that I think it was everything from disbelief to what the heck's going on here? How are we going to survive this? For many people, it was a life-and-death situation. For some, it was like they had to kind of grow to believe that there was something that was happening.

DJJ:
Did you ever think this would happen in these modern times or even in the US?

David:
I've watched movies, so I've seen *Contagion*; I've seen all those things. And so, I suppose in the back of my mind I'm thinking it could happen. But then you walk out of the movie and it's like, it's gone, right? But I know that there are a lot of people whose lives are built around studying that and being informed, being prepared, and making sure that our country and that the world is prepared. So yeah, I was not amongst them. I was just an average person that was caught off guard.

DJJ:
How did you see donor habits affected because of COVID-19?

David:
Two things basically happened with donors. They either kept coming or they stopped coming. And we're extremely grateful for those who continued to come. And we understand why some people didn't feel that they could. I think a lot of people forget that you can't manufacture blood. Nobody can just go out and make it. Someone has to give it. And we're regulated by the Food and Drug Administration.

And so we're considered an essential service, but I think we were all surprised during the pandemic that very often we were not treated like an essential service. And that was perhaps a big surprise for me because many people I knew in the community that I was asking to please help, schools were shut down, we couldn't do school drives. Over 10 percent of the country's blood supply comes from high school students. Churches were closed, people were worshipping virtually, and we understand that. But we had only a few churches that we were able to do drives with. Businesses, people were working remotely, right? And so, all the business people that we used to do blood drives with, not all, I shouldn't say all, many, just their employees were not there for us to do the blood drives. So, it was a shake-them-up situation.

DJJ:
Was it safe to donate blood during the COVID-19 pandemic?

David:
It was safe. It was safe. I mean, again, we're regulated by the Food and Drug Administration. We adhere to the CDC guidelines. We're in step with the local county health department, the state health commission. Anybody that could provide any guidance, we were following every bit of that. And people forget, it's sort of like, you think about going to a donor center to donate, and we were doing all the social distancing. We were doing all the sanitization; we had the sanitation stations; we had the masks. We had everything that we were expected to have. But when you do a mobile drive, you can only have so many people on a bus. And so, where we used to go and do a blood drive and we could collect 20 units, now we would go, and we could only collect 10 in the same period of time. So, we were taking every precaution, including where it meant we had to do less in order to continue to collect something.

DJJ:
What concerns did donors have about donating during the pandemic?

David:
I mean, any person going through a pandemic, people are going to have questions and concerns. And I had mine, my family had theirs. People that I work with had concerns. It was like, yes, do we want to keep our donors safe? Absolutely. Do we want to keep our employees safe? Absolutely. So, it was trying to keep everybody safe, and people did have questions and they

did have concerns. And there wasn't always clear guidance, but you just went the extra step, you went the extra mile to make sure that we were doing everything we could to keep people safe. But it was safe to donate.

DJJ:
What steps are being taken to protect the US blood supply from COVID-19?

David:
I mean, again, being regulated by the Food and Drug Administration, blood banks, just in general, they're all following guidelines. I mean, when somebody donates blood today, a sample of that blood is taken, and it's sent to a lab, and it is screened and tested for safety purposes. So, they're testing and testing and testing. By the time we get the results back and we can actually label the blood as safe and that a volunteer donated it, and we can then deliver it to the hospital, 48 hours have passed. So, you'll hear us talk a lot about, it's the blood on the shelves that saves lives. If some catastrophe happens today, it may be 48 hours before what is donated today by people who want to rush in and help, it might take 48 hours before that blood is actually available to help a patient. So, it is a never-ending request of people to please give and to give as often as they're allowed to give. And so, when we're working with hospital partners, we are just constantly communicating on a day-to-day basis just to make sure that we can supply. I want to say it's probably almost like that scene out of *It's a Wonderful Life*. Tell me what you need right now. Tell me what you need right now.

Diversity in the blood supply is important because certain blood types are unique to specific groups. Blood from a donor of a similar ethnic background is less likely to be rejected by a patient and often results in fewer complications after a transfusion. In addition, some people have rare blood types and need transfusions of compatible blood. Having a large, diverse pool of blood donors ensures that all patients will have access to the blood they need, when they need it. Despite this, America's Blood Centers estimates that less than 20 percent of all blood donations currently come from communities of color.[34]

DJJ:
How have communities of color been impacted?

David:
So, on that, I watched the news, and perhaps I got a lot of my information from the news. My friends, coworkers, but I know it was very difficult for communities of color for many reasons that I can appreciate, but maybe I can't completely understand. I'm not a person of color. So, I understand that. I understand that there are differences in how people of color might view a pandemic and what was happening in their community where it was disproportionately impacting their community and having a more devastating impact in their community. I don't know.

DJJ:
How have blood donations from communities of color been impacted?

34 (ASH), A. S. for H. (2022, August 4). HHS announces new campaign to increase U.S. blood and plasma donations. HHS.gov. Retrieved April 14, 2023, from https://www.hhs.gov/about/news/2022/08/04/hhs-announces-new-campaign-increase-us-blood-plasma-donations.html

David:
So as a historical reference, communities of color have not traditionally been a significant percentage of blood donors. So nationally, it's somewhere approximately 15 percent, and that's what it is in Memphis, Tennessee. It's less than 15 percent in a community that's 60, 65, 67 percent African American. So, there is a challenge that we face in engaging the African American community without COVID. Overlay COVID and it just becomes, increase the degree of difficulty in terms of connecting and making the case for really rolling up your sleeve and saving somebody's life.

DJJ:
What donor campaign strategies did you implement to ensure adequate blood inventory to supply contracted hospitals during the pandemic?

David:
I mean, I can just tell you that, you work the phones, you're on Zoom, you're on Teams, you're on every platform you can use. You're on social media. You're just appealing to humanity to care about fellow human beings, make a difference, and save a life. We did create a virtual blood drive where somebody could have a blood drive, and instead of us rolling up with the bloodmobile and people piling on and all that, the virtual blood drive, they could sign up and they could go to a donor center at their appointed time. They could pick their time. They could pick their day. And so, a bank, a church, a business could say, we're going to do a virtual blood drive this week and encourage their employees to go by and donate. So that was one way.

DJJ:

> The need for blood initially decreased because surgeries and medical treatments were postponed, ensuring hospital capacity for COVID-19-specific treatments. Blood banks worldwide still report a significant shortage in donations since the pandemic started. [35]

How have planned surgeries affected supply?

David:
So, before COVID, so I'll put this in perspective, Memphis, if I'm allowed to just talk about Memphis itself?

So, Memphis, for every four units we deliver to a hospital, only one of those units is donated locally. So, 75 percent of our community's blood supply comes from other communities that are part of our national network, other communities who give more than their community needs. So, we are technically what we would call, say, an importer city as opposed to an exporter city. People don't think about FedEx and other companies that know logistics. I mean, we have to know logistics, too, because we have to get blood to where it needs to be.

And so, we're constantly having to move blood to where it's needed most. If there's a shooting in El Paso, Texas, or in another situation, the blood supply may be moved around in order to meet that need. But with Memphis, it's every day. Every day we have to have support from our national network so that we can supply patients. So, you overlay that with a pandemic, and I mean, we think about what the stock market does. We watch those graphs. Take a look at March 2020 and

35 M;, V. B. S. S. (n.d.). The impact of covid-19 on blood donations. PloS one. https://pubmed.ncbi.nlm.nih.gov/35324952/

blood donations. It was the big crash of blood donations. And we have not recovered from that.

At the risk of dating this, it's like today, right now, our blood supply is half what it was this time last year. And so, when we're working with hospital partners, we are just constantly communicating on a day-to-day basis just to make sure that we can supply. I want to say it's probably almost like that scene out of *It's a Wonderful Life*. Tell me what you need right now. Tell me what you need right now.

DJJ:
What did funding look like doing the pandemic?

David:
Right. So even though we're a nonprofit, we have not actively been raising money. We've been so focused on volunteers and volunteer blood donations. So, I think that will be changing. But for now, we've really just focused on blood donation.

DJJ:
Is there a "new normal" for this business industry? Or have things relaxed and we're back to pre-Covid-19?

David:
You know, I think we're all hopeful that we can move past this and that we can, I don't know what the switch, I don't know where the switch is, I don't know what the lever is, but we're searching diligently to find a way to break through and to be able to communicate that this is something that is so important and so desperately needed. I mean, it's not that we want people to donate to us. It's that we want people to donate to help a patient. We're an intermediary. We're the middleman, so to speak. Don't do it for us. Do it for mom or dad or sister or

brother, or the person you go to church with or your neighbor or do it for a complete stranger.

One unit saves up to three lives. I mean, if you think about it, I mean, I used to be fascinated watching the news, and there are people who will run into a burning building. It might be a first responder, but it could be somebody, a next-door neighbor, and they run into a burning building to save somebody. Or there's this thin ice and there's somebody that's fallen through, and somebody just kind of glides out on that thin ice and they put that hand out there, and they're risking their own life to save someone else. Someone recently did that. They jumped into, it was a rain-swollen culvert, and they dived in to save a child. And they did save the child, but they didn't make it. And so those are all very heroic things. But so is just rolling up your sleeve and feeling a little bit of a pinch and donating a unit of blood that's going to save somebody's life.

DJJ:
What affect did the COVID-19 pandemic have on your personal life and that of your family?

David:
So, I mean, I think everybody in America, everybody in the world has a story to tell about how it impacted them personally. For me, it was working remotely. For me, it was trying to figure out a new routine of how to do what I needed to do and how to be responsive in everything from taking care of staff and those that were interacting, whether it was with leadership methods or with blood bank. My wife is a first responder—she's a nurse practitioner. She was on the front lines. She was doing drive-through COVID testing. And there were weeks that she was doing 200 people a week, and her day would start at 5:00 a.m., and I can remember she would be calling patients at 10, 11, 12 o'clock at night because people so wanted to know, did I test

positive? Did I test negative? What do I need to do with my family?

So, we became kind of part of a lot of families just because of the role that she was playing. And what were the risks that we were taking in terms of, I can remember a picture of her where the only way I knew it was her, she was all gowned up and had every piece of what, PPE, is that what they called it, personal protective equipment. She had every piece of that on. But I recognized her tennis shoes, then I knew it was her. But it takes a toll.

It takes a toll just physically, emotionally, mentally. People that you know, people that you learn to know. And so, we had to live carefully in terms of if she thought she might have been exposed, and then how did we have to adjust our life accordingly? So, there were things like that. There was my mom and dad, my sisters. My mom and dad were living in a retirement community, and we know what happened with a lot of retirement communities. And a lot of the communities were trying to protect their residents, and things began to shut down. And just being able to access my parents became a bit of a challenge.

And I was the one that provided their medications. I was the one that did the grocery shopping. And my sisters, they had their responsibilities. We all had certain things, roles that we played to take care of them. And my mom, my dad was very, very social people. And my mom had had a health condition and could not, when it actually did come time where they could get a vaccine, she couldn't have the vaccine because of her health condition. So, they had to remain in isolation. And my dad passed away a year and a half ago, and my mom is in hospice at this point, and I know that they would be, I think my dad could easily still be with us today if they hadn't been so cut off.

He'll never show up as a statistic. They'll never be part of the total number of people who passed away as a result of COVID.

But COVID nonetheless had an impact on them. And it cut their lives short. And it'll end up being that for my mom too. She could have gone—she's got 20 lives. Cats get nine lives. My mom got 20 lives.

DJJ:
On September 15, 2022, the World Health Organization reported deaths dropped to the lowest number since March 2020 and that the end of the COVID-19 pandemic was approaching.[36]
Is the COVID-19 pandemic ending?

David:
This pandemic probably is over, but it doesn't mean that it won't keep coming back. It's like if . . . Let's say it ends up being the flu-like thing. But even with the flu, you have people that don't take the flu shot. You have people that don't wash their hands. You have people that don't do those things that we're told every year will save lives and keep people healthier, so is this one done? I think so. We'll find out.

DJJ:
Do you think we are better prepared for the next pandemic?

David:
I think if it's a pandemic like this pandemic, then we're better prepared. If it's a pandemic of another type, then I think it's anybody's guess. We went through something that probably technically wasn't called a pandemic with HIV. Were we better prepared this time? And how much time goes by between now

36 Croft, J. (2022, September 15). 'end is in sight' for covid-19 pandemic, who chief says. WebMD. Retrieved April 14, 2023, from https://www.webmd.com/covid/news/20220915/end-in-sight-for-covid-19-says-who

and the time that there's a next pandemic? We tend to forget, right?

I'd love to think that we'll be much better prepared. Yes.

David Williams, Blood Bank Regional Director

Like the blood supply, we never think about oxygen until we need it, or we can't get it. Likewise with our ability to breathe and use our lungs. We breathe approximately 20,000 times a day. But when there is any interruption of our breathing, it is a serious matter. Well, imagine depending on great lung capacity for your livelihood. I am talking about a musician playing an instrument. Specifically, a saxophone. A musician opens up in the next chapter about the fear of contracting COVID-19 and losing lung capacity.

Chapter 11

A MUSICIAN'S STRUGGLE TO PROTECT HIS CRAFT

Music gives a soul to the universe, wings to the mind, flight to the imagination, and life to everything.

—Plato

Broadway, casinos, film and television production, and live performances all fell victim to the shutdowns due to COVID-19. Not only were the shows and the venues shuttered, but the many performers, support staff, and adjacent businesses were dealt a death blow. The entertainers and actors couldn't work. The makeup artists and set and costume designers all found themselves out of work. The roadies who build stages and monitor sound could not work. The venue owners could not open, and all the associated staff were without jobs. There is a huge ecosystem supporting the entertainment industry, and the virus crippled that infrastructure. Restaurants, subcontractors, car services, etc. were all devastated and may never be the same. Musicians were susceptible to the virus just like the rest of us, but the effects could have profound consequences on their ability to perform, especially those that sang or played instruments that depended on their lungs.

The COVID-19 pandemic caused major changes to how musicians and performers practiced and rehearsed, as well as bringing live performances to a halt. COVID-19 was center stage. Aside from being depended on to do our jobs, go to school, do shopping, and keep informed and connected with others during COVID-19, the internet also became the main source of entertainment. Artists stepped into the digital universe with great resilience during the pandemic. The world was heavily dependent on musicians and artists to create a new entertainment source. During the height of the pandemic, creatives turned to digital platforms more than ever, not only to offer relief to their fans and followers but also to regain some of their lost revenue, as their paid gigs and performances came to a staggering halt.

It was a pleasure to interview Mr. Brian "Breeze" Cayolle, world-renowned jazz saxophonist/clarinet master/singer/songwriter, at the Circle Music Store. We were surrounded by all types of horns, guitars, pianos, and other musical instruments. Breeze shared his thoughts on how he adapted when COVID-19 stunned the world.

DJJ:
Breeze, tell me what was happening in the music industry across the country, specifically in New Orleans.

Breeze:
Yeah. New Orleans totally shut down, and the problem with New Orleans is New Orleans's economy is based on entertainment. It's music, it's food, it's the restaurants, all that. So, you eliminate that, the music stops, the riot stops, it's over with, basically. No one in the city was working. No one in the city was working. So, I mean, it turned into almost like a wasteland. The French Quarter was empty. When's the last time you heard about the French Quarter being empty? Yeah, Bourbon Street was barren. There was nobody on Bourbon Street at all. There was nothing going on. There were no carnival parades. That was it. There was nothing.

So, no one was working. And there was nothing to fall back on. That was it. Everyone's job, for the most part, well, almost everyone's job, has something to do with that industry. Either you're in music, you're in food, you're in something that caters to those two industries. You're the guy that provides the paper products, the napkins, and the tables. You're the company that brings all of the tables and sets up all of these . . . You're gone. You're done too. Yeah, everybody. Everybody.

DJJ:
Things were shutting down rapidly. What were your initial thoughts when concerts and performances were canceled, venues closed, and travel suspended? Where you when all the pandemonium started?

Breeze:
Yeah. For New Year 2020, I was in Italy. I played the Winter Festival in Umbria. I left the States the day after Christmas and I came back the day after New Year's, and I was like, "Man, that was great." And then all of a sudden, I'm seeing, hearing all these news feed and clips and stuff about what's going on in Italy. And I'm like, "Oh, wait a minute. Is that the canary and the coal mine? Is that going to come here?" And sure enough, they started saying about New York and it was coming across the country and things were shutting down. And it's like, "That's it, that's the end of business. There's going to be no live playing. There's going to be no events like weddings and parties and all that. Everything's going to come to a grinding halt."

And one of the indications I knew about everything coming to a grinding halt was when my son's school closed. They closed for spring break. They extended the break for a week, and then they just didn't go back. So, if I'm not playing live and I'm not doing anything in that capacity, the only other stream of income I had was teaching private lessons. So, first thing I did was go and get a brand-new tablet with all the new operating systems in it. Because I figured if I had a chance of doing anything, there was going to be teaching virtually. And it was like some people were teaching virtually, but it was like someone you wanted to have a lesson with, and they lived across the country or in another country. That was really the state of virtual lessons. It wasn't like what it was about to be, which was every day teaching my students that I was normally in person.

But now the parents wanted whatever shred of a normal life that they could have for their kids. So, it's like, "Well, at least the band lessons are going to go on, so we're going to have that. So, I know at 3:00 or 3:30 or 4:00 or 4:30, you're going to have your lesson. So, get online, and we're going to go on with Mr. Breeze, and we're going to give you your lesson." And it was a strange year. There were lots of competitions that would've normally been in person, were done virtually. Yeah. So that was the saving grace for me was the fact that there was just such a yearning for something for the kids to be at least kind of normal. So that's pretty much where I was—I was in my music room.

After I would sit in helping my son virtually with his teachers, I would go into the next room and turn on my tablet and continue with virtual music lessons. So, I spent a lot of time in front of a screen, from like 7:30 in the morning till 6:00, 6:30, sometimes 7:00 at night. So, I was in front of this. I was teaching. I did a jazz camp that way. I learned about how to work all of those things. That conference call, you've seen multiple screens and have two and three kids at one time and try to teach jazz to them. It was interesting. Where was it? Teams and Zoom and Skype and Duo. I was already familiar with Skype, but Teams and all that multi screens at one time, that was a new game. That was a new game. Yeah.

DJJ:

Did you ever think this would happen in these modern times and especially in the United States?

Breeze:
No. You would never think that everything would come to a grinding halt. It was like, "Okay, well, we're going to have to do some alterations, some configurations. We're going to adjust to this." Not "Just going to pull a plug out the wall, and we're just going to stop. Everybody go home."

DJJ:
Did you think it would last for as long as it did?

Breeze:
Yeah. No, I never thought that was going to happen. I never thought it would go on that long. You figure, "Oh, eventually." And there were so many false starts. "We're going to open, we are going to set a date for this, and we're going to set." All right. And then "No." "Well, we reset the date for here. Three months down, four months down the road." "No." "Okay, well, next year. Same time next year we're going to have the festival." "No."

DJJ:
What were some of your immediate concerns and personal day-to-day changes?

Breeze:
My concern was not to get sick, not to catch it. And that was because this is before they came out with any kind of shot for it. And I'm watching on TV, people that are dying and having long-term effects if you did recover. It's all about your respiratory system. Well, being a horn player, anything like that, I'm out of business. If I survived, that's it. Party's over. You might survive. Are you going to have long-term effects afterwards?

So, what exactly does that mean, long-term effects? Are you going to be able to play, or you going to be able to sing, or you are just going to be left to the point where you just can sit there and just barely breathe and that's it. Or you can breathe, but then you got stamina problems or any kind of other issue that might arise from long term. You can't stand up there and play two hours. You can't play a wedding, you can't play a party, you can't play a festival because you don't have it in you. And you will never have it in you again. To have the stamina to pull that off, to stand outside in the heat in a festival and play, that just won't happen no more. You're done.

DJJ:
What did you fear the most about COVID-19?

Breeze:
Yeah, you can't teach a lesson if you can't play. You can't demonstrate what this is supposed to sound like if you can't play. It doesn't even matter about playing a job or a club or anything like that. You cannot play, period. So that ends all of it. That ends teaching, that ends playing, that ends all of it. Performing. You name it, everything is done. You're done.
It was—they all had fear in their faces. That was one of the hardest things to deal with. Every day to get up and have this totally new environment of seeing all your people that you see every day, but now you're looking at them on the screen—the teacher, all your classmates. That was day in, day out. Watching the teachers deal with that. I still have such high regard for his teachers because they were thrown in. They were just pushed into it. Like, "Here you go, do it." And that went on and on. I remember Christmas, you'd normally have a Christmas party. So now it's all virtual, so everybody's wearing their little Christmas hats and stuff. And I went and got my saxophone and started playing Christmas songs for them virtually. So, everybody was sitting, listening to me playing Christmas music for all of the kids.

DJJ:
I know that you have a special-needs son. How did you explain COVID-19 to him and ease any fears or concerns that he may have had?

Breeze:
Yeah. It was okay for him. Because I was with him and he kind of got used to that thing of being virtual and helping him do his work and all that. But when it ended and when it was time to go back, that's when it got hard. That's when it got hard about getting him to wear a mask and being in that environment and not being just totally full of fear because of just what he had seen and what he had heard and people getting sick. That took a long time to get that fear out of him.

So, it took a long time for him to not be totally fearful of going to school. And it wasn't just him, it was all of them. It was just a hard thing. And it was also hard because of how long this lasted. Now not only did he miss his junior year, but he missed almost half of his senior year. And then we had a half a year, and it was the graduation. So, there was so many programs and so many things that he should have been able to have a chance to be a part of that just didn't happen.

DJJ:
What digital platforms did you use during this staggering period?

Breeze:
Because of helping my son with school, I had learned about Microsoft Teams. That was like training central. I knew more about a computer after that than I had ever known before, from dealing with Teams. And then I was already familiar with Skype because Skype was one of the first programs when you would be overseas, you could still talk to someone and not get home and

have an astronomical phone bill, because you were still using the internet. Then there were other ones that I got accustomed to using. Duo, and there was Zoom, Skype, and Teams, and then there was another one, Meet-something. And then also I got used to calling people through, what was it? Facebook. Calling people on Facebook so I could see them. Yeah.

That's how a lot of the musicians were keeping in touch with each other, through Facebook. And some people were like, "Okay, well, check me out. I'm on Facebook. I'm going to have a virtual concert." And my friends who play piano, they would have a concert. If you wanted to come check it out, if you want to donate something, you can do it through Zelle or Venmo or PayPal. I learned about all of that stuff too, that went hand in hand with all of that. The Zelle and the Venmo and the PayPal and all that stuff. It was a world of education.

The funny thing is everyone thought that "Okay, when we get back to the world and the world starts up again, we're going to go back to the way it was." We didn't go back to the way it was. It is kind of a blend now. I'll have students that I'll see maybe once, maybe twice a month in person, but the rest of the lessons will be virtual. Which it helps the parents—there's no travel time involved. Now "Here, log on at this time and I'll be there, and I'll give you a lesson." Yeah. Some of them never stopped. Some of them just stayed virtual.

DJJ:

> The collapse of the live industry affected not only artists but the thousands of people who work alongside them. This includes everyone from road crew and sound engineers to security guards and transport and equipment companies—not to mention all the venues and the staff they employ. Then there is the fact that during the rolling lockdowns, many artists globally couldn't even

get into a studio to record to take advantage of the shift to digital.[37]

This had to be very frustrating. What can you tell us about this, and how did this affect you?

Breeze:
Wow. Like I said, all of my friends who, well . . . First of all, let's just talk about how it affected everyone that I worked with that wasn't a musician, like chefs and bartenders and barbacks. It was so far-reaching. It was like people that you wouldn't even think about. If you have a venue, well, what about the people that cleaned the place? What about the valet park? The guys that parked the cars. What about security? What about the barmaids? And what about everybody else that's involved in that? The guy that drives the shuttle bus to bring people around. I mean, it was just so far-reaching. And that's a club. When you think about the large venues, the large halls, and all the people that are involved in the upkeep and cleaning, and then just the staff to put on the events. I mean, all these people, it was so far-reaching, way more than just musicians. It was the road crews.

I was in touch with a lot of my friends, like I said, through Facebook. And everybody was just . . . Some of them were dumbfounded. And then you get news of somebody that you knew that didn't make it. Road crew people that didn't make it. Musicians that just, they didn't make it. A couple of club owners I knew, they didn't make it. They didn't come back. They caught it, and that's the last thing you heard, that they weren't doing well. And that was it. Somebody calls you up for a little while, or you see a posting on Facebook about rest in peace. They let you know they didn't make it.

37 How covid-19 exposed music industry fault lines and what can be done. UNCTAD. (2021, September 28). https://unctad.org/news/how-covid-19-exposed-music-industry-fault-lines-and-what-can-be-done

DJJ:

> COVID-19 had a major impact on singers and other musicians worldwide. It can affect the voice and can lead to paralysis of laryngeal nerves to long-term changes in respiratory function. There is a risk from aerosolization/droplet formation transmission with singing and with playing wind and brass instruments.[38]

This had to be of great concern to you. Can you share what your concerns were and how you managed?

Breeze:
Well, one of the things I do besides play instruments is I repair instruments. So, you had to figure out how were you not going to contaminate yourself with an instrument if someone had it and didn't know it. The horn's infected, but they didn't show any symptoms. Now you got this horn in your hands. What are the protocols? Then you're searching online for different—how do you avoid catching it? Okay, so you're going to let the instruments set out for how many days, so it's dry and there's no chance of infecting yourself, or you're going to use a disinfectant on the instrument and swab the instrument out to not infect yourself. Or you, you're going to use gloves, you're going to have a mask on, just in case. Yeah. So, I would have people from music store, they bring the instruments that needed repair to my house and drop them off in front of my house.

I would open a door, I'd pull them in, and I'd put them on the side and let them sit there and whatever. Cool out, you know. "Whatever you have on you, let's reduce the chance of

38 RT;, V. D. S. P. S. (n.d.). Covid-19: Impact on the musician and returning to singing; a literature review. Journal of voice : official journal of the Voice Foundation. Retrieved April 14, 2023, from https://pubmed.ncbi.nlm.nih.gov/33583675/

me catching it." It was a real thing because, man, I've caught colds from instruments. You can just, like, the flu, head cold from the instrument. So, you have to be careful. You don't play the instrument. Oh no.

So, they were bringing the instruments, I'd put them out, I'd let them air out. I try and disinfect them, wear gloves, fix the instruments. Call them, say, "Hey, okay, I got this one done." "Okay, we're going to come by and pick them up at this such and such a time." "Okay, I'll put them out front, and I'm going to stand there and wait for y'all when y'all come." "Okay, y'all come, I'm going to close the door. You take them and you go there." So that was just that side of it, the repair end of it. The repair people all over the country that were trying to figure out, how do you deal with an instrument that someone's blowing into? How contaminated is it? What are the real precautions? What are the chances of you catching COVID from that instrument?

DJJ:
What sustained you during this period?

Breeze:
Friends, being in touch, talking to my sister, being with my son. Being with him all day, every day. There was no replacing that time that we spent together. We were the two amigos hanging out. So, something good out of something bad is I got to spend so much time with my son. There were no interruptions. We got to spend a lot of movie time together, watching all those streaming services and all kind of crazy movies and just hanging out there, sitting down, having meals with him, watching *Star Trek* every evening. It was having Christmas with him, because you don't think about the holidays, sitting there with him. I preordered the meal from the grocery store. So, I go pick it up,

press the button on the car. The trunk opened up by itself. They put it in there. I paid for it.

Your trunk closes. You can bring it home. You turn on the oven, you put all that stuff in, and you're just heating it up. Because I wasn't going to cook all that stuff for, he and I. Then we just sat there and watched the rebroadcast of the previous year's Macy parade because they couldn't have the parade. Everything was a rebroadcast. And watching movies all day. Same thing for Christmas. Watching all those Christmas rebroadcast and all of the traditional movies, things that normally you wouldn't have time to do because you'd be so busy going and trying to do stuff that you actually did have time this year to sit down and watch that goofy Christmas movie with him. Watch the Grinch.

So that was the one saving grace of all of that was being able to spend so much time with him.

That was the heartbreaking, bad part about it when life came back, and we had to go back to school; he didn't want that to end. That part of that connection of he and I sitting down and me making hamburgers and pizzas and all that stuff and hanging out, watching TV over the weekends. It's like, "Sorry, man. We're going to try and get the world started again now." Yeah.

> Most performing artists are portfolio workers. The introduction of social distancing measures shut down large then small gatherings, public venues then small-scale bars, cafés, and restaurants. As a result, the multiple income streams on which many performing artists rely all disappeared. This includes performance occasions such as concerts and soundtracks, private bookings such as weddings and parties, etc., and then their parallel work (waitressing, casual admin). From a more complex perspective, parallel creative careers that many combine with their work as performing artists

(freelance producing, sound engineering, technical and roadie work, private tuition, as well as participatory arts work) also disappeared.[39]

DJJ:
Tell us about the worry, stress, and grief involved in trying to navigate this "new normal."

Breeze:
Yeah. The new normal was just surreal. Some of the clubs that I played tried to reopen. So now you've got tables spaced apart in the living room, looks weird, and everybody's trying to be at ease, but it's not quite there. Everyone looks slightly weirded out, and you're kind of weirded out, and they're staying away from you, and the tables are away from each other and the bartenders and all that. Some of them are wearing masks. It was a strange environment, and they didn't want to take a chance because if you have too many people come in, then there's a health code violation and now you get shut down, which is now you're starting back at ground zero trying to reopen. So, it was really tough. And being close up on someone was just scary. It really was. Everybody was being checked.

I would still, to this day, how has this changed? I still play for assisted living facilities. When you go through those facilities, you have to show a vaccination card and they're going to take your temperature before you get past the front gate. They are going to take your temperature and give you a real hard look. Because we can't have what happened before happening again.

As far as virtual teaching, that tried to evolve back into one-on-one teaching, but this was also before the kids could get vaccinated. So that was still very dicey, very limited. "Have you

---

39 Performing artists in the age of covid-19: A moment of urgent action ... (n.d.). Retrieved April 14, 2023, from https://pure.qub.ac.uk/files/204727792/Performing_Artists_in_the_age_of_COVID_19.pdf

had your shot?" And "How we're going to do this?" And "We're going to go into a well-ventilated area. We're going to do this in an open area. We're going to do this in a gym. We're going to do this."

And it's just the two of us in this huge room so that it reduces the risk of somebody getting sick. That was the new normal of them trying to reestablish some sort of in-contact lessons and in-contact performances. Some musicians just didn't want to do it. I mean, some of the guys I knew who were up in age, older than I was, they were like, "I can't take a chance." And they just didn't go back. They didn't come back. They still aren't back. Some of them now are finally coming back, but they're very wary of it. They're wearing masks even after all of this time. What is it? Two years down the road now and it's still not back.

DJJ:
Do a lot of the musicians believe in the vaccine or getting the vaccines? What's the general consensus?

Breeze:
I still have a few musicians I know that didn't get it. Some of I know that that just didn't trust it. Most of them took it because we all had to witness all of those notices on Facebook about who didn't make it. So, when the vaccine came out, yeah, I went and did it. Yeah. It was like, "Well, I'm going to take a chance." Because I said I'm just at that point in the game, only thing I could do, take a chance, because you don't know what the future's going to hold. If we're going to open back up, what we're going to do, what's going to happen. Yeah.

DJJ:
Many say we're looking at COVID-19 through the rearview mirror. Is pre-pandemic live entertainment back?

Breeze:
It is not back to where it was. It's trying to get back. I'm playing so many parties now that were events that were postponed or canceled indefinitely, and now they're finally coming back. I've had more jobs that were supposed to happen in 2020 and in 2021 and now they're happening. The weddings, conventions, and parties—all of that stuff just got put on hold. And I know more weddings got put on hold and the bride and grooms have said, "We can't do it. We can't have everybody get together. So, what sense does it make to get married now? So, we'll wait until we can get everybody together." Hey, and it's trying to come back. The fact that events that I'm doing would never be done on a Wednesday or a Thursday night. A wedding party, that's always a Friday night, a Saturday night, the wedding's on Sunday. No, now it's the middle of the week.

So, they'll let you know that everybody's trying to come back at the same time. It's still dicey. I played a festival not too long ago and people made the rehearsal, and it came time for the performance, and they weren't there because they tested positive. So somewhere along the way they tested positive. So, the lineup was constantly changing because someone was testing positive. It is the new normal and some people, it's like a cold, but some people are really getting pretty sick still. Now it's an individual thing of how sick people are going to get, even with the vaccine. So, it's like, "Yeah, you had the vaccine, but nah, I just spoke to you on the phone, and you sound like you are flat on your back." Yeah.

DJJ:
What convinced you to come back in and feel the rush and excitement of a live audience?

Breeze:
Being a band leader and you know; you got people out there that want you to perform so that they can get back out there. So, I was just, "Come on back and play." Yeah. And that's how I ended up going back as far as live performing.
Then eventually some students really wanted to have an in-person lesson. Yeah. So little by little now I'm starting to see more of them starting to come back. At least once or maybe twice a month, like I said, and the other lessons will be virtual. The gigs, they're coming back. I check out friends of mine on Facebook, and they're trying to go overseas and do some things, but it's nowhere near what it was before the pandemic, as far as I can tell now. It's not the same. It is a new normal, a new reality. And who knows how long if it'll ever be what it was again. You don't know.

Brian "Breeze" Cayolle, world-renowned jazz saxophonist/clarinet master/singer/songwriter

Breeze talked about the fear and threat of COVID-19 compromising his ability to play his saxophone and perform. He did not want to contract the virus and risk his lungs being destroyed. There were others who weren't as fortunate to avoid the virus and experienced a range of issues, from difficulty breathing to death. The next chapter exposes what it was like on the front lines in hospital COVID-19 wards.

Chapter 12

LIFE'S BATTLE ON THE FRONT LINES FROM THE COVID-19 WARD

You may encounter many defeats, but you must not be defeated. In fact, it may be necessary to encounter the defeats so you can know who you are, what you can rise from, how you can still come out of it.

—Maya Angelou

The beleaguered nursing profession has endured a decrease in numbers and a reduction in those entering it. There have been many contributing factors, and COVID-19 added to the toll with its harsh realities and mental and physical demands. According to the American Nurses Association, 51 percent of nurses feel overwhelmed. "Preliminary findings from International Council of Nurses' (ICN) new survey of its 130-plus National Nurses Associations (NNAs), coupled with studies by its NNAs and other sources, suggest that the COVID-19 Effect is a unique and complex form of trauma with potentially devastating consequences in both the short- and long-term for individual nurses and health care systems they work in."[40] McKinsey's data showed that of the 22 percent of nurses who suggested they would leave their current positions, 60 percent

---

40 The COVID-19 effect: World's nurses facing mass trauma, an immediate danger to the profession and future of our Health Systems. ICN. (n.d.). Retrieved April 10, 2023, from https://www.icn.ch/news/covid-19-effect-worlds-nurses-facing-mass-trauma-immediate-danger-profession-and-future-our

stated they have been more inclined to leave since the pandemic began.[41]

Many health care professionals are drowning under their workloads and increased patient-to-nurse ratios, which is taking an emotional toll. Nurses are under severe strain, and mental exhaustion has become pervasive in their ranks. Nursing shortages have become critical across the country, which for some communities has created a complete crisis. Emergency rooms and COVID-19 wards were staffed with courageous individuals that risked life and sanity as they mounted a strategic battle to care for patients afflicted by the deadly coronavirus. Taking care of patients under the best conditions can be challenging. Try to imagine the daily routine of nurses, doctors, and other health care professionals at the height of the pandemic. Wearing a full complement of robust personal protective equipment (PPE) for the duration of their long shifts was formidable in itself. Protective clothing, N95 masks or higher, gloves, eye protection, gowns, face shields, shoe covers, and in some cases, respirators were essential to protect health care professionals from infection and illness. Conditions were unbearable and took on the characteristics of an active war zone. At the end of the day, looming in the minds of these professionals was the thought that they didn't want to expose or infect any loved ones when they went home. There was a focused and intentional ritual of disrobing in the garage and sanitizing the body before entering the space with family. In some cases, these health care professionals lived apart from their families to protect them.

Come walk with me through my discussion with Mrs. Kathryn Wiggs, Administrative Director of Nursing, Methodist

41 Berlin, G., Lapointe, M., Murphy, M., & Viscardi, M. (2021, May 11). Nursing in 2021: Retaining the health care workforce when we need it most. McKinsey & Company. Retrieved April 10, 2023, from https://www.mckinsey.com/industries/health_care/our-insights/nursing-in-2021-retaining-the-health_care-workforce-when-we-need-it-most?cid=eml-web

Le Bonheur Healthcare North, as she recounts the frightening attack of COVID-19 and the extraordinary measures taken to mobilize for the war against the virus. The valiant efforts of her team and nurses across the country should never be forgotten.

I was able to tour the facility and talk to Kathryn about what she witnessed on the front lines during the height of the pandemic.

The COVID-19 pandemic was not yet in sight when the World Health Organization (WHO) declared 2020 the *Year of the Nurse and Midwife*, with a goal to raise awareness of the need for "nine million more nurses and midwives to achieve universal health coverage by 2030." [42] Neither the WHO nor nurses could have imagined how the profession would be thrust into the spotlight during massive public health crises. The COVID-19 pandemic, Black Lives Matter and social justice movement, unemployment, financial crisis, environmental disasters, and politics have exposed the fragility and inequities of our health care and nursing education systems.[43]

DJJ:

Even though your experience as a health care provider has allowed exposure to a number of tragedies, diseases, illnesses, and even deaths, I'm guessing the scale and global impact of COVID-19 was an anomaly to you as well. What were some of your concerns and fears during this time?

---

42 The importance of midwives in achieving Universal Health Coverage. Wilson Center. (n.d.). https://www.wilsoncenter.org/event/importance-midwives-achieving-universal-health-coverage#:~:text=However%2C%20the%20world%20will%20need,legislated%20and%20regulated%2C%20said%20Knutsson.

43 Ojin homepage. OJIN. (n.d.). Retrieved April 14, 2023, from https://ojin.nursingworld.org/table-of-contents/volume-26-2021/number-2-may-2021/the-impact-of-covid-19-on-the-nursing-workforce/

Kathryn:
Oh, they were great. How long is it going to last? How sick are the patients going to be? How can we provide the best, safest care for these patients? How do we support our nurses and health care workers during this? There was a lot of unknown.

DJJ:
Did you ever think we would see the level of deaths experienced with COVID-19?

Kathryn:
Never in my life would I ever have dreamed the magnitude of the death that we experienced. So far Methodist North has had 410 patients die of COVID in just two and a half years. That's extraordinary.

Even on the worst surge, which was in August 2021, we had the most, 77 patients. And then 22 of those were in our critical care areas. And then 17 of those were on ventilators. And then, when the patient would go on the ventilator, their chances of mortality was really, really great. Very few of them ever came off the ventilator and discharged. So, the death was just really high.

And then came another big surge in January 2022. Then we had, like, 63 patients in the hospital with COVID, with 17 in critical care and 15 of those on a ventilator. So, you can see, once they made it to ICU, a lot of them got placed on mechanical ventilation.

And then our morgues were full, and we had to look at alternate sources and places to place the bodies. We even had a refrigerator truck on standby, in the event that we needed to use those. It was just a very trying time for everybody.

DJJ:
Did you ever think this would happen in these modern times and especially in the United States?

Kathryn:
Never. Never. Because the United States has such advanced science skills. They do such advanced research. We started hearing about COVID, and then we thought, "Oh, it's in China. Now it's gone to another country. Is it going to make it to the US?"

Well, knowing people travel internationally, we figured it was coming to the US; we just didn't know when. It makes it to the US. "When is it coming to Tennessee?" It gets to Tennessee and then it's like, "When is it getting to Memphis?" And then Methodist North had our first patient, and that's when our COVID journey began.

DJJ:
How were community closures and lockdowns communicated at the hospital, and how did the hospital try to prepare the staff for this novel COVID-19 virus?

Kathryn:
Great question. We work collaboratively with our local county, state, and federal government. We follow the CDC guidelines. And then we would communicate daily to the associates. Michael Ugwueke, our corporate CEO, would send out a daily email.

And then we instituted our Incident Command Center because we're always in a state of readiness for a disaster. So, we instituted that system-wide, and we would meet every day. We started tracking data and all this other information.

And then Dr. Florence Jones, who is the North CEO and president, would send out communication also to the North associates. And then we would have our daily shift huddles and stuff. That information was also disseminated to the associates.

DJJ:

Kathryn, tell me a little bit more about this Incident Command Center. What was that?

Kathryn:

It starts at the system level, and then each facility has their own, and the system incorporates different physicians and entities as they work together and do the planning for the COVID, and then within the incident command center you have different section chiefs. You have the incident commander that kind of oversees it, then you have an operations chief, you have a financial chief, you have a planning chief. And then they meet and talk about what updates, ideas, troubleshoot, what do we need, you know, throw ideas out, and just work together on how to best meet the needs of what's going on.

DJJ:

COVID-19 was new for many in the medical community. What type of questions did the doctors, nurses, labs, etc. have?

Kathryn:

Oh, they had plenty of questions. "What is COVID? How long is it going to be here? How can we provide the safest care for our patients? What are the long-term effects from this going to be?" And then "How do we protect ourselves? How do we protect our families?"

And we had some associates that would stay somewhere else. They would not go home to their families. And then we had some associates who would disrobe in their garage and take their shoes off. The first thing they would do would be to go take a shower before they touched anything in their home.

Yeah, we've used and utilized our subject matter experts to help us with those answers that we didn't know. And so, then they would put out talking sheets of talking points for us to use to help best get the same message across the whole system, so everybody heard the same message.

DJJ:
Kathryn, tell us about the supplies and the lack of, or what you experienced across a full spectrum of things.

Kathryn:
Oh, the list is endless. PPE or the personal protective equipment was huge. The N95 masks, quickly we had to store them in a secure spot so that everybody would use them appropriately and stuff. So N95 masks, the face shields—we had other associates within the system even making face shields, making cloth masks, because if you worked in the hospital proper, you couldn't wear a cloth mask, had to be a hospital-grade mask. And then ventilators, we were short on ventilators, which we rented what was available, but that quickly got exhausted with every hospital in the city needing more ventilators. I think the day we had the most on ventilators was 22.

So, as you can see, our CVICU, that was our COVID unit, we had to expand, which surge planning was huge. We had to plan on where are we going to expand our bed capacity to take care of these patients. And we did have to implement a lot of that plan. So, the ventilators were short. And then that put the providers, "What are we going to do?" They worked with the ethics committee. It's like, "Do we not put this patient on the ventilator?" Or "Okay, so we've put them on the ventilator, so does that make them an automatic 'no resuscitation'?" Because that can prolong the patient's length of stay trying to do all these heroic measures. Therein, just trying to create more bed capacity. But we didn't pull the trigger on either of those. We left that with the families to make that decision. But it was a topic that we had to discuss. We had to look at all options.

Very few patients that had COVID came off the ventilator. Now, if you're on a ventilator and you don't have COVID, yeah, we get those off all the time. But with how the disease process goes with COVID, it makes it difficult to come off of the ventilator. We saw about two, maybe three. We've had 410 deaths over the last two and a half years. So low frequency of survival with it on a ventilator.

DJJ:
Medical workers were tired but kept showing up for the same simple reason most sought out this field in the first place: they wanted to help people. They witnessed immense pain and wanted to provide comfort. The media often referred to health care workers as heroes or angels, but you and other medical personnel were actually human beings who were not immune to the pressure, grief, and relentless crush of misery this pandemic caused.
Tell me about a typical day in the hospital during the height of the pandemic.

Kathryn:
Oh, it was intense. It was very intense. People had to be able to change processes on the fly because everything was changing so fast. But what we did at the height of the pandemic was cohorted the patients, which is where you section them off away from the non-COVID patients, so that you minimize the cross contamination of the virus. And if you couldn't section it off by doors, we would use walls. Or even if we used part of a hallway, we would use a temporary wall and then move it as we needed it to, to cohort those patients. We had a cohort on for Med Surg, a cohort for step-down, and then CVICU was our critical care cohort, which was a 12-bed unit.

And so, they would be dressed out in their PPE, which is their protective personal equipment, which would be the gown, the gloves, the N95 mask, and the face shield. And they would be behind that wall the whole 12 hours of their shift, except when they had to leave to have their meal break or restroom break. So not only were they hot and tired at the end of their shift, but they were pretty isolated from the rest of the staff. And then they also bundled their care, which is they would try and take everything that they needed to do to care for that patient when they went into the room, so they didn't have to keep coming in and out of the room, to minimize their exposure and opening the door and closing it a lot.

But with that came the added duties of taking on the roles of other departments like environmental services and dietary. So, the nurse would go in there and take her meds, do her assessment, and then she'd disinfect the side rails, the tables, and empty the garbage, take the trays in, discarded the meal tray. So, the nurse also took on a lot more roles, but that also provided the opportunity with a little bit more time with the patients because the patients are here for a service and we're the guest in the patients' lives, and we wanted to be that friend, that family member, and show that compassion because they couldn't have visitors at the time. And so that brought a lot of moral distress to the staff. And so, then the life of a day.

And when I mentioned the meal breaks and the restroom breaks, that was a luxury that day. Most of these nurses did not have time to eat. Most days, we were lucky if they got a chance to use the restroom. And then because of wearing the N95 on their face all day, a lot of them would develop pressure ulcers, always bruises on their face. The back of their ears would get sore. They were warriors, but they were also humans too.

DJJ:
Tell us about your experience with the patients and families.

Kathryn:
That was a really, really, really hard time. It was heartbreaking, absolutely heartbreaking, to be standing at the front door of the hospital and have to tell a family member, "I'm so sorry, you can't come in." Because initially when COVID hit, we stopped all visitations. We stopped all visitations. We even stopped our elective procedures. And then we were worried because you've got these healthy patients out there, but even the doctors' offices were closing. They couldn't figure out how to manage it. And they did eventually start using the telehealth as well. But in that gap of time, we were worried for the other patients. And then the patients quit coming to the hospital because they didn't want to get COVID. So, then the ones that came were really, really sick, and so having to have those conversations with the families.

Then it starts opening up a little bit. We start doing some procedures, and so then we start having patients coming in for outpatient procedures, CT, MRI, those type of things. By then we had put screeners in our hospital lobby, and so they had a sheet of every outpatient procedure and test that was being done that day. And the patient would have to say, "I'm Kathryn Wiggs. I'm coming in for a CT today." The screener would verify, "Yes, you are." And if she wasn't on the list, they would call to verify that maybe they were an add-on or something.

And then the COVID patients could not have any visitors. The only time they could get visitors was at end of life. End of life was death is imminent. Imminent death is the only time that we would have the patients' families come up, for their end-of-life visits. And then we would communicate to the screeners because the screeners knew which rooms were COVID. So, we would have to let them know this patient can have visitors. It was a really tough time.

DJJ:
From what I've read in the research and what we've talked about and seen, the relationship between the patient and the nurse really became the two-way linkage between the patient and the family.

Kathryn:
The nurse was the liaison between the patient and their family members. Mother's Day hit, Father's Day hits, holidays hit. And so, we utilized iPads and used FaceTime to help those family members talk to the patients. And then we would even use Zoom with some of them that didn't have an iPhone so they couldn't use FaceTime. Got very innovative, very creative. And even for those patients that were at end of life and that either the family just could not bring themselves to come to the hospital, either because of COVID or because they knew they were saying goodbye to their family member, we would still offer Zoom. We did. We had family members that took us up on that. And so, they would Zoom, and they would talk to their loved one, even though the patient couldn't talk back, so that they could have that final closure moment.

Yeah, we would get quite a few of family complaints, and we'd do service recovery for it. And that was actually what prompted us to start doing Face Timing with patients and their family members. And then we broadened it to other technological resources.

DJJ:
Can you tell us about the roller coaster of emotions experienced during the various surges due to holidays and family gatherings?

Kathryn:
We dreaded holidays, we dreaded big sporting events, and we dreaded all of that because we knew in two weeks there's either going to be a spike, or there's going to be a big surge. Because is this going to be a super-spreader? There was so much fear in there, and it's like, "All right, we're breathing now. But give us two weeks, we're going to be at it." We dreaded those type of events because we knew we were fixing to get a spike again. And we did.

Because nurses come in and we take care of the patients. They're just so resilient that they really don't decompress until after the event. And when we talk about all those deaths, there was one day in January of '22 that CVICU had four deaths in one day, and that's a unit that only has 12 beds, so a third of their patients died that day. That's hard for them to deal with. So, providing them a lot of support.

DJJ:
How did you see health care services change?

Kathryn:
Yeah, some of those changes are still in place and a lot has changed. The visitation policy changed based on what was going on with COVID at the time. So, we went from absolutely no visitors to non-COVID patients could have one visitor a day, but they couldn't swap out. And it just kind of revised as the COVID situation changed.

And then, yeah, so then we had to start also screening our emergency department patients when they came in, because that service, that didn't change. And then we did start using Zoom and conference calls for our staff meetings, for our town halls, in some of our other meetings, so that we could still get the participation of everyone without them actually having to come to the hospital. Because of one, trying to minimize exposure, and two, trying to still keep them informed.

And so, another big thing that we did is, when the associates that were not direct patient care, if they could do their job remotely, we allowed them to work remotely from home, trying to minimize their risk. And then we also skilled-up the nurses that were not in direct patient care, so we could use them in patient care. Because when the patient volume dropped off when COVID first hit and patients weren't coming to the hospital, we had to be good stewards of our finances, so we didn't need agency nurses as much. So, we were canceling contracts, but then as the patient volume was returning, we needed those nurses.

And so again, trying to be good stewards of our money, we used our skilled-up nurses, which means we trained our step-down nurses to take care of critical care patients, not necessarily ones on a ventilator, but stable critical care patients. And then other nonclinical nurses, we skilled-up to be a nurse assist on the floor, so they could help with starting IVs, taking an Accu-Chek, blood sugar, and other skills that they were competent to complete. Hadn't done it in a long time, but they were still a great set of hands to help those nurses on the floors.

And even though we had all these things that changed, one thing that did not change is the foundation of who we are. Our pursuit of excellence. We did submit a Beacon application, which is for our critical care areas, showing their excellence in care, excellence in patient outcomes and patient satisfaction. Still pursuing and keeping with what the core of who we are was important to us to maintain.

DJJ:

Kathryn, can you tell us about the anger the nurses felt, especially during the Thanksgiving and Christmas holidays - and then the increase in patients with COVID-19?

Kathryn:
Yeah, they felt anger. I felt anger. It's like you've got this big sporting event, you've got this big celebration. It's like we're looking at death in our face every day. And it's like, "Do you not care about your neighbor next door? Do you not care who you might be getting it from? Who you're going to give it to? Do you not care that you might be giving it to my family member?" Yeah, there was a lot of anger.

DJJ:
Tell us about the interaction with the patient's family and their frustration with the inability to visit their loved ones.

Kathryn:
There was. They would get very angry. We'd have to do a lot of service recovery. And in fact, that was why we initially first started doing "Here, let me FaceTime your family member" then. Because we had started FaceTime before we started using all the other technology sources.
People were having big family events. They'd go to these big sporting events, there'd be the holidays, and at first the small holidays, like Fourth of July and Labor Day, which wouldn't be that big a deal for people. But some of those, the Thanksgivings, and the Christmases, when they would go to all those big events, it would create some anger. It's like, "Do you not care that you might get COVID? Do you not care that you might give it to your neighbor? Do you not care that you're going to give it to my family member?" We're looking at death in our face every day. Do these people not care? And I know that some people didn't believe it. They thought it was a joke, but we lived and walked it every day, and it was not a joke.

DJJ:
Let's talk a little bit about the blood supply and blood demand. How did that affect the hospital? Because I know there were a number of things that were going on. Elective surgery may have discontinued, but then you still had those surgeries that were required. So how was blood supply affected?

Kathryn:
Blood supply was really extremely low. In fact, we added the blood supply to the data that we were tracking in our incident command center so that we would know what are critical shortages that day. And then we changed the parameters in collaboration with the medical staff on what would be an acceptable blood count to give a patient a transfusion.

DJJ:
Another question is, we didn't ask you about the vaccine, but how did the vaccine affect the numbers? Do you think the numbers in ICU went down after the vaccine? Because we still know we had patients that contracted COVID-19 even with the vaccine. So, was that also a level of frustration for the nurses because they thought maybe the vaccine would have decreased the numbers?

Kathryn:
Well, it wasn't the end-all because even vaccinated patients were coming in the hospital and dying from it. But the moral distress that it would . . . That was an added component of the moral distress for the nurses because it's like, "Man, if this patient had just gotten the vaccine, maybe he wouldn't be as sick. Maybe he wouldn't be on a ventilator." And we would never know the answer to that question. But the unvaccinated patients, it did hit harder.

DJJ:

> According to an article published by the Kaiser Family Foundation in February 2021, among the many impacts of the COVID-19 pandemic, its effects on mental health have proven to be widespread and substantial. The impact of the pandemic on the mental health and well-being on health care workers has been well documented, with anxiety, depression, and post-traumatic stress disorder being reported in nurses, along with increased risk of burnout and emotional exhaustion. Some health care workers, including nurses, have also been subject to bullying and stigma, partly due to the perception that they are more likely to contract and spread COVID-19.[44]

What can you tell us about the mental anxieties and stress felt during this period by you and your staff?

Kathryn:
Several for that, but the number one would be the moral distress. They were distressed because of so much death that they were encountering. And then you would have these patients at the end of life. And majority of the patients, when they were placed on mechanical ventilation, they would expire. They wouldn't make it. And some of the family members just were not ready to make the patient a "no resuscitation." So, it would be hard for the nurses to resus those patients. But nursing is a calling, and so we're going to do and abide by the family's wishes. And

---

44 Ashley Kirzinger. Follow @AshleyKirzinger on Twitter, A. K. F. @audrey__kearney on T., & 2020, A. (2020, April 20). KFF Health Tracking Poll – early april 2020: The impact of coronavirus on life in America. KFF. Retrieved April 14, 2023, from https://www.kff.org/coronavirus-covid-19/report/kff-health-tracking-poll-early-april-2020/

then other components of the moral distress are just we're here to save and to help patients. And there were times when they felt like it was futile care, and they want to save the patient—they want to save every patient. And it was hard because they couldn't.

DJJ:
Did you or your nurses experience any long-term difficulties with depression and stress—after you've gone through pretty much a war zone?

Kathryn:
Yeah, and that's exactly what we would refer to it as at times—war zone.

DJJ:
A war zone?

Kathryn:
Yeah. Lot of nurses have the PTSD from it. And then we would have employees' assistance programs when it would be at its height, and they just needed that extra support that would come in and have sessions with them. And then I would come in and other leaders would come in on off shifts to provide support to them. And then the added component of the moral distress was when we would have our own associates that would pass away from it. We had three nurses and one environmental services that passed away from COVID. And I actually had to go and tell the nursing staff. The nursing staff knew this nurse was really sick, not doing well. But right after she passed, I went up to the nursing unit and had to share that with the nursing staff. And that was really hard.

DJJ:
What did you find to be the most extremely stressful, disturbing, or traumatic experience due to COVID-19?

Kathryn:
Number one is the deaths. Number two is the moral distress that was caused to the associates and to the leaders. And then the third one is the staffing that was impacted from it.

DJJ:
Are you aware of any new support systems established for nursing staff because of the COVID-19 pandemic?

Kathryn:
Yes. We have the employees' assistance program. So, we have counseling on-site at each facility. And then there's the spiritual care helpline that associates and patients and community people are welcome to call. And then, like I said, the support that they get from the leaders. Yeah.

DJJ:
Due to the COVID-19 pandemic, how is nursing recruitment expected to change?

Kathryn:
It's changed along with everything else that's changed. We still hire for our culture. We're not going to hire anybody just because they're a body. We do still hire for our culture. But executive leaders have gone internationally to seek to hire nurses.

DJJ:
Is it harder to get nurses?

Kathryn:
Oh yes, it is. It's hard to get nurses, and it's hard to get nursing assistants. Used to be we could get a lot of applications for nursing assistants. We get very few of those now. And nurses are really hard to get too. They're seeking employment elsewhere.

DJJ:
Has the COVID-19 pandemic resulted in earlier than expected retirements among nursing staff?

Kathryn:
Absolutely. Those that were nearing retirement did choose to go on and retire. And then we also lost a lot of nurses because they were tired. Day in, day out to come in and go through this moral distress. We lost a lot of nurses to go to a less stressful job, whether it be a doctor's office, a surgery center, or to be a travel nurse, because travel nurses were making mega-bucks and they were following the money. So, we lost a lot to be travel nurses.

DJJ:
The COVID-19 pandemic has presented death, devastation, and disruption—but also an unprecedented opportunity to leverage lessons learned from the pandemic and truly transform US health, health care, and health delivery.
What do you think were some of the immediate lessons learned?

Kathryn:
It validated the culture that we had and worked on for many, many years and truly showed the resilience because we knew we had a strong team, but this made our team even stronger. Everybody had everybody's back. But that's really the core of what we are here anyway, so it just really intensified during all this.

DJJ:
Instead of simply reverting to business as usual, and from your vantage point, what are some of the things the health care community might be doing to seize the opportunity to transform or innovate in the next normal?

Kathryn:
It's an opportunity for us to reimagine, just to make it what we need it to be, what we want it to be, and meet the needs of our patients, meet the needs of our staff. And personally, I'm a really positive person, but I really have a very positive attitude toward the trajectory that we're going for. We've decided that now's a great opportunity for us to pave our way forward to what we want it to be.

DJJ:
If I may ask, how were you personally affected by COVID-19?

Kathryn:
So COVID really hit Memphis and the United States in March. My elderly parents at that time were 81, 82. They always go to Venice, Florida, which is in the lower part near the Everglades in Florida. And that year they flew back and forth. So, they were down there in Florida, and then Florida became a hot spot. And then they started talking about closing the border of Florida. And I thought, "Oh my goodness, we've got to get Mama and James out of there before they closed the border." Because we didn't know how long this was going to last. And they have pretty high comorbidities, so I surely didn't want them to get it down there and surely didn't want to be that far away from them if they did get it. So, my husband and I drove down to Florida, helped get them packed up, and drove them back home.

And so then came Christmas of 2020, and we were one of those Zoom families, because I see death every day. I'm not going to take a chance. So, the family members that felt comfortable getting together gathered together; they all social distanced. And then we offered Zoom for those family members that didn't feel comfortable coming, so that they could still participate in the activities. Lot smaller, much more low-key than what we had ever done. And so that was a different Christmas. And then fast-forward to Christmas of 2021, and my brother was in the hospital with COVID. He had started as a sinus disease, but he has sinuses. Didn't think much of it. He just felt really bad, felt really bad.

Got some medicine to help his sinus infection. Went to the doctor on that Monday because he was feeling really worse, and the provider said, "Well, you've got pneumonia." So started him on stronger antibiotics. And then by Wednesday, and by now it's December 20th, five days before Christmas. And they also tested him for COVID on that Monday. But come Wednesday morning, he's dropping his O2 saturations, which is the amount of oxygen saturation that you get to your tissues. And so, his was low. So, I said, "Robby, you've got to go to the hospital. I don't care how bad you feel, you've got to go to the hospital." And so, then when they were in route to the hospital, they received the results that he had COVID.

So, I met him in the ER parking lot, and his wife, Shannon, was driving. And so, they brought the bag of personal items and stuff for him. I said, "Well, be sure that you hug him really good because he's going to be in the hospital for a while." And she said, "Oh, I thought it was a couple of days." I said, "No, he's a lot sicker, I think, than you realize. Be sure you hug him really good." Because by then she had COVID too. And I kind of kept my distance. And so that was hard. That was hard to see my brother as sick as he was. And so, he gets admitted. And he's admitted to Med Surg, and then he deteriorated pretty rapidly for what I was seeing. He had to go to step-down the next day. And then he was in step-down for about a week. And I made sure . . . Because him not being able to maintain his oxygen levels—he should have been able to maintain his oxygen levels by then. I knew it was probably not going to have a favorable outcome.

So, I told his kids that "If you want to take balloons to your dad or take his Christmas presents up there," they could bring them to the screener's desk, and the screeners would get them up there to him. Or I could take them to the nurses' station, but I couldn't see him because remember, COVID patients can't have visitors. And it was so important to me not to break the rules, because the other COVID patients couldn't have family members. It wasn't fair for my brother to get family members. I just couldn't do that. So that created some moral distress for me. And they did. They brought him balloons and I brought his Christmas presents up, and he opened them Christmas. So that was a sweet moment because at that time, he was still able to talk on the phone.

But we tried not to talk a lot because we wanted him to preserve his breathing. And so, then he did deteriorate to where he had to be transferred to CVICU on December 30th. And then they called the family up, and we were able to go in there and spend some time with him while we waited on his room in CVICU. Because remember, this is getting on the edge of that big surge again. So, we had to wait for a room to come available. And so, we got to spend some really sweet time with him, really sweet time with him. And then the time came for him to be placed on the ventilator.

At first, he didn't want to do it, but then he changed his mind. And knowing once he's placed on the ventilator, what that meant, it was so hard. But he was so healthy, so healthy, had no comorbidities. He was a healthy 51-year-old. And so, they put him on the ventilator. And then God's perfect number is seven, and there were seven times that the nurses called Shannon, his wife, up to the hospital. And it was that seventh time that he did pass away. She and I were in the room with him, and it was just a really sweet moment, really super sweet moment. And it was really hard for me to go back in the unit and to see that room that he was in. But I knew I had to do it because CVICU is one of the units that I cover. So, I knew I had to do it. And I had taken a really sweet angel music box that I had engraved, and I gave it to the staff one day. And that was the first day that I'd been back into the unit.

So, it was the compassion. The compassion that those nurses . . . I mean, everybody that touched us was just extraordinary. And it wasn't because he was my brother, it's because that's who they are. And I had made a poster board and put all these different pictures of Robby's personality on it so that they could see and know the Robby we knew, so it wouldn't be a patient in the bed. But the staff always do such a great job at making a connection with patients and family members. They would've known who Robby was anyway, but being that it was COVID, excuse me, they didn't have the opportunity to interact with him after he got placed on the ventilator. But those nurses fell in love with him even before he got placed on the ventilator because that's just who he was. So that was a really hard time. That was a hard time, but it . . . it was just hard.

COVID is no respecter of persons. It doesn't matter. My son is morbidly obese and has high blood pressure. He got COVID, and of our family members beside my parents, he's the one that I did not want to get it the most because I knew he would have the biggest chance of not having a good outcome. Man, he breezed through it. So yeah, COVID doesn't matter who you are.

DJJ:

Tell us, why is the survival rate of ventilated patients for COVID-19 so low?

Kathryn:
It's multifactor why COVID ventilated patients have a much lower survival rate. One, it depends on what their comorbidities are that puts them at a higher risk of mortality, and then just the general way that COVID acts if you would. You've got the different lobes of the lung, and you can kind of think of healthy lungs are like slicing a fresh-made loaf of white bread, and then COVID lungs would be cutting through a piece of liver.

So, you've got these lobes of the lung, and then within those lobes you've got air sacs, and then within those air sacs you have smaller air sacs. And so, all of that is inflamed. Inflamed and angry. And then you've got mucus that's thicker and stickier than your normal mucus that you would have produced from your lungs. So that's why it's harder to oxygenate when you've got your lungs in that state. So, some patients respond better to the medications that are given than others, and some the COVID inflammation is just overwhelming, as was the case with my brother. His inflammatory markers never came down. So, all that inflammation and that thick, gooey mucus really makes it hard to oxygenate. And then when it's hard to oxygenate, it's not just your lungs that makes it hard to oxygenate. Then you're getting less oxygenation to your other vital organs, which over time can be negatively impacted as well.

DJJ:

> There will come a time when we speak of COVID-19 in the past tense, when it will be subject to retrospective analysis and debate, rather than being something we continue to live through. However, the pandemic's

repercussions will be felt for years to come in society, in health care, and in nursing. [45]

Given everything you have experienced, how optimistic are you about the future?

Kathryn:
I'm very optimistic. More research has been done. More people are vaccinated. I think that will help calm it down some. But I know that there's other strains that are out there. We're in the middle of one now. Luckily, this one's even more contagious, not as deadly. And then because our numbers in the hospital right now, we only have seven. And none of those are in critical care. So, I think we're going to be dealing with this for the rest of our life. It's a matter of how are we going to manage it? And I think that we have great strategies in place and great research and everything. But I feel really good about what the future's going to be. And because we have gone through this for the last two and a half years, we're better equipped for it the next time. I pray we don't have a big bad surge, like we've had several over the last couple of years. But if we are better equipped because of what we've learned from what we've done.

---

45 Barrett, D., & Heale, R. (2021, October 1). Covid-19: Reflections on its impact on nursing. Evidence-Based Nursing. https://ebn.bmj.com/content/24/4/112

Kathryn Wiggs, Administrative Director of Nursing, Methodist Le Bonheur Healthcare North

In the midst of the battle raging in COVID-19 wards across the country, there was a huge yearning by fitness fanatics to get back in the gym to continue daily routines. However, fitness facilities, boutique gyms, and studio gyms were severely affected by the spread of COVID. Local government safety measures mandated all facilities be closed. These were harrowing times for gym owners. I had a chance to speak with an owner who opened his boutique gym during COVID-19, all in the spirit of maintaining fitness.

CHAPTER 13

MAINTAINING YOUR FITNESS

Physical fitness is not only one of the most important keys to a healthy body, it is the basis of dynamic and creative intellectual activity.

—JOHN F. KENNEDY

The fitness industry has experienced a meteoric rise over the last ten years, riding the growing numbers of health-conscious consumers who desire to live longer, healthier lives. Research has shown that physical movement, cardio training, and strength training can contribute to improved health. According to Harvard Medical School in Harvard Health Publishing, "Exercising regularly, every day, if possible, is the single most important thing you can do for your health. In the short term, exercise helps to control appetite, boost mood, and improve sleep. In the long term, it reduces the risk of heart disease, stroke, diabetes, dementia, depression, and many cancers."[46]

Another factor driving the increase in gym and boutique gym memberships is the desire to lose weight and have a more fit-looking body. Looking good in your clothes and feeling good about yourself is a huge motivator. Although big-box facilities have dominated the industry in the past, boutique gyms are now growing faster than their big-box counterparts. "Between 2013 and 2017, membership at traditional gyms grew by 15%,

---

46 Exercise & Fitness. Harvard Health. (n.d.). Retrieved April 10, 2023, from https://www.health.harvard.edu/topics/exercise-and-fitness

while membership to boutique studios grew by 121%. Vying for an even larger share of $25.8B fitness market, studios are ramping up expansion."[47]

Boutique or studio gyms offer a more intimate and personalized training environment. Members usually enjoy the smaller classes and specialized trainer attention. The small group workout sessions are also conducive to social interaction, where bonds form over time with other members and coaches. A camaraderie develops, and you don't want to miss your daily class. This has been my experience at the boutique studio I attend.

However, when the pandemic hit, everything changed. COVID-19 committed a full-frontal assault on the fitness industry. Government social distancing guidelines, mandatory shutdown orders, and members' fear of being exposed to the virus led to the shuttering of many gyms, studios, and health clubs. "The U.S. fitness industry lost $29.2 billion in revenue from March 2020 through June 2021, and 1.5 million gym and studio employees lost their jobs due to mandated health club and studio closures, according to the National Health & Fitness Alliance."[48]

Mr. Nate Vanderburg, Owner/Fitness Expert and Coach, Grind Central Fitness Center, took me on a tour of his new boutique fitness club. Nate spoke with me about the challenges of being a boutique gym owner and the mental fortitude he exhibited to remain true to his business plan during the pandemic.

---

47 Vennare, A., LinkedIn, & Twitter. (2022, October 5). *The numbers behind the Boutique Fitness Boom*. Fitt Insider. Retrieved April 10, 2023, from https://insider.fitt.co/boutique-fitness-boom-numbers-statistics/

48 Staff, C. I. (2021, August 10). *22 percent of gyms have closed, $29.2 billion revenue lost since COVID-19 hit*. Club Industry. Retrieved April 10, 2023, from https://www.clubindustry.com/industry-news/22-percent-gyms-have-closed-292-billion-revenue-lost-covid-19-hit

DJJ:
My pleasure to come out and talk with you. Tell me a little bit about yourself and Grind Central Fitness.

Nate:
Well, I'm a fitness coach and owner of Grind Central Fitness. We do a lot of individualized training, and we do a lot of group classes as well. So, we specialize in two different types of classes. We have a high-intensity class, and we have a class that's more built around building muscle and getting strong, man. So whichever one you prefer.

DJJ:

> The COVID-19 pandemic hit the fitness industry hard, largely due to its reliance on in-person facilities. From early 2020 to the spring of 2021, the pandemic rocked most industries to their core, but it had extreme effects on the fitness industry. Mandatory lockdowns forced gyms and fitness clubs to join restaurants, bars, and other service businesses in shutting down indefinitely, causing crippling losses in revenue and resources such as staff.[49]

What is your lockdown experience?

Nate:
Well, we opened in 2020 of October, so we knew it was going to be a challenge kind of going into the thing. We felt like we

---

49 Taylor, N. K., Faulks, M., Brown-Johnson, C. G., Rosas, L. G., Shaw, J. G., Saliba-Gustafsson, E. A., & Asch, S. M. (2022, November 22). Pandemic through the lens of Black Barbershops: Covid-19's impact and barbers' potential role as public health extenders. Journal of immigrant and minority health. Retrieved March 31, 2023, from https://www.ncbi.nlm.nih.gov/pmc/articles/PMC9684895/

had a pretty good plan moving in. We had an open house before we had opened our doors officially, so people could reserve spots online to keep capacity safe, and they could come in and kind of check the facility out. And during that time, they could kind of decide if this was going to be a safe environment, which that was our number one goal to make sure we had if they wanted to join or not.

So, we felt like as a team, that was our number one goal, was to keep equipment clean. Gyms spaced out on the flooring, safe, and everything like that. So, I think clients kind of picked up on that, and that helped us moving forward. So, our number one thing was just keeping it safe, keeping it clean. And a lot of the things that we did after the pandemic were things that should have probably been going on before the pandemic, as far as just the cleanliness of everything and then equipment and spacing on the floor. So, a lot of stuff has stuck with us that we decided beforehand to do.

DJJ:
Do you still stress the COVID-19 cleanliness protocols?

Nate:
Absolutely. So, you can probably look around the gym, and at every corner you'll see a hand sanitizer, sanitation wipes. We have new mats placed in the showers, front doors—every week they come in. We have a cleaning crew as well that comes in, on top of the coaches cleaning. So, cleaning in the gym is just, that's always key. That's always number one. COVID, no COVID, but that's just the biggest thing for me is just keeping it nice and safe.

DJJ:

> Worldwide, restrictions varied from capacity limits on gyms to complete lockdowns and stay-at-home orders. Some governments didn't allow gyms to provide outside exercise facilities or classes, and in other areas it was far too cold to do so. So aside from gyms that offered online services, the shutdown left most gyms—especially larger corporate facilities—without a revenue source, while fixed expenses remained.[50]

How has the COVID-19 pandemic affected your fitness business?

Nate:
I would say being a small fitness studio actually played into our favor a little bit. I believe clients were more comfortable coming into a controlled environment with less people or a community they knew, compared to a bigger gym with, I'd say, one hundred random strangers. So, someone you interact with day-to-day that you can trust versus coming into an environment that's just not as controlled, that's not very well spread out, with a ton of people, I could say.

DJJ:
Were you able to generate any new source of ongoing income by moving training online or outdoors with appropriate social distancing measures in place?

---

50 Business, T.-B. (2022, January 26). Fitness Industry Analysis Post-coronavirus: 3 surprising takeaways. Two. Retrieved April 14, 2023, from https://twobrainbusiness.com/fitness-industry-analysis/

Nate:
I'll say marketing definitely, or my marketing skills definitely increased. I feel like during the pandemic we had to advertise a lot of classes online as far as what we were doing here, how we ran things, and what type of classes we offered. So, in the past, people would be able to come in and kind of just talk it up with you and try out a class, and everything kind of switched to where it was online via email, text, or Zoom to see if this is something they could do or if they had the options to stay at home and do it at their own place. So yes, we definitely could try to, or we tried to touch everything, I could say, from indoor, online, you name it—we were Zoom calls, live, everything.

DJJ:

> Reports indicate around 40,000 US gyms and fitness clubs were operating in 2019 (with approximately 201,000 clubs worldwide). The shutdown cost the US fitness industry $29.2 billion in revenue from March 2020 to June 2021. Unfortunately, Congress did not include the fitness industry in economic relief packages. This fact is part of the reason 22 percent of American gyms closed permanently. I know you opened your club in August 2020 and probably were in the planning process long before the COVID-19 lockdowns.[51]

What made you proceed with opening your fitness center in the middle of a pandemic?

---

51 Business, T.-B. (2022, January 26). Fitness Industry Analysis Post-coronavirus: 3 surprising takeaways. Two. Retrieved April 14, 2023, from https://twobrainbusiness.com/fitness-industry-analysis/

Nate:
Okay, so that was definitely a tough one. So, we'd had a lot of thought on this, but we believe that health and fitness is the number one thing that could combat COVID. I believe the CDC released the statistic that people that exercise daily were less likely to be or hadn't as bad effects with COVID as far as being hospitalized or risk of death. So, I know people that did exercise more fought COVID at a better rate. So, if we had any chance of helping people that wanted to get in shape or lose weight, then I mean, that was our number one goal. That's what we were going after.

DJJ:
Several reports predict that boutiques, high value-low price, and digital would bounce back from COVID-19 sooner than traditional health clubs.
How have you seen this play out?

Nate:
I think it's been good. I think being a smaller gym, like we talked about earlier, definitely helped. And being a smaller gym as well with the boutiques is you get in with your community, you get in with each other, and you kind of can push each other and help, and you kind of keep each other accountable. So biggest thing with fitness is you don't have to do it alone. So, you can get your friends involved, and we're here as coaches to help you. So, moving forward, it has helped. And I think, just like we talked about earlier as well, all of the things that we put in place as far as spacing on the floor and being a controlled environment that's clean. That helps a lot of people to ease their mind a little bit when they walk into those doors.

DJJ:

> Although imposing lockdown or quarantine for the population was a widely used measure across the world to stop the rapid spread of COVID-19, it had severe consequences too. Recent multinational investigations have shown the negative effect of COVID-19 restrictions on social participation, life satisfaction, mental well-being, psychosocial and emotional disorders, as well as on sleep quality.[52]

How did physical activity improve emotional health during the COVID-19 pandemic?

Nate:
I'm going to be a little selfish and say it actually improved mine a lot too. So yeah, it is. Fitness has been a part of my life for a very long time, and I just know if I'm ever having a bad day or stressed out, not having that option to work out was tough. I remember we were in the lockdown sitting at home, and I believe they may have said it was the COVID 15 or COVID 20, the pounds you put on, and that was real.

I remember coming out of that, and it was just trying to open up a place that people could come and train and have fun and be safe, because we're kind of figuring out the pandemic together. And I'd say to this day, we're still probably trying to figure it out as well, so.

---

52 Kaur, H., Singh, T., Arya, Y. K., & Mittal, S. (2020, October 29). Physical Fitness and exercise during the covid-19 pandemic: A qualitative enquiry. Frontiers in psychology. Retrieved April 14, 2023, from https://www.ncbi.nlm.nih.gov/pmc/articles/PMC7673425/

DJJ:
Do you think the last two-plus years presented a shift in priority, and people realizing the importance of focusing on health and wellness?

Nate:
Absolutely.

DJJ:
What do you think some indicators of that are? What do you see happening here?

Nate:
It's just like we had talked about. I believe that people realize that the healthier side of people that exercised daily had a better chance maybe, if they were to catch COVID . . . I guess you could say the thinking was, the better experience, or they would have a better battle with COVID than people that didn't exercise daily. So, it's definitely going to be tough either way if you contract COVID-19, but if you have an opportunity to better yourself, why wouldn't you?

DJJ:

> In the COVID-19 pandemic, government intervention was the common scenario for all sectors. Governments imposed different rules, regulations, and guidelines to control the spread of the virus. Several business owners believe that some interventions/lockdowns were not implemented properly due to a lack of proper

monitoring, which caused the virus to spread out more extensively.[53]

What are your thoughts on how the shutdown was communicated, what businesses had to close, what businesses were allowed to remain open, and then the entire reopening process?

Nate:
I think it that's a very, very tough one because I know a lot of businesses shut down and weren't able to reopen. And kind of looking at the timeline, we were close to being one of those businesses. So, we had planned this business, probably 2019, before all the craziness happened. So, we were blessed enough to have not had opened, and opened up a little bit later, because if we would've opened up during the lockdown or right before it hit, we probably would not be here today. So, I do find a blessing in that.

DJJ:
What governing body provided the guidance to the fitness facilities? Were there multiple organizations, and did you have to discern independently which had the most updated and/or accurate information?

Nate:
So, it was left to the state, I believe, to decide how we opened up and how much capacity you could have and what businesses could open and what could not. I remember following the state level, and I remember also just communicating with other

53 The territorial impact of covid-19: Managing the crisis across levels ... (n.d.). Retrieved April 15, 2023, from https://www.oecd.org/coronavirus/policy-responses/the-territorial-impact-of-COVID-19-managing-the-crisis-across-levels-of-government-d3e314e1/

businesses in the area. We were a brand-new business, so we were still kind of the new kids on the block of figuring things out. So we did lean on a couple other businesses as well to see how they were doing things and how they went about the entire process. So that was a lot. That was very helpful for us.

DJJ:
Did you find some of the information conflicting or had to sort through it yourself?

Nate:
It definitely wasn't easy by any means, but since we weren't operating before, we were kind of just coming into it all new and all at once. So that probably made it maybe a little bit easier for us because we were just learning as we went, so we were still just new to everything.

DJJ:

> In the US, mandated closures caused 1.5 million fitness professionals to lose their jobs. These individuals accounted for 47 percent of the fitness labor force. According to Professional Trainer Development Center, 58 percent of trainers lost some or all of their income. Unless they trained clients online, many coaches had no source of income except unemployment. In some countries, government benefits were extended to affected workers, but employment status—contractor vs. employee—prevented some from accessing certain benefits.[54]

---

54 Business, T.-B. (2022, January 26). Fitness Industry Analysis Post-coronavirus: 3 surprising takeaways. Two. Retrieved April 14, 2023, from https://twobrainbusiness.com/fitness-industry-analysis/

How did job loss affect your business during the pandemic?

Nate:
Well, it did because it obviously slowed everything down just a little bit. So, we had spoken with a bunch of clients, and I had been a trainer for a couple years beforehand, so I had known that I would have a pretty good amount of clients coming in, but definitely not as many as I thought due to the pandemic and due to people's uncertainty. And I won't lie to you, I had many a night—this is a little off topic. But I had a many a night thinking, moving forward when we had opened up that will we go into another lockdown, or will we be shut down again, and will we lose everything that we've done and worked hard for? So, it was a little scary, but I mean, all you can do is just trust in everything going on and the people that we're going to move forward and get through it together.

DJJ:
What was the impact of COVID-19 on gym memberships?

- 60 percent of Americans plan to cancel their memberships [Freeletics, July 2020].
- 59 percent of Americans don't plan to renew their gym memberships after COVID [TD Ameritrade, 2020].
- 59.06 percent of gym members are considering canceling or have canceled their memberships [Runrepeat, September 2020].[55]

Nate:
Well, everything originally went into lockdown, and then we saw a huge shift from group classes into individual personal

55 Rizzo, N. (1970, August 6). Covid's impact on the fitness industry [35+ stats and facts]. Athletic shoe reviews. Retrieved April 14, 2023, from https://runrepeat.com/pandemics-impact-fitness-industry

training sessions. So wasn't surprised, but we had a huge spike into personal training, and then we had a slight decrease into group, which makes sense. You could see. But all in all, I think the biggest thing was just people still finding a way to exercise and stay healthy.

DJJ:
What was (and potentially now) member attitudes toward returning to gyms?

Nate:
It was a little skittish at first, which you could see. For the longest time, we did have people come in and it was tough because we're trying to build that relationship, but at the same time we're having to cheer from afar. In these types of workouts and things, it's a lot of moving parts. So, we want to make sure everyone stays safe, whether they're exercising to do the right movements and stay with the right form. But we're not able to necessarily get in that personal space because of CDC regulations of keeping your distance and keeping everybody in a safe environment. So, cheering from afar was definitely something new.

- 25 percent of Americans don't plan to go back to the gym [Lifeaid, June 2020].
- In a Morning Consult poll, only 20 percent of Americans are comfortable going to the gym as of July [Morning Consult].
- In April 2020, 68 percent of Americans stated that they are much less likely to go back to the gym based on what they know about COVID-19 [Statista].

- In April 2020, 18 percent of Americans stated that they're not anticipating going back to the gym or exercise classes for the next six months at the very least [Statista].[56]

DJJ:
What do you think COVID-19's impact has been on exercise behavior?

Nate:
It definitely affected, and I know multiple family members that knew people that had lost their lives to COVID, and majority of them may have been overweight and that could have played a big factor in their battle with COVID. So, it was kind of eye-opening for a lot of people that this is our time to get in shape and do what we can do. You don't have to come in and be Mr. Olympia or anything like that. It's just exercise daily and change your eating habits will go a long way with the battle. So, I think it definitely was an eye-opening experience for a lot of people.

- There's been an 88 percent average increase in exercise for people who normally exercise 1–2 times per week [RunRepeat].
- In a survey, 37 percent of a thousand fitness club users state that they will work out more after COVID. Over 50 percent said that this is due to their "renewed appreciation for their health and well-being" [Harrison Co.].
- 50 percent of Americans say that they are less active during the pandemic-related shutdowns [IHRSA, 2020].
- 65 percent of respondents report that working out at home alone during the lockdown boosted their confidence [Freeletics, July 2020].

---

56 Rizzo, N. (1970, August 6). Covid's impact on the fitness industry [35+ stats and facts]. Athletic shoe reviews. Retrieved April 14, 2023, from https://runrepeat.com/pandemics-impact-fitness-industry

- 60 percent of men said their top reason for working out during the pandemic was for their mental health [Freeletics, July 2020].
- Reducing boredom (52 percent) was the top reason why women are working out during the pandemic [Freeletics, July 2020].[57]

DJJ:
Did anyone you know personally pass away due to COVID?

Nate:
I personally did not, but I had a lot of clients that I had worked with that did. So, it was . . . And like I said, we're a big community gym. We're all family in here. So, I felt like we kind of went through that experience with them, and it's just a tough pill to swallow.

DJJ:
How has COVID-19 permanently changed the fitness industry?

Nate:
I think it has increased the fitness industry a lot. I think, like we talked about, people realize that exercise, eating right, and health should be one of your number one priority. Thirty to forty-five minutes out of the day can change your life in the long run, just every day with that consistency. So, I think that we will continue to see an increase in gym memberships and in people getting into this industry. And I can even say from experience around town, we've had three gyms open up. So, we've had a lot of people getting into that field and wanting

57 Rizzo, N. (1970, August 6). Covid's impact on the fitness industry [35+ stats and facts]. Athletic shoe reviews. Retrieved April 14, 2023, from https://runrepeat.com/pandemics-impact-fitness-industry

to help others. And I mean, I know I'm a gym owner, but I love to see it. So anytime somebody's exercising or bettering themselves, I love it.

DJJ:
If I may ask, how were you personally affected by COVID-19?

Nate:
I say the same as everybody, man. It's been tough. It's been a journey that we've all gone through together. The unknowns are probably the biggest scare. But I mean, I believe in people, so I believe if we can all figure it out together moving forward, that's our best bet.

Nate Vanderburg, Owner/Fitness Expert and Coach, Grind Central Fitness Center

Fitness centers were mandated to shut down during the pandemic. They faced incredible challenges on how to stay in business and comply with local laws. Social distancing and mask mandates required completely new operating procedures when, and if, a boutique gym would be allowed to reopen. These circumstances were dire. But there is another industry that arguably had to contend with worse ramifications that threatened its livelihood. The restaurant industry, or at least the dine-in portion of it, suffered stifling impacts as the COVID-19 pandemic completely dismantled the normal flow of business. Thinking about the phrase "Bon Appétit" at your local fine dining establishment would take on a radically new perspective. It would no longer exist as the virus spread rampantly across America. Restaurant owners and patrons didn't know whether things would ever return to normal.

Chapter 14

BON APPÉTIT FOREVER CHANGED

Success is to be measured not so much by the position that one has reached in life as by the obstacles which he has overcome.
—Booker T. Washington

Dining out has become an integral part of our culture. It is essential to our way of life and how we share and commune with family and friends. The local diner, pub, and bar are fixtures in communities across the country. It's the way people wind down for the day or the weekend. It's where people share and get up to date on what's happening in each other's lives. The ubiquitous "happy hour" has become an after-work ritual to unwind or socialize after a grueling day at the office. Or a way to cap off the day and have a nice dinner. It has become the expected norm, and none of us could have imagined that experience being curtailed, radically modified, or completely stopped. But that's what happened. Dining-out dollars for full-service restaurants spiraled downward when the COVID-19 pandemic began, and a national emergency was declared. Restaurant owners were faced with the Herculean task of trying to save their businesses. This struggle continues, although some improvements have been made with the introduction of vaccines and increased restaurant traffic. However, this industry has not seen a full recovery to pre-pandemic levels. According to the National Restaurant Association, "40% of operators say they are not open to full capacity for indoor on-premises dining; 7 in 10 report it's due to staffing shortages. 90% of operators say food costs are higher than they were prior to COVID-19; 8 in

10 say labor costs are higher and costs will likely continue to rise in '22."[58]

Restaurant owners have adapted their business models along with rethinking restaurant design. Supply chain disruptions have also caused changes to what a restaurant could order and when. On top of those challenges, the effect of inflation on product prices made matters even more difficult.

Many of these entrepreneurs introduced online and take-out services to create revenue streams, even at fine dining establishments, due to the preference of consumers to pick up the same food but dine in the comfort and safety of their own homes. Chef-owners have had to be very intentional on splitting their focus between the culinary aspect of the business and the hypersensitive economic conditions brought on by the pandemic.

I sat down with Chef-Owner Ben Smith at Tsunami Restaurant, a sleek eatery specializing in innovative Pacific Rim small plates that change with the seasons. We had an enlightening conversation in which he shared how his restaurant adapted. He also discussed how the spirit of survival helped his team face the threats to his business precipitated by COVID-19.

DJJ:
Tell me a little bit about Tsunami and what you do in the restaurant.

Ben:
So yeah, chef-owner here. We opened July 1998. I'm a graduate of Culinary Institute of America. I was born and raised here in Memphis, culinary school graduate. Did a good amount of traveling after culinary school. Worked in San Francisco for

---

58 *Report: Pandemic leads to long-term industry changes*. NRA. (n.d.). Retrieved April 10, 2023, from https://restaurant.org/education-and-resources/resource-library/new-2022-state-of-the-restaurant-industry-report-projects-trends/

three years, took some time off and spent six months traveling the South Pacific, all over the South Pacific. Picked up a lot of influence from that. Worked three years in Hawaii, so picked up a lot of real strong influence there with the seafood and the Asian ingredients and the different cultures. And then came back to California for a little while.

And then ended up back in Memphis and was sort of testing the waters of what's going on here. And was half a foot out the door to go back to California or someplace else. And at the urging of friends and family decided to open my own restaurant. I had this vague idea, brainstorm, that I've been working on for months, years really, about my ideal restaurant. And for years it was like, "This is a place I want to work. This is a kind of environment I want to work in." But that just morphed into "This is the kind of place I want to own." And that's what happened.

And then once I put, just like anything, I put a hundred percent my focus into that, and things just started falling into place. And a space came available, and some people came into my life that were very influential in helping me get this place open. And it happened. And like I said, opening this restaurant was a very selfish act on my part because I wanted to create the kind of environment that I want to work in, the kind of food I like to cook and eat. And it was different. In 1998 to open a seafood-forward restaurant right in the very belt buckle of the Barbecue Belt was, it was a crapshoot. But it works. And here we are 24 years later. Never thought I'd, I'd be sitting here saying, now 24 years of business in the same place. But here we are.

DJJ:

The coronavirus (COVID-19) pandemic caused an unprecedented change to many sectors of the

US economy, with commercial foodservice being no exception. Following the national emergency declaration on March 13, 2020, many states began to issue emergency measures, including closure and restrictions of on-premises dining at restaurants and other foodservice businesses. Things were shutting down rapidly, and I assume Tsunami was also required to close and remained closed for some period of time.[59]

What were your initial thoughts when food-away-from-home or restaurant dine-in services began to close?

Ben:
Well, when this whole COVID thing started to hit, we recognized pretty early on that it was going to be impactful. We didn't know to what extent or how, but we had an inkling. We felt first from my staff, this level of heightened concern from my staff about safety issues regarding health. And because we're in a business where we're in contact with, close contact with lots of different people. We were concerned about that . . .

Early on, we didn't know how this was spreading, what was causing this, what were the danger factors for this COVID. So early on, there was a heightened concern, first of all, from our staff. And then we started hearing some rumblings from customers. Mostly just asking questions, but we sensed a level of—heightened level of concern. So, we would meet on a regular basis, myself, and my management team. And in fact, we came to the conclusion—and we felt this looming issue—and we came to the conclusion early on that we would shut down before they mandated that. We were worried. I was concerned about my staff. So, we decided before the mandate came down

59 Covid-19 working paper: The impact of covid-19 pandemic on food-away ... (n.d.). Retrieved April 15, 2023, from https://www.ers.usda.gov/webdocs/publications/103455/ap-100.pdf?v=350

to shut restaurants, shut dining rooms down. And we made that call and I met with my staff. I had a full staff meeting and told them what was going on and that effective immediately, we were going to shift into curbside, pickup, delivery system. And we had no idea what that was going to look like. No idea.

That was March 2020, yeah. I don't know the precise date, but it was a few days before I think they mandated shutting of dine-in. So, we preempted that because we felt that was the right thing to do. We wanted to be ahead, we wanted to be in control of our own, how we dealt with this. We wanted to take the lead.

DJJ:
Did you ever think this would happen in these modern times and especially in the United States?

Ben:
No. No. You know, anticipate a lot when you own a restaurant or any business really. You anticipate, you hope for the best and plan for the worst. And everything we've been through in the 24 years we've been open, 24-plus years we've been open, I felt like we'd seen it all. And believe me, anything that can go wrong in a restaurant does . . . will go wrong. But this is one of those things that we just never could have anticipated. There was no precedent for this. There was the Spanish flu. Yeah, sure. But it's the twenty-first century, right? We have eradicated things like this. This can't happen here. So yeah, we were caught a little bit off guard for sure.

DJJ:
What did you fear the most about COVID-19?

Ben:
Yeah, it was first and foremost from a health standpoint. Concerned about my staff, concerned about my family, concerned about my customers. And I didn't want to be a part of perpetuating the spread of this thing. And as you know, early on there was not a great deal of information about how to deal with this, how to safeguard yourself or your family or your general people in your circle. So, some people say we were overly cautious. We got a lot of pushback from people when we decided to close the dining rooms and pushback when we stayed closed even after they said we could reopen. We absolutely erred way on the side of caution throughout all of this. And the silver lining of that dark cloud was that I think we gained a deeper level of trust with our regular clientele. And we have a tremendous loyal, long-standing clientele, and they were very supportive and very understanding.

DJJ:
How did you communicate the closure to your employees?

Ben:
Well, I'm blessed I guess to have a small staff, 20 people top on the staff. So, it's easy to get that many people together. We've always been really open about communication here. I feel like knowledge is strength, and I don't hold anything back from my staff. And we were facing what could have been, or yeah, turned out to be and still is a major crisis. And I felt like it was important to have frequent meetings and updates on, again, whatever information we could get, wherever we could glean it from. Updates on how to keep things sanitized, how to keep ourselves safe, about mask mandates, and etc.

So, we met frequently as a management team. We had discussions every day. We have a regular weekly lineup with the front of the house staff, traditionally about menu changes and about the specials for the week. But we expanded that into a full staff meeting and communicating all the latest. All the latest—here's what we know now, here's how we're dealing with this, here's what we're doing next. And to the credit of my staff, from that very first meeting when we preemptively said we were going to shut down, and I stood in front of my whole staff of 20 people and said, "We're shutting down the dining room, and we're shifting to curbside, delivery, and pickup only," every single member of that staff was like, "Okay." There was no pushback. No "What do you mean? What does that mean? What about my job? What about . . ." It was like, okay. And they came in the next day, every one of them, and they were ready to go. They didn't know what we were going to do. We didn't know what we were going to do or how we were going to do it. But they 100 percent were with it. They were down for it.

DJJ:
In the COVID-19 pandemic, government intervention was the common scenario for all sectors. Governments imposed different rules, regulations, and guidelines to control the spread of the virus. Several business owners believe that some interventions/lockdowns were not implemented properly due to a lack of proper monitoring, which caused the virus to spread out more extensively.
What are your thoughts on how the shutdown was communicated, what businesses had to close, what businesses were allowed to remain open, and then the entire reopening process?

Ben:
I again, go back to this preemptive stance we took early on, and we did that because, and we had so much communication amongst my management team and the staff in general because there was no communication, very little communication coming

from anywhere. And even that communication that was coming out seemed conflicting. And there was no one entity, no one source of information. It seemed like nobody wanted to just stand up and say, "Here's what's going on. Here's what we need to do. Here's how we're going to deal with this." We're hearing from CDC, we're hearing from local health department, we were hearing from the president of the United States. And all of it was conflicting and uncertain. And so, it was frightening. It was disconcerting to us to not have any leadership, we felt like. And so early on we figured out to get through this, we're going to have to make the decisions; we're going to have to figure out our path forward through this. And again, we felt like erring on the side of caution was the right path to take. And that's what we stuck with. That was my gut feelings. That we got to protect our staff, ourselves, our families. Because we're around a lot of people, then we're going out to be with our individual families and circles. And until we could understand more how the trajectory of this was going to play out, we played it really cautious.

DJJ:
Were you thinking this was a crisis of two weeks or two months?

Ben:
Yes. When I had that first talk with my staff March of 2020, I said, "Look, this looks pretty serious. We're going to shut down effective tomorrow. And look, we have to face the reality of we could be in this for six weeks, a couple of months. We got to be prepared for a long haul here." Which to me, two months. And here we are, what, two and a half years later? We're still in it. We're still in it.

On top of the angst of just preservation of our health and well-being, there's this added level of angst and stress and anxiety with that sense of apathy that a lot of people have of, "It's fine. It's over." Mixed in with the whole politicizing of this thing, of its freedom. "I have the freedom of choice not to wear a mask." And people have become so polarized with that, and it's gotten very political. And as a business that welcomes everybody, we have to walk this path of non-offensiveness to everybody here and yet still balance that with, we have our number one priority is to keep everybody safe and healthy. And it's gotten really uncomfortable at times during the height of it from my staff when we are going through mask mandates. People that would just very flippantly come in and said, "I'm fine. I don't have it. I don't have any symptoms. I'm not wearing a mask." And for my staff to become police, in a sense, on top of the tremendous responsibility of being a server and all that goes along with that, now we are being asked to be the police to enforce these policies that somebody has put on to control this COVID.

So, it hasn't gone away. It's gotten, I think, increasingly more stressful for us and this business. For those reasons to being on top of trying to protect ourselves and each other and our clientele. We also, on top of that, have to police them, which is very uncomfortable.

DJJ:

> COVID-19 was not only a devastating public-health crisis; it was, and remains for some, the restaurant industry's greatest challenge to date. Never before had so many restaurants been forced to cease operations, and some will never reopen. COVID-19's economic toll on the restaurant industry hasn't been evenly distributed. Whereas pizza chains maintained or even increased sales during the pandemic and casual-dining and fine-dining

restaurants saw their revenue decrease. For some fine-dining establishments, revenues fell to zero.[60]

DJJ:
What new policies and processes do you have in place because of COVID-19?

Ben:
For a while, we were, during the height of it, everybody, front of the house, back of the house, masked up. Everybody that came in the door, mandatory temperature. We took everybody's temperature, recorded that, and tracked that. Anybody, of course, who was feeling symptoms, mandatory stay at home. Those masks, temperature, stay at home if you have any symptoms. Front of the house still wears masks here. We encourage testing when people are feeling symptoms. We don't mandate it.

I think moving forward, I think the mask thing is just, it's just impossible to police that. People are going to do what they want to do. We've eased off that a bit because we feel like hopefully, we have some confidence in the whole vaccination process and hope that'll play out and work. I think moving forward, there's always going to be a heightened sense of concern about flare-ups and about the variants that are coming along. And I don't think we're out of it yet. I think we might still see a time when we'll get shut down again.

DJJ:
How did you have to reconfigure your space?

60 Haas, S., Kuehl, E., Moran, J. R., & Venkataraman, K. (2020, May 19). How restaurants can thrive in the next normal. McKinsey & Company. Retrieved April 14, 2023, from https://www.mckinsey.com/industries/retail/our-insights/how-restaurants-can-thrive-in-the-next-normal

Ben:
We went, once we did after the first mandate, we were about 50 percent capacity, which took out half our tables. Took out all of our bar seats, so no seating at the bar whatsoever. We lost 15 seats there alone, just at the bar. Obviously, that was extremely impactful for us in a negative way. And it wasn't until really just about a month ago that we built back up to a hundred percent. And we immediately felt that too. That was impactful after being used to certain level of business and putting all the tables back. It was like boom, we're back. And it felt good to be having, doing old numbers, pre-COVID numbers again. It felt really good. But for a minute it was just almost overwhelming.

DJJ:
Is there a "new normal" for this business industry? Or have things relaxed and we're back to pre-Covid-19?

Ben:
No. I think any smart operator moving forward is never going to think. There's no going back. There is no going back to normal. I mean, this is an impactful, historically impactful thing that's happened. To move forward we have to recognize and acknowledge that, and any path forward has to take into consideration what we've been through and what we could go through again. And anybody who hasn't learned that lesson in the past two and a half years is not going to be well armed to go forward in this business. Yeah, I think the new normal is that we all have a heightened sense of awareness and caution when it comes to public health issues like this. We have an obligation; we have a duty.

DJJ:

> While COVID-19 didn't discriminate in who it affected, the impact wasn't so evenly or randomly distributed among restaurants. Full-service locations (like Tsunami) who were less equipped to pivot to takeout and delivery represented the tip of the spear. They had to not just try to rearrange business practices, but also to bring along customer bases that have historically looked elsewhere for off-premises consumption.[61]

What did you do to engage with your customer base and to bring them into your new business model (i.e., online ordering, curbside pickup, delivery, etc.)?

Ben:
We have a really grassroots marketing if you want to even call it that. We have, as I said, a very long-standing, very loyal, very supportive, regular clientele. And we did engage more in social media, but we also did a lot of personal reach out to calling long-standing customers and explaining, "Here's what we're doing; here's what's going on." We got a lot of calls. The support we got from our regular customers was outstanding. When we shut down, we had people calling. People had standing orders, weekly orders, people coming two, three times a week to get takeout.

We had people . . . One customer, regular customer called two different times from out of town and said, "I want to order a thousand dollars gift certificate. Here's my credit card number." "Okay, thanks. We'll be here for you. Pick up whenever." He said, "Now tear it up." He did that twice.

61 Covid-19's impact, from the perspective of restaurant owners. QSR magazine. (n.d.). Retrieved April 14, 2023, from https://www.qsrmagazine.com/consumer-trends/covid-19s-impact-perspective-restaurant-owners

We had one incident where we were doing pickup, and people were coming in the front door picking up their orders. We used the bar as a staging area. It was a busy day. People in and out, in and out, in and out. At the end of the night, we locked the door, exhausted. There was just three of us working that day. There was an envelope on the bar that said, "Tsunami staff." And we were like, "Where did this come from? What is this? Whose is this?" None of us knew. None of us saw anybody leave an envelope. We opened it up. It was 10 crisp $100 bills somebody had just left on the bar.

We had somebody anonymously send us three large pizzas one day with . . . We had still to this day, don't know who did that. So yeah, the support and the outpouring was really good. And I think that speaks to just how supportive our regulars are and that personal outreach was impactful. And some of these people are still, they're still regulars. We still have regulars that have not set foot back in the restaurant, but they're ordering takeout every Friday night, every Saturday night. They have their nights.

DJJ:
So, Ben, you mentioned there are some regulars that have not come back into the restaurant. Do you think that's because there's still some fear of COVID-19, or the fact that some people just became comfortable with takeout ordering?

Ben:
I think there's a little bit of both of that. I think there's a new business model going forward. And we've seen how impactful that takeout has become . . . Even now, we're back to a hundred percent. We still do a significant amount of takeout. And when we look at that, it adds up. So we know . . . What we've learned is that takeout, which is something that before we weren't, we just weren't set up for that. We didn't do a whole lot of takeout. We

felt like our food is meant to be eaten in restaurant . . . There's a presentation aspect to our food that is lost in the translation or in the transportation, if you will.

DJJ:
What percentage of your business is attributed to takeout?

Ben:
Right now, probably, it spikes on the weekends, but 15 percent some nights, 20 percent maybe. It's significant.

We also have had a great deal of success. I and my lead chef, Kevin Sullivan, host what we call a chef's market every Saturday on the patio out here. And we do prepared meals, take, and reheat meals, soups, and side items. It's kind of a little side hustle for me and Kevin. But that's been really successful as well. So, I think that makes me think of ways to build on that as we go forward.

I think that's a lot of people, as you said, are not comfortable with eating out because of health issues. But a lot of people too, were like, "Man, I can still get this good food, but I don't have to dress up. I don't have to worry about parking. I can do it in the comfort of my home. I could eat in the comfort of my home." So, I think that is an impact that's going to be, have some legs. It's going to be a lasting impact from COVID.

It's a new business model moving forward. And I think we all need to pay attention to that, including, especially fine dining. Because you said that the pizza places have raked it in because that's how they're set up. And I think we need to educate ourselves on how we can take that takeout model and make it work and make it sustainable.

DJJ:
The COVID-19 pandemic caused major changes to how the food service industry operated.
What were your biggest challenges due to COVID as it relates to?

a) **Food cost or supply chain issues**
b) **Keeping staff safe**
c) **Unable to pay staff**
d) **Unable to pay bills.**
e) **Transitioning to a new business model with online ordering**

Ben:
That's been a nightmare. That's been a nightmare. And that is something that causes me sleepless nights because I understand there's been disruptions to the supply chain. Cost of fuel has gone up. Cost of everything. There are labor shortages. All these factors, I understand. And they're real and they've been extremely impactful. The prices continue even after two and a half years, prices are still going up. Restaurants are already, under the best of times, the best of circumstances, working on sometimes razor-thin margins. It's ridiculous. When you look at the P&L of a typical restaurant, it's like, why? Why does anybody do this? And it's really cut into the bottom line a lot.

What has helped us, and this goes back many, many years before COVID, is we . . . Basically, our specials menu are small plates, smaller portions. And I did this years ago because I wanted . . . Honestly, when we first opened, I was getting in fish that people had never had before, never tasted before. And people were apprehensive of, "I don't know what that is." So, they were sort of reluctant to spend entrée price on something they'd never tasted before. I was still building trust with my clientele. So, I said, "Well, what if we did smaller portions, smaller price, smaller cost to get people to try these things, to try these new fish that I was bringing in?" And I got pushback from my staff. It was like, "Well, it's going to lower the check average and tips are going to go down" and all this. But as it turned out, people were supportive of the small plate. They got people to try the fish, and then they were like, "Okay, this is cool. I like this." And instead of check average going down, it actually went up because people were like, "Okay, we got a smaller portion. We can get a salad and a small plate, and we can still have dessert cause it's still in our budget."

So, I think we've maintained that small plate/lower price point on our specials menu. And in the mix of things, the small plates are a huge part of our sales. So, I think having established that smaller portion sort of thing, there's more profit in that for us with a smaller portion. Portion control is extremely important right now. With the prices, we've had to tweak our prices up a little bit. But it's getting to the point where it's starting to get uncomfortable for me as an operator and uncomfortable for some of our clientele. So, it's a worry. That's a worry.

The supply issue has been difficult as well. There are some things we've taken off the menu just because of supply issues. We also took some things off that we didn't feel traveled well for takeout. But again, because of our reputation as having a small plate specials that change weekly, people are used to coming in and seeing something new every time they're in. So, we're able to utilize that concept and get whatever. We can be real flexible. My seafood purveyors would call me at the beginning of the week and say, "Here's what's coming in. Here's what we got." And I'll look at things at a good price point, which are maybe not the most popular things that every restaurant in town has, but the price is right. So, I'm not locked into this static menu that I have to have all these items every week. I can be flexible with the prices. And that's how we get by. That's how we get by.

DJJ:
Are there any extra things you're doing to keep your staff safe?

Ben:
The thing about working in this industry is . . . And I have everybody on my staff, they're veterans of this business. They've been in the business years, and this industry has a reputation for you show up no matter what. And joke, the running joke in the kitchen at least is if you're calling in sick, you better be either in jail or in the hospital because no other excuses are allowed. And that's not cool. But it's that, that's this industry. It's like it's drilled into you that you show up no matter what, no matter how many shifts, how many shifts you've worked, how late you were up last night, how much you drank. You got to be at work the next day. So that's ingrained in people who've been in this industry as long as I have, and a lot of my staff have that. That thought process is ingrained in people, and it's hard to overcome. So, what I've been trying to drill into my staff is that if you're not feeling it, don't come to work. We got this—we can function without you. We got this. We can all step up and make it happen.

And at times we have two or three people out. And this goes against any business principle, but we'll control reservations because I don't want service to be compromised because we're short-staffed. And I'm not going to fill up a restaurant and have a restaurant full of people not getting great service and great food because we're short-staffed. And that's a hard decision to make as a business owner. It's like I'm going to mitigate the flow of revenue, flow of potential revenue because I want to maintain this certain level of service and food quality.

So, what I try to drill into my staff is, it's okay to take a day if you're not feeling it physically, and even more importantly, emotionally. And that's another thing that's a hard sell on the staff that's so ingrained to show up and show out. It's okay to not be okay. And that's a hard thing to get across to my staff. But it's starting to work. And many people have taken many personal days, which is good. And I think that's something we all need to carry forward, too, as mental health is important as physical health.

> A 2020 article by McKinsey & Company stated that of the 650,000-plus US restaurant locations that were in business in 2019, approximately one in five—or more than 130,000—will be permanently shuttered by next year (2021). It noted that independents would bear the brunt of the closures, both because of attributes that made most independents more vulnerable in this pandemic (i.e., minimal off-premises presence, limited digital capabilities, low emphasis on value-based menu items) and because of their unfavorable economics (thin margins and poor access to capital).
>
> 69% of restaurants updated and pared down their menu for online ordering
>
> 66% become more engaged with their guests on social media
>
> 33% of restaurants surveyed (33%) relied on third-party delivery
>
> 20% of restaurants started their own food delivery service
>
> 24% of restaurants sold pantry or grocery items out of their restaurant or online

8% of restaurants created wine or cocktail subscriptions

6% of restaurants created grocery or food box subscriptions[62]

DJJ:
What were you able to do financially to remain afloat? Some of the restaurants, specifically, fine dining restaurants, automatically put the 18 percent gratuity onto the payment.

Ben:
Hate it.

DJJ:
Some of them even put an additional 18 percent surcharge.

Ben:
Hate it.

DJJ:
Did Tsunami have to utilize any of those financial tactics, or did you mitigate through other supply chain strategies

Ben:
No. No, we don't do that. We would never do that. And that's a point of contention with me. I get it. And there's, throughout this whole episode, there's been a lot of talk about pay and compensation and why do we even have a tipping system? Why don't you just pay your servers a living wage like in Europe. You don't tip in Europe. And it's a reasonable question; it's

62 Haas, S., Kuehl, E., Moran, J. R., & Venkataraman, K. (2020, May 19). How restaurants can thrive in the next normal. McKinsey & Company. Retrieved April 14, 2023, from https://www.mckinsey.com/industries/retail/our-insights/how-restaurants-can-thrive-in-the-next-normal

a reasonable argument. But the reality of it is, are you as a consumer prepared to pay 15, 18, 20 percent more for when you dine out? Because that's what it's going to take. That money just . . . it's not like we're just hoarding money and refusing to pay our servers. This system dates back, as you know, many, many years. And that's a whole other story. That's a whole other documentary you can make. So no, I don't see . . . Never will we put a mandatory 18 percent gratuity.

DJJ:

Ben, during the pandemic when you had to pivot to curbside and delivery, revenues were much lower than in-dining service. How did you manage to pay your bills and meet payroll?

Ben:

It helped that a lot of people, when we were just doing the curbside, a lot of my staff wanted to disengage. They wanted to stay home. Some of my staff have kids and they wanted to be at home, and that was cool. So, we limited our menu. Some nights we only had two guys in the kitchen, and we would do it that way. We'd have two people in the front, one person taking orders, one person organizing the orders and taking payment, and two guys in the kitchen slinging food. So that's how we worked that.

I didn't lay anybody off. I kept everybody on staff during the pandemic. In fact, put all the servers all in front of the house on hourly, much higher hourly wage than normal. And they tip pooled. And that's how they got by. In fact, they did pretty well. Because as I said, our customers have been very loyal and very supportive. And besides ordering gift certificates that they never used and dropping off envelopes full of cash, they were very generous with their tips too. So, it was very heartening to see that sort of behavior. We did get a PPP, which helped a lot. So, we made it through so far.

But it's still, as I said, we're still in it. It's still a challenge. And I hope that these prices, these elevated prices, these costs of goods and this supply chain thing gets resolved. And I hope that the providers don't get used to this high level of cost of goods, and hopefully prices will go back down when the supply chain issue gets a little bit more resolved.

Staffing is a challenge. Again, I'm lucky to have a very little turnover historically in this place. Plus, my staff has been virtually unchanged since the beginning of this. We lost three or four people. But yeah, the supply, really supply chain and the cost of goods are the biggest issues.

DJJ:
You've been here in this midtown area, and there were other restaurants around. How do you think they may have been impacted? Were they as successful? Did they pivot? Did they shut down? What can you tell us about that?

Ben:
We've had some shutdowns, not all of them entirely COVID related. But I think one thing that happened is we have a text thread of about 20 restaurant operators here in Memphis that we're on the same text thread together. And communication with that has been really helpful and really uplifting because we all sort of chime in about, "Hey, I need a dishwasher tonight" or "Where are you buying your seafood from now? Are you having delivery issues?" And sometimes it's just things like, "Man, how are y'all holding up? How are you dealing with these people walking with no masks?" So, there's been a real strong level of support within the Memphis restaurant community, really strong. And it's made me really, really proud to be a part of a group of such generous, outreaching people.

So, we've all dealt with it differently. But there's also been a lot of communication, a lot of support, a lot of "We're going to make it through this, we got this, we're going to do this." And that's been instrumental to, I think, all of us in helping push through this.

DJJ:
So, you pivoted from being competitors to actually networking and working as a community?

Ben:
Yeah. I think even before there was always a good camaraderie among this group, at least that I'm with. And this just heightened that. I think this whole lack of a source of communication and leadership and guidance for this COVID thing, we all started leaning on each other and asking each other for advice. "How do you do this? How do you do that? How are you managing this?" And so, we just figured out ourselves. Just like a group of people lost at sea. We just all banded together. We're going to make it; we don't know how. But if we're in the middle of the ocean, if we just keep going one direction long enough, we're going to hit land again. So yeah, it's been good to have that sense that we're not alone in this. We're all going through this. Again, the bigger picture is that we're all impacted by this. Not just restaurants, everybody. But we all got together to figure out a way to get through this.

DJJ:
If I may ask, how were you personally affected by COVID-19?

Ben:
I don't know how many years off my life. It's been tough. I've got three kids; I've got elderly parents. My mom passed in March of 2020. So, all that attention I've had to focus on

the restaurant to get this through, I feel like I was . . . I felt neglectful in other aspects of my life. So, it's been a tremendous amount of introspection. And why am I doing this? Am I doing the right thing? Is this a sign that I've done this long enough? I've exceeded my wildest dreams in operating a restaurant 24 years. God, I've done it. Is this a sign that I just need to call it quits? So, there's a lot of mixed emotions, a lot of anxiety and stress and apprehension about the future. There's a lot of sense of guilt. Like I should have spent more time with my family, my kids, my parents, my mom before she passed. There's also a tremendous sense of pride in my staff and my fellow restaurateurs who have been there and lifted me up and helped push us through this.

So, the impact from a financial standpoint, sure, it's been significant. From an emotional standpoint, also very significant. And I think lesson learned for me through that is the importance of acknowledging that. Again, in an industry that prides itself in stamina and you keep pushing and nothing, you don't let anything get you down. And now it's like this is, hold on. The message here is you got to take time to acknowledge the fact that things are really messed up and realize the emotion. It's okay to not be okay. And we need to recognize that. And I think that is a lesson that we're all taking from this, is that we got to figure out a better path forward for this industry that is more supportive of physical and emotional health and more supportive of balance of life. And we don't have to give everything we have for this job. There's life outside.

DJJ:

I think many business sectors are realizing the importance of mental and physical health and work–life balancing. It's interesting that I'm hearing you say the same thing. But one of the things I wanted to ask, it sounds like you're optimistic about the future as a restaurant owner. Is that correct to say?

Ben:
Yeah. Yes. Just with this group I've been in this text thread with, the underlying theme, the current running through it all is that we're going to get through this. And again, so much introspection and so much self-questioning of how we're doing business, how we're managing things, and why we do this. And a lot of these people I've been in touch with and in conversation with have been doing it for many, many years. And we're all coming to this realization of—why? Do we have to work this hard? Do we have to do this? Does it have to be this way . . . And I think we're learning. And this is why you see restaurants that are shut down on Mondays and doing shorter business hours and closing at not necessarily their regular times. I think it's realization of how important self-care is in this industry, in any industry. But really, especially in ours where we've been driven so hard for so long to just, you got to just show up every day and do it.

DJJ:
How optimistic are you as a restaurant owner about the future?

Ben:
And I think it's, optimistically, I think it's invigorating. It's getting, tapping into that creativity that was largely lost a lot during this pandemic. Where we were forced to challenge all that creative energy for creating food got shifted into creative energy of how to manage under these new circumstances. So, we're starting to get back into a more creative-for-creative-sake mode. And that feels good.

DJJ:
Instead of simply reverting to business as usual, what are you doing or how might you be seizing the opportunity

to innovate in the next normal (i.e., rethinking restaurant design, reinventing the menu, assessing the store footprint, and digitizing the customer experience)?

Ben:
Well, I think we've been doing things different. We've learned a lot. It's been a big learning curve for us to transition from seated restaurant to takeout. But we've learned a lot. We've learned . . . We've seen that that's now a valid trend and we have to recognize that. So, we have plans that involve, first and foremost, maintaining our original concept of a seated sit-down in-house restaurant. But build on that with a mixture of takeout, chef market, retail. That's something we're exploring. We have space here that we want to turn over into maybe more of a retail outlet. We're looking at maybe expanding into different hours. So, we got a lot of things we're . . . a lot of projects we're kicking around.

Ben Smith, Owner/Chef, Tsunami Restaurant

We all long for the time when we can go out to our favorite restaurant and share a wonderful meal with family, friends, and other loved ones. Sharing time over dinner with family is a part of American culture. Helping us get back to this state is a whole host of public health professionals monitoring the data surrounding the health of communities across the country. They are working with health care professionals and government officials at the local level to put in place policies and procedures to keep us safe. In the next chapter we will speak with one of those public health professionals about his experiences and perspective on the outbreak.

Chapter 15

COVID-19 ATTACKS THE BIG APPLE

To become "unique," the challenge is to fight the hardest battle which anyone can imagine until you reach your destination.
—A. P. J. Abdul Kalam

New York City became the nation's hot spot for COVID-19 in aspects ranging from overcrowded hospitals to ventilator and PPE shortages. These were all prime-time topics on every major news network. Not to mention the politics that were displayed in day-to-day, theater-like fashion as politicians, government officials, and medical experts sought answers to bolster public policy. Additionally, key individuals were on the ground in local health departments and public health organizations, working in conjunction with the government and coordinating efforts to help community members as they struggled to navigate the pandemic. "Since its arrival in the United States, COVID-19 has presented a daunting challenge for local health departments (LHDs) fighting the highly infectious and sometimes fatal disease on the front lines of public health. The stakes were especially high at the pandemic's start in New York State (NYS), which emerged as the national epicenter of the disease in March, with roughly 5% of the world's confirmed cases."[63]

---

63 New York State Association of County Health Officials. (n.d.). New York State Local Health Department Preparedness For and ... : Journal of Public Health Management and Practice. LWW. Retrieved April 14, 2023, from https://journals.lww.com/jphmp/Fulltext/2021/05000/New_York_State_Local_Health_Department.6.aspx

Public health workers are at the tip of the spear when fighting a pandemic, and they have a great responsibility for educating communities about these diseases. They have to explain how an illness is spread, who is most at risk, and what steps to take to reduce the risk of catching it.[64] Public health organizations also conduct sophisticated data analyses that provide critical information to assess the spread of a disease and how to mitigate its presence in communities. Additionally, these algorithms and software programs can assess the effectiveness of treatments and provide vital feedback. Experience has shown that science, medicine, and public health all have to work in concert to combat a pandemic.

I spoke with Dr. Ashish Joshi, Dean and Distinguished University Professor of the School of Public Health of the University of Memphis, former City University of New York Senior Associate Dean, at his office. He shared his perspectives on public health policy and its importance for fighting COVID-19 and preparing for potential future pandemics.

DJJ

New York City was arguably the epicenter of the fight against the COVID-19 pandemic at its peak in the United States. Many strategies and tactics were employed to fight the spread of the virus. What was your role with the New York City government during the peak of the pandemic in New York City?

64 Impact of covid-19 pandemic on Public Health. Monroe College. (n.d.). Retrieved April 14, 2023, from https://www.monroecollege.edu/news/impact-covid-19-pandemic-public-health#:~:text=The%20Role%20of%20Public%20Health%20During%20Pandemics&text=Since%20pandemics%20are%20often%20-considered,risk%20of%20catching%20these%20diseases.

Dr. Joshi:
Thank you so much. It's been such a pleasure to be here among all of you. I think I was at the City University of New York School of Public Health. My academic role was, I was a Senior Associate Dean for Academic and Student Affairs, and my responsibility was at that particular period of time to really look at helping the city with implementing the Test and Choice Program for the city of New York. And the goal of that program largely was to basically provide the communities across the city of New York with the resources, access to the resources like food, housing, tenant help, eviction. And our role was really, frankly speaking, it was all the School of Public Health students who were employing that kind of responsibilities and delivering great work. So, I think we were really contributing toward connecting the communities back to the resources, what they needed the most.

DJJ:
Can you describe what you saw with regard to the death and the spread of the virus?

Dr. Joshi:
Yeah, it's been a tough thing, and obviously, I think that was a moment of really showing your strength. I would say, frankly speaking, anyone, not only those people who got impacted, but also the people who were taking care of those who were getting impacted, from my perspective. And coping, I would say, was a very important element. Adapting to the tough situations and the real realities of where the world is heading to, so I think adaptability was an important element. Resilience is something which I keep on talking a lot about because I think that was a moment when people were feeling, not knowing what exactly is going on. So, I think how best to communicate the evidence-based information back to the people is another one. So that's

how I feel that coping, adaptability, resilience, and empathy, understanding what people are going through . . . I think all those things were self-reflection of really what we were hoping to look upon and see and reflect upon a day-to-day basis. These were tough times, but at the same time, I think the strength came from within.

DJJ:
What behaviors did you see among New York City residents as the lockdowns were in place and mask mandates took effect?

Dr. Joshi:
I would say that New York City did pretty well, to be honest. And frankly speaking, we have never experienced such a thing ever before. So, something like physical distancing, social isolation, you can call it, masking mandates, I could also experience, and I can share my own personal experience. There was a lot of, I would say, information. We were trying to get more and more. I think people were more curious to know exactly what this is all about. What precautions do they need to take? Work-from-home policies were being institutionalized. I think people were very responsive, I would say, to the new environment which was getting set up. And I would also say that there were some challenges at the same time. It was not that everybody's going to follow the same protocols. There were folks who were skeptical about what this is all about. And so, I would say largely, the city was being very responsive, but at the same time, there were certain challenges, which understandably were different than when the pandemic actually earlier started. And a lot of things came into reality as the time went on.

DJJ:
Can you tell me about your current role?

Dr. Joshi:
In my current role as a Dean for the School of Public Health at the University of Memphis, I would say that I am so excited and motivated in this role, and I feel strongly that I would love to see that the School of Public Health becomes a resource that can serve the community, a source where the community can always count on, also a source which says that we are here to be a solution-centric institute. How can we become an anchor to the community to help them on the very long-lasting problems which have been there?

But at the same time, I would say, how do you really advance education in a way that actually can translate research into action and community impact? So, I think the best thing which I feel is, how do you make School of Public Health at the University of Memphis a model for public health and a solution center as a global village, where we can actually be a knowledge generator for the world in this global setting?

DJJ:
You bring a unique combination of academic training and medicine, public health, field experience, and informatics. Your research is focused on developing multifaceted, cost-effective, technology-mediated interventions that address user needs by combining principles of social, cognitive theory, and human-centered approaches to improve population health outcomes. That's a mouthful. I tell you, that was amazing when I read that about you. You have such an extensive background in epidemiology and informatics.
Tell me about your research and how you're applying these principles to combat COVID-19 and in other areas.

Dr. Joshi:
No, I think, to be honest, I would say that the COVID-19 was a central point to the implementation of human-centered

design, what I call. So, my research basically is all revolving around how do you translate research into actionable items for the communities to get the benefit of it. And I think, a couple of examples I would like to share with you specifically related to COVID-19, was that a lot of problem was like people didn't know, you know, what the real data is, what the real numbers are, and how to get the best possible information. And that was not just in the United States but globally, frankly speaking. So, I think one of the things what I was doing was, how do you really bring the data together in a way that is understandable to people, so people can understand the numbers?

The second very important element was, especially in my global work also, that there was a lot of misinformation and disinformation going on. And remember, internet is not everywhere, and not everybody has access to the technologies. You'll be surprised to know that there were a lot of rural populations around the world who may have no access to any kind of evidence-based information. So, one of the initiatives, which I also did using my research, was to use podcast as an intervention in a multilingual way. So, people who could not read or write, they were able to hear the podcast in a local dialect or a language that they could relay to them the most evidence-based health information.

There are several areas of how I've been using informatics. So, for example, on very unique intervention or innovation, what we've been doing is to implement Health ATM in the urban poor settings. It's a unique model because people are looking for access to the right information at the right time. And I think my focus of research has been, how do you bring data and evidence-informed decision-making to the people who need it the most?

DJJ:
What was a typical day like for you at the height of the pandemic?

Dr. Joshi:
I think like everyone, I would at least say this, that I was very grateful, to be honest, first of all, to the things which I could do compared to the people around the world who could not do that. So, I think that is very important to say, that I was always thankful every single day. So, if you ask me what my day started, was to be grateful that I'm there around my friends and my family. I think from the perspective of being in my academic role, my major, major focus was how do you ensure that our students have the utmost resources to succeed professionally as well as personally. Everyone was going through tough times, so the goal was really to provide them with all the possible assistance, help, resources, what they need to succeed during that difficult period of time.

On another note, as you know, it was a remote work. It has its pros and cons. So, I think juggling between the kids, between the work, between the pressures of responding to the needs of not just the professional level but also at the personal level, I think all was playing a lot of roles. And I would also say every single morning, I used to reflect upon how this is all impacting the community at large. There was a lot of reflection. A lot of people might say, "Oh, I did this, I did that," but I think for me personally, it was a lot of reflection about where things are.

DJJ:
Were you personally impacted by COVID-19? And if so, may I ask how?

Dr. Joshi:
Yeah. In my role, I think there were several aspects. As an administrator of a school of public health, you are responsible to take extra responsibility in terms of providing all the support what is needed. Because I was engaged in the providing of the services with the New York City, I think I was experiencing to talk to a lot of students, to a lot of family members, to communities. I think sometimes that would also put a little bit of an extra thought process in your mind, your own personal well-being. And also, I happened to get COVID myself, to be honest. And I would say that I was fortunate enough that the vaccination was there. I was able to, yes, get through the symptoms, but I didn't have to go to the hospital. So, I wish that there were people who could avail that thing.

But I think in all, I would say, I think resilience, being understanding, having the empathy. I think a lot of time we talk about the disease or the health, but I also feel that it was an overall well-being that was a very important component. There was a social aspect. There was a physical aspect. There was a mental aspect. So, I would say that meditation was very important element of myself, and I think reflection on a day-to-day basis of "What more can I do?" played a very important role in bringing those elements of strength as we were navigating through this pandemic.

DJJ:
What were some of your fears and concerns during this time?

Dr. Joshi:
I think the very important thing, which I personally feel which was very important during this moment, was to inform, educate, and empower the people at large because the more than the virus, also there was a lot of misinformation, a lot of disinformation. So, I think the most important fear, which I

had in my view, was how do you respond and counter to the misinformation which is out there? So, I think the more and more I was listening, the more and more I was wondering, how do you and what tools you can bring to the audiences at large, so that you can inform them in the most evidence-informed way? I think that was one of the ways—I think the manifestation of a disease and its symptoms, they are one thing, but manifestation of misinformation is unknown. So, we just don't know how to counter the misinformation.

So, I think for me, the biggest fear was, how do you communicate and translate the right information to the people, so that there is more trust and more supported by evidence? I think that was my biggest fear. I think the second fear, which may not have a short-term, but a long-term impact was also the economic impact. How does it impact employment opportunities? How does it impact those students who are in the college, who are in the middle of graduating? How does it impact day-to-day people who are living on daily wages? So, when you start to see something like this, as a public health professional, I just don't think about just health. You start to go thinking beyond health. And I think those were the things which were coming into my mind.

DJJ:

Did you ever lose faith in our health care system and our ability to fight the virus?

Dr. Joshi:

No, not at all. I think being a physician myself, being in this public health, I have to say that we have to give a lot of credit to our health care professionals. The amazing work that they did during these tough times, I think, in itself reflects how committed, dedicated they were. So, I would say that never, ever, at least my faith got shaken up in any way. Not at all.

DJJ:
Dr. Joshi, virtually every country in the world was stunned and crippled by the COVID-19 pandemic to the extent of being shut down physically. Life was paused, and economically, every part of commerce was brought to a complete halt.
What is your perspective on how countries attacked the pandemic differently and used various approaches?

Dr. Joshi:
I think each country responded based on the resources what they had. Things which was applicable in the United States may not be applicable in Nigeria, or things which were applicable in Nigeria may not be applicable in Brazil. And it was not just related to the COVID. It's related to many of the factors, so for example, the infrastructure which might be there, the kind of health care access which might be there, the kind of workforce which might be there. So, I think countries responded based on the availability of the information, the ability to use the data, the resources at their disposition, and also very important is about their own belief about the condition itself. So, I would say that countries responded. Some did early. Some took some time. And I would say that instead of saying that this country did better than the other country, my view on this is basically that each country experienced a different level of challenge, and each country responded to that challenge differently based on their own current scenario. But one of the things which I would really want to emphasize is the importance of using the data and the evidence as a way to make an informed decision-making is something which should be a common thread across, no matter which country is responding how.

DJJ:
Do you believe accurate information and data were shared at the onset of the pandemic?

Dr. Joshi:
It's a mixed response. Yes and no. To be honest, it depends on who you ask, and it depends how people respond to it. I think there was a lot of skepticism about what this is all about, its origin, its translation, its variants, its treatment response. But I think I would also say that this was also the biggest challenge to our human existence, frankly speaking, at this point, and countries responded based on, as I mentioned earlier, the resources what they had. But I would also emphasize here is that very importantly, the way the information was being shared and the way that was being communicated could have been far more responsive. I think it could have been more . . . but I think it would have been relayed to the community at large different levels that would actually make sure that people's doubts about a particular condition would have been alleviated. So that's how I see that.

DJJ:
Do you have a perspective on how China is handling the virus today with the COVID-19 zero tolerance?

Dr. Joshi:
Yeah. Especially since we have known so much about this right now, I don't think that the countries can have a zero policy, frankly speaking. And in my view, the best strategies are to vaccinate, mask, depending on the population, who's at high risk, proper tracking of the cases, testing wherever required, able to bring in preventive measures. But saying that a zero-tolerance kind of a COVID-19 policy might be very, very difficult. And actually, it not only just hurts economically, but it also starts to create that kind of a fear of the outcome of this condition. So, I think from my view, institutionalizing more preventive measures and monitoring measures to the burden of the disease and its response by providing them the right information so

that people are getting vaccinated, and I think that's the only best way right now.

DJJ:
Can you tell us about what your research showed as it relates to India?

Dr. Joshi:
Remember, India is a country of 1.5 billion people. And I would say largely that it did well in terms of managing, keeping in mind the scale and the scope of the population it has with the resources what it has. I think the larger challenge of the COVID-19 was its impact on people who were living on daily wages. There was an economic impact. I would definitely say something to look at is going to be the school closures. How does that impact the children coming back to the schools and how to engage the kids back into that kind of an activity. So, I think India, specifically, with such dense populated but, also, I would say that the policymakers, the government, the private sector did come together to really bring the vaccination pretty rapidly. So, I think it depends how you want to view it. If you're looking at a country of 1.5 billion, just imagine that COVID-19, how best to respond to that. I think from that lens, I feel that India did a pretty fair job.

DJJ:
I know as you watched the media and what have you, you saw all of the deaths that were occurring in India. In your estimation, what was happening? And you talked about 1.5 billion people. **Can you expound upon what was happening in India with the widespread deaths and policies to vaccinate citizens?**

Dr. Joshi:
I think what happened was, I think, as a caution, yes, there were early closures. And probably the time when it still should have been continued, it seemed that they were being relaxed, and I think that's when the peak was there. My understanding is that also, to be honest, the people were living with a lot of comorbidities, the challenge of lack of resources in the hospitals. I think, also, the availability of the PPE kits, the health care infrastructure at large, I think attributed to that particular aspect a lot. And I think the lack of information. A lot of people did not know at what particular period of time they need to go to the hospital. So, I think that was a virus which was so transmissible, and I would also say that the population who was getting impacted largely was living in densities where the availability of the hospital beds was also a problem.

I would view this as a lot of contributing factors, external contributing factors, like, say, lack of infrastructure, overwhelming hospitals with limited bed capacities, response by the health care professionals, the lack of workforce, and also lack of information on when you should go to the hospital. So, I think people who really needed the cure may have taken a lot of time to reach to the hospitals. So, I think all these things did at least impact the worst part when you saw a widespread of death. And also, I would like to highlight here that there's a lot of cultural contexts to this, so people tend to get a little bit more worried about what they were seeing around the world. And because it did not impact the population in the early phase, the people tend to become a little bit easy. So, they thought that it's getting over, and I think that's when the hit was the most.

DJJ:
What were some vital lessons learned?

Dr. Joshi:
This is a very important question, I think, because we can keep on talking about the COVID-19 problems, but I think it also, at the same time, really emphasize the importance of public health. It also talked about how important it is for us to prepare both not as individuals but as countries at large about the infrastructure in health care. The third thing, which was very important, is, to be honest, how do you prevent, plan, prepare for the future pandemics, to be honest. Another aspect I would say which had a huge economic impact. And sometimes we are talking about so much of the health impact that the economic impact means, I think, people started to really take care of the health also a little bit seriously. I would also say from my own personal experience, not that there wasn't any such data, but the people who I knew who were not saving the resources for their future started to save the money. This was something which was not seen earlier.

And another thing was how technology can play such an important role in both the prevention, both in the monitoring, both in the distribution of health care services, reaching out to people through use of drones. What is the role of artificial intelligence in COVID-19? I think it also opened an era of how technology and data can play such an important role in both the prevention and the prediction of these diseases. As much as we are talking about the COVID-19 and its impact, at the same time, I strongly feel that it also created an opportunity for the individuals, the families, the communities, as well as the policymakers and of governments, on how best to prepare themselves to respond to these urgent, emergent, and acute needs.

DJJ:
Do you believe the medical community is better prepared for the next pandemic?

Dr. Joshi:
I would say that it has alerted them. I would also feel that there has been lot of investments by the different governments around the world, but to be honest, there's a lot to be done, frankly speaking. Pandemic, nobody prepared or thought about it. That means we need to prepare our workforce for the future. We need to sensitize more people about how and what are the important measures they need to take care of this. And I like to communicate one more very important message there. How do you build your immunity? How do you stay healthy and not wait for any disaster to happen? So, I think it also emphasized the importance of exercise, importance of eating healthy food. These are important elements, how to manage your chronic noncommunicable diseases because a lot of people who became victim to the COVID-19, sad outcome of being dying out of that, were also people who had chronic noncommunicable diseases like diabetes and hypertension. So, I think overall, I would say that I hope it motivates in a way where people start to take care of their health in a much better way.

DJJ:
Are there any other perspectives or information you'd like to share regarding this once-in-a-lifetime event?

Dr. Joshi:
I was asked this question, what did COVID made you learn? And if I look as an educator or if I look like a father of two kids who are currently in the schools or if I look from the lens of the community, there are four things which come to my mind: that coping, adaptability, resilience, and empathy. If someone asked me, I mentioned to them I would like to create a clear curriculum that should prepare our kids, our communities, on how to cope to uncertain situations, how to adapt in difficult environments, how to be resilient. And very, very important is

how to be empathetic because to be honest, if somebody tells me, "How did you overcome this period?" or "How did you respond to this?" I would say, "Yes, I had the knowledge. Probably I had the skills. I had the education. But you know what? COVID challenged everything." What came into help was these four words. And I will say from the lens of being an educator and now as a dean is that we can talk about all the skills. Those are great. But I think teaching our kids and students about these four elements, I think, are going to be the pillars.

The second component is COVID-19 has reflected that world is a global village. It's all interconnected. Someone like me, living in the United States doesn't mean that I if not take care of my surroundings will be safe, but somebody sitting in India or in Bangladesh or in Nepal, in Brazil, in Mexico will get impacted. So, I think the COVID has shown how interconnected the world is, and I feel that it is a collective responsibility to act to any such future or even as we are experiencing through this COVID-19 to be responsive and be responsible toward prevention and the management of this thing. So that's how I think. I think science, use of data, bringing more evidence, and also the people on how to bring the information, which is understandable to them, these are the important aspects.

DJJ:
Given everything you have experienced, how optimistic are you about the future?

Dr. Joshi:
I'm a very optimistic person, and I always believe hope sustains life. And I think this is a moment of we need to just spread optimism, positivity. Personally, I would say I think people have had too many challenges, and too much has been lost in all this. I think we can keep on talking. I think as long as we are reflecting upon what went wrong, but at the same time we can't

just lose hope. So, for me, and I would say only one thing, that optimism, spreading positivity does play a very important role in how we cope, we adapt to the difficult challenges. So, I think not only me, but I would encourage everybody, to be very frank, being optimistic, and actually be grateful that we have been given another chance now to contribute to making the world a better place.

DJJ:
What are some of the things about COVID-19 we don't know today and should be concerned about?

Dr. Joshi:
Obviously, as much as I think science has shown tremendous gains, but COVID-19 is an evolving scenario. There's a lot of variants which is happening. I think the only thing which I would say is to be watchful, be cautious, but at the same time, be very optimistic. Have faith in the health care system. Have faith that today also science has played a very important role and will always continue to play that important role. So I think, yes, being cautious and able to track and monitor is key, but that doesn't mean that we need to live in any kind of fear. But what we need to do is believe that there is going to be always a solution to every problem.

DJJ:
Do you believe COVID-19 is in the rearview mirror, or is it still lurking with us, waiting for an opportunity to unleash a new deadly strain that will shock the world again?

Dr. Joshi:
I would say stay vigilant. Follow the basic things. But at the same time, I would also say that do things which makes you feel happy. Do things that gives you the optimism, the confidence

in your health care, in yourself, in the communities, and that we are all here together into all this. I think as much as we might be getting misinformed, I think it is well important for us to become more self-informed in the best possible way. So, I'm pretty optimistic. I think I would hope that everybody becomes more optimistic.

Dr. Ashish Joshi, Dean and Distinguished University Professor of the School of Public Health of the University of Memphis, former City University of New York Senior Associate Dean

Talented health care, government, and public health professionals fiercely worked in concert to fight COVID-19 and save patients. However, their best efforts couldn't save everyone. The pandemic stole lives from a great number of families on a scale rarely seen before in this country and around the world. Loss of a family member is tragic and creates a huge void in the family unit. It became apparent during the pandemic that every moment with family, friends, and loved ones should be cherished and never taken for granted. We never know the last time we will be able to get together or have an opportunity to kiss our spouse. The next chapter shows how the last kiss is priceless when your loved one passes away.

Chapter 16

THE LAST KISS IN THE PARKING LOT

The risk of love is loss, and the price of loss is grief—But the pain of grief is only a shadow when compared with the pain of never risking love.

—Hilary Stanton Zunin

The death and destruction of COVID-19 has been well documented. Millions of lives have been lost around the world. However, the individual pain that families and spouses experience with the loss of a loved one is inexplicable. When someone is ripped away, an irreparable hole is left in the lives of family members. It's hard for those on the outside to understand how the absence of an individual shatters the family dynamic. We really don't know how a person's presence, personality, and contributions play such a significant role in the day-to-day lives of others. Every individual is unique, and what they bring to the world has different effects on the people around them. The loss of a spouse captures and crystallizes this mental pain and anguish. Isolation, separation, and the feeling of helplessness all contributed to the roller coaster of emotions that surviving spouses experienced as they watched from afar while their loved one withered away in a hospital room. This next interview highlights the emotional trauma. Yet it also shows the nature of perseverance and resilience in the face of tragedy.

I sat down with Mrs. Shannon Bellamy in her home to talk about her amazing husband, Robby Bellamy. She shared precious moments in their wonderful life together and how special he was to his family and the broader community.

DJJ:
What were your initial thoughts when businesses, churches, schools, and everything we considered normal, in our day-to-day lives, started closing and COVID-19 was called a global pandemic?

Shannon:
I think our initial thoughts weren't exactly fearful. We wanted to be part of the solution, and so we were willing to do what needed to happen for a period of time. We were very concerned for us. Closing the churches was a huge issue. That is our strength, and that was our social, that was our everything. That's what we did. Work was incidental church was everything. And that was our family. And so that was hard.

Staying home, I'm a stay-at-home mom. I homeschool my kids. We're home. We do a co-op for homeschoolers here in our home. So, staying home wasn't really that big of a deal for us. We weren't overwhelmed with that like a lot of people were. But the churches closing, that was tough. That was really hard. We were concerned in how long that was going to be. Because they said that it was only going to be for two weeks. We knew, before they even said that, that it was going to be longer. We knew instinctively that it was going to be longer, and we were concerned about how long that was going to be. So, I think that was our first initial responses of, how long is this going to actually be?

DJJ:
Did the term, "global pandemic", give you any pause? Did you think this would be far-reaching?

Shannon:
Yes and no. I homeschool, and it just so happens that we had, two weeks before this all hit, had just studied the Spanish flu. And when we study, we go all in. And so, we had just studied it, so we had seen this happen before. This is just history repeating itself. Right? And the flu that we get now is the Spanish flu, or a version of. And so, we had already kind of seen it. So, when it was global, we got it. We understood that it traveled faster because our travel is faster.

DJJ:
You said, you knew this thing was going to last longer. What was the source for your thinking?

Shannon:
Absolutely, actually, yes. Because you had the Spanish flu—it hit, it was huge, all these people were getting sick. And then they thought it was cured, and then they had this huge gathering, and it was five times worse than it was. And I could see that same thing playing out again. Because most schools don't cover this. I know when I went to school, the Spanish flu was barely touched. And so, if you don't know history, you repeat history. And even when you know it, you repeat it. That's just what it does. History repeats itself.

And so, I knew that we were probably going to go on lockdown. We were probably going to get a little bit ahead of it, and then we were going to let up, and people were going to gather. And it's a virus. Viruses mutate. They're going to do everything they can to stay alive. They're going to mutate, and then they're going to get worse, and so people are going to die. And then they're going to back off because the virus doesn't want their host to die. They want to survive. And the virus is going to do whatever it can to survive. And if their host dies, then they die.

And so, then it gets less, and that's it. It's this cycle. And so, we had just studied all of that. So, we talked about that quite a bit, of how is this mimicking that? Everything is a learning moment.

DJJ:
What changes did your family have to immediately make?

Shannon:
As a family, not exactly a whole lot. As I said, we homeschool, we're at home, most of our stuff. Our music, I teach voice. And so, you could teach guitar and piano and some other instruments online. Voice is not one of those things you can really teach online. It just doesn't work. So, I lost my job, basically. Robby came home from work, which was wonderful. We loved having him here. That was fun. And it was easy to set up. We already had an office set up, so that was an easy transition.

The only other big thing: our co-op, we had to figure out what we were going to do. The way our co-op works is that we meet on Mondays, and a whole bunch of families get together. And each family teaches a different class, so it's not all on one parent. Because I am fantastic at literature and American government and history, and I am not touching science or math at all.

And so, I need help with all of that. And so how were we going to facilitate that? We had to get very, very creative with all of that. We did some Zoom. We took a break for a minute. Everybody needed a break. This was such a change. This was such a change for everybody. And you had to catch a breath. And so, we took a little bit of a break, which homeschooling allows you to do. And it was kind of nice for all of us. And then we, "Okay, how are we going to do this?"

So initially it was mostly, how are we going to do the schooling? Because we had to keep schooling. A lot of schools shut down for quite a while, and they really couldn't just immediately deal with that number, volume . . . We only had 12 families. So, with 12 families, we were able to jump back in very quickly and figure out how we could do this, much more quickly than I think most people did. So, for us, it was not a huge anything.

DJJ:
Did you ever think this would happen in these modern times and especially in the United States?

Shannon:
I don't know that I was surprised. I believe that it became very political very quickly. Let me rephrase that. I believe that the political parties in the United States, who are so at odds with each other, because we have two, instead of, as it was originally intended, we were supposed to have many different political parties. It was never supposed to be a two political party. And because we have that, it's so volatile because it's two. If we had three or four or five, it would balance out much better. Because we have two, they're so at odds with each other. They used the whole situation, I think, very quickly to both of their advantages, which I think caused things to last longer than they had to have. So, was I surprised? No.

DJJ:
Were you ever afraid during those early days when everything was being blasted on television? And did fear ever enter into your thought process?

Shannon:
I don't think so. Honestly, the only person that the family was most concerned about was me because I have some autoimmune responses to things. And that was, everybody was

blasting, "People with autoimmune, you're really in trouble." So, I think they were maybe a little hesitant for me to go out and do anything, the rest of the family. But as a whole, your days are numbered. Your days are numbered. So, you live them as beautifully as you can, to the best that you can, as full as you can, for as long as you can, and then you don't regret it.

DJJ:
In that same vein, if you did or if you had to, what conversations did you have with your children to ease their fears?

Shannon:
Yeah, my two youngest ones, at that time, were still at home. Robby is the fun one. They were thrilled that he was home, and that's all they cared about. They really did not care about much of anything else. The fun one was home.

And he was absolutely the fun one. And he could get them out of a lot of stuff, so they were fine. My oldest was in college. She had gone through her first year of college. This was starting her second year of college. And we had some difficult decisions that we had to make for that, of scholarships and lack of scholarships, and do we take a loan or do we not, if they're not even going to be able to finish it? And all of those questions. And she ended up going because they said they could work some things out, and then they couldn't.

And so, she had to come back, which was good because they did shut it down, and she would've taken a loan out for what she couldn't even have used. And that's not good either. So, there was a lot of emotions for her. My oldest was . . . That's the one. It wasn't fear of the virus. It wasn't really fear of if we were going to get sick or not sick. It was more she wants to go into the FBI. She wants to be a chemist for the FBI. And this was stopping her forward momentum, and it was changing her path.

She's very type A. Opposite of me in every way. And so, she really struggled with that. So that was hard. That was hard. I'm not sure exactly what words we said other than, "God directs our paths. And so, if He was shutting doors, and we allow Him to shut doors, and we figure it out from there." She's actually married now and working as a chemist in an agricultural lab and loving every minute of it.

DJJ:
Did COVID make a lot of people change plans and do different things?

Shannon:
It did. It changed a lot of paths very quickly.

DJJ:
Shannon, you have a special story to share as it relates to COVID-19 and one very similar to far too many others during this time. Tell us about Robby.

Shannon:
I don't even know where to start. Robby was so busy. Robby was incredibly smart. He was incredibly friendly. Robby would approach just about everybody. And you probably know this, with, you would say, "Hey, Robby," and he'd say, "How can I help?" That was almost always his first thing. "How can I help?" And his next answer would be, whatever you said, was "Absolutely."

Now, there's times I'm sitting beside him, looking at him, going, "And exactly how are we going to do that?" But he did it most all the time. "Absolutely, let's do it." Which is great, right? He was involved with so many things; it was hard to narrow down who was going to talk about Robby at his funeral because there were so many avenues that he did and so many things that he did. He just was busy and involved and cared. And there was nothing that he wouldn't help you with, ever.

DJJ:
Tell me about his faith, volunteerism, barbecuing, and involvement with the Boy Scouts.

Shannon:
Yes, very much. We were actually on the cusp of being involved with a political campaign for a friend of ours, and Robby was going to be helping spearhead that. So, he did . . . The activities that he did, some of the things. He was an Eagle Scout. Him and his dad got their Eagle Scouts together way back in the day. He was an electrical engineer. That was his actual degree. He was incredibly, incredibly smart. The first and foremost thing about Robby is that he was a strong Christian. And so, everything they did, he was on the Men of Faith team, which would pour into the Bartlett football team. And they would go to every single game, and they would do all the jobs that parents would do because there weren't always parents involved. There weren't always parents there. And if they were, they wanted to watch their kids.

But more than that, they were on the sidelines, and they were loving on these boys that didn't always have strong men in their lives. And that was probably one of Robby's favorite things. We had Memphis State football tickets for 30 years. Good, bad, ugly, horrible, awful, beautiful. All the good, all the bad, we were there. We were there. Let's see. He was volunteer for, I think, 15 or 18 years at the St. Jude Golf Tournament.

I'm probably missing stuff. He just did so, so much. And barbecue cooking team. He was the pitmaster, the whole hog pitmaster for Anna Dale's Pork and Fireside Smokers. So, he did that for about 10 years at Memphis in May. And Anna Dale's Pork is actually the oldest team on Memphis in May. And they don't compete in the circuit. That was Fireside Smokers. And Fireside Smokers, we're actually third in the nation right now in our pulled pork. So, we've been enjoying that. Now, we haven't done a whole hog since Robby died because Robby was our hog person. So, we're not really sure what we're supposed to do about that. But he just did so much.

I was into music, and so he ran sound. Because he was going to be there anyway, so he might as well run the sound. Because "How can I help?" "Absolutely." We were chaperones for 10 mission trips. I may be wrong in the numbers. They all blend together. I think it was 10 mission trips with the youth in the choir and the youth groups. And we went to San Francisco, New York, and Las Vegas, and . . . I don't know. Philadelphia. We went all over the place. And Robby was the one toting all the sound equipment on subways. That was not fun. So, all the things. We just did all the things.

DJJ:
Tell me about him as a father and as a husband.

Shannon:
Robby was incredible. I was beyond blessed. He made me feel incredibly loved, very beautiful all the time. He was always home. I never had to wonder where he was. He was always home. He was at work, or he was home. He was home. And he would prefer to be home. When COVID hit and he was home, he was happy. He would prefer to be home with us, which was great. That's not always the story. And so, we were very, very blessed with that.

We had fun together. We had fun as a family. As a father, his girls adored him. His son idolized him, absolutely. We enjoyed each other. We had fun together. Board games, we have a whole closet full of board games. That was every Christmas we would get a new board game. And board games and card games were our thing.

And so, we would go camping, and we would leave all the electronics behind and just take four or five board games, and that's what we would do. And it was great. So, we enjoyed each other. I will tell you. I will tell you one thing, because he sounds like the saint person, right? He was a classified genius. His parents did not tell him that because he barely studied as it was, and they didn't want him to stop studying anything. So, he did not know he was a classified genius until I told him after we got married. His mother told me and never told him. I don't know if he told his sisters or not, but he didn't know it until I told him, after we got married, that he was a classified genius. But he was a horrible teacher. Horrible teacher. We homeschooled. He's a math genius. He's an electrical engineer. He should be able to teach math. It did not happen.

When Robby was teaching you math, he could not just teach you one way. He had to say, "Well, you can do it this way." And then before you could even process what that way was, he would tell you four or five "Or you could do it this way, or this might be easier too." He would tell you four or five different ways to solve the same problem, and you haven't even figured out the first one. I had to just shut that down. It was awful. So, he was a horrible teacher. But he was a fantastic worker. Horrible teacher.

DJJ:
You lost Robby in January 2022 because of complications due to COVID-19. Tell us about Robby's journey with COVID-19.

Shannon:
So, we got exposed in our home in a group and really didn't have any symptoms throughout our family, and two weeks later, we were still doing all of our normal things, getting ready for Christmas. And then on a Sunday, Robby really did not feel well. He was very sick. Sleeping on the couch because he could sit up, fever, all the things, coughing, and just miserable. My grandmother was here at the time, my 89-year-old grandmother. We were incredibly concerned. We hadn't tested positive at this time, but we all had headaches, coughing, fever, all the things. So, we figured we probably had COVID.

I took Robby into Minor Med to see what was going on. They diagnosed pneumonia, but his rapid COVID test came back negative. Came home with medicines for pneumonia, and he just kept getting worse. My grandmother had COPD and was on oxygen, so she had the oxygen monitor, and we were using that on Robby.

By Wednesday, his oxygen level was in the mid-80s. Oxygen levels should be around 99, 98; most healthy people are about right there. When you start getting into the 80s and you have a fever and not doing well, it was obvious he was getting sicker at this point. We were like, okay, let's go to the hospital. Robby did not exactly want to do that. We knew that meant we were not going to see each other probably through Christmas, if not longer. Because at that time, the hospitals were still shut down. They did not allow family in unless it was end of life.

And so COVID patients had to go in by themselves. Robby's sister, Kathryn, is an administrative nurse at the hospital we chose to go to because she was there, so somebody could be with him at times. She met us in the parking lot, and he was just going to go in because he felt so bad, and she stopped us and she said, "You need to hug, and you need to kiss because it's going to be a long time before you can do that again." It was the first time it really dawned on me that I was not going to see him through Christmas. I was not going to see him for a while, and that was hard.

That was hard. We did, we hugged and kissed, and Kathryn took him inside, and I sat in my car and sobbed. That's when fear hit. When we talked about fear earlier, that's when fear hit, the realization that he was very, very sick. I didn't even say this. On the way to the hospital, we got a call from the Minor Med. They had done a long COVID test, and his COVID had come back positive. So, on our way to the hospital, we got the positive results that this was COVID, so it was COVID pneumonia. He was getting sicker, but we knew that the hospital was where he needed to be able to have any chance of getting the treatments that could possibly help us combat this. So that was a very difficult ride home.

DJJ:
In our conversations, you described Robby as a fighter, but he experienced a lot of difficulty in the hospital. Can you tell me about that and what that was like for him?

Shannon:
Yes. He was incredibly sick. They were giving him medicines. He got into the ER. As soon as he moved to the ER, he went to a regular room. Within 12 hours, he was in a step-down unit on high-flow oxygen. His oxygen level just kept decreasing. They were putting all the different medicines. We were doing all the different things. He would have a little bit of a rebound here and there sometimes, but his oxygen levels just kept going down. They would test one particular marker that would tell us what his inflammation levels were. And they kept going up even with all of the antibiotics, all of the antivirals, all of the things. They did their treatments, the hospital did. I am an advocate. I've been through some medical things before with other family members as their advocates. So, I knew to ask questions. And

so, we had so much information being thrown at us. I would go to the doctor. You can't say, "I want you to do this." Doctors totally shut down. That does not work. But if you go to a doctor and you say, "I've heard this works. Can we try this?" And they'll say, "It's actually not proven to work." And then my answer would be, "Well, but his inflammation markers keep going up and his oxygen keeps going down, so he is dying. If it might work, I know it's not proven to work, but it could work. Can we try it? Will it hurt him?" And so, we actually did three different things that the hospital did not typically do because my way of going to them was, "Will it hurt him?" It might not help, but will it hurt him? And at this point, if it won't hurt, let's try it.

At one point I told one of the doctors, "I need to know that I have done everything I can in this journey to advocate for him to get all the treatments that could possibly work." And they were willing to do that. So, we did some things in the hospital that they didn't typically do. Unfortunately, his inflammation markers kept going up and his oxygen kept going down. His heart stayed strong. That's actually heart issues, your kidneys shut down, your liver shut down. There's lots of things that typically occur, because COVID is a full-body disease. It doesn't just hit your lungs, it hits everything. It hits your mind—there's just so much. We didn't have to face any of that. Robby did not have any comorbidities prior to his COVID diagnosis. Once he was diagnosed with COVID, his blood sugar was high and his blood pressure was high, which were two things that had never previously been an issue.

DJJ:
Can you tell me about that last day and those last hours?

Shannon:
I have to back up a little bit to do that because it was a very unique time for us. We had hundreds of thousands of people

following Robby, all of those activities. I was posting on Facebook, letting everybody know. I did everything public, so anybody and everybody could see they were sharing and praying. There was so much. I actually got called in, over the course of two weeks, I got called in to the hospital seven times, exactly seven times, for end of life. The first end of life was when Robby was still in the step-down. He was on high-flow oxygen. That was not working, and they were about to have to put him on external respirator, which was even more flow. And then the next step would've been the ventilator. And Robby, at that point, had refused the ventilator. And so, they called me in because they were saying, "If he doesn't do the ventilator, then today is the day."

And so, I got to stay with him for about four hours, and we talked, and we prayed, and he rested some. He rebounded a little bit with me there, which hurts my heart. He was agitated, which isn't him, right? He's very compliant. He was very agitated. When I was there, he immediately calmed down. His blood pressure calmed down. His respirations went up. He was doing so much better with me there. And that was very hard when they're saying, you have to leave. And I'm like, "But he's doing better with me here. Why do I have to leave?" That was very difficult. But they called us in several times. We talked to the doctor. We asked the percentages, "How many people that go on the ventilator with this COVID come off the ventilator?" They gave us the percentages. And I'm like, "Okay, Robby, what do you want to do? It's your call." And he's like, "Those sound like good percentages. I'm willing to fight." It was 50/50.

He said, "I'm going to fight. I will keep pushing." And I said, "So if we go to the ventilator, that means that you need to rest, and we can still do." So, when I left, they were taking him to ICU, which I could not go, and the plan was for him to go on the ventilator that night. But he rebounded for two or three days because he was a fighter. He was going to do everything in his power to fight this. And so, on January 1st, he was tired, and he said, "I'm tired," and he was ready for the ventilator. So, they called me back in. I don't even remember what day. I think that was the third time they called me in, second or third time. I can't even remember.

And so, I was able to be with him before they sedated him to go on the ventilator. And I was able to sing with him, him, and his sister. Me and his sister were both there. We were able to sing and pray and worship, and it was very peaceful. It was very, this is what we're doing, this is the next step in the battle. We can do this. It was very positive. It wasn't what we wanted, but it was positive. And he went to sleep, resting well and at peace with that.

So, from January 1st to January 13th, it was up and down. The roller coaster is intense. You have small rebounds of, okay, he's doing better, and then you have crashes of, he's going to die today. And so, through it all, it was seven times they called me, "He's going to die today." And on that seventh day, his respiration was very, very low. His heart was still strong. We were a little worried. He's stopping breathing, and his heart is strong as anything. That heart, that big heart that Robby has was just so strong.

His sister and I were there. Normally, in this COVID, I would've had to be there by myself. The only reason she was there is because she worked there in administration. That's wrong. I cannot imagine. I can't wrap my head around. My heart went out to so many of the people on that COVID unit that as I was walking past them, that were fighting alone and had no one in there with them. That was as hard for me as watching my husband die. That was as hard as anything. The nurses were so tired. The nurses were exhausted. They were defeated. They were defeated.

They said it was 50/50. But in this particular strand that Robby had, it was more like 80 percent that went on ventilators died. These nurses were devastated. The nurse that was in there with us when he died, we had worship. The Bible tells us that when a believer goes home to be with the Lord, that Jesus himself comes and takes them home. We were in the room with the angels and with Jesus when they came and got Robby. The peace that filled that room in that moment is something that is indescribable. But as soon as that spirit of Robby left, we could feel it. We knew it. It was instant. Neither one of us, his sister or I, either one wanted to stay in the room at all. We left very quickly because it was so obvious that Robby's person, him, who he was, was gone, but Jesus had him.

Right? Jesus had him. So, it was a hard day, but the nurse was sobbing. She was sobbing more than we were. She was inconsolable. They were so rooting for Robby. They wanted so much for him to be the exception and the miracle. They were following my Facebook. I didn't know that until later. But they were all following my Facebook, and they were rooting for him. We had pictures of him on poster board his sister had made, so they could see his personality and who he was.

And when he wasn't sedated, they got to meet him to some degree, and they wanted so badly for him to be that exception. And the nurse and the nurse manager, both the nurse manager met us outside the door, immediately hugged his sister Kathryn and just lost it. They were more emotional in that moment than I think Kathryn and I were. We had just had worship. We had just been with Jesus. They didn't experience that. They had the backlash of another patient that they've lost the battle. So, there was so many emotions of that day of for us, for him, for the nurses and the doctors, and it was hard.

DJJ:
How did your faith sustain you?

Shannon:
Oh, it was absolutely the only thing that sustains us, right? Early on in this battle, and I was told by a beautiful, beautiful woman that had lost her husband when she was 42, and she is now 93, I think, she said, "You need to choose a promise of God that's in the Scriptures, that's for you." Because not every promise in the Scriptures is for us, right? "Choose a promise of God that is for you and hold on to it with everything you've got. You can't hold on to them all. You need to focus on one." And so for me, that I held on to was all things work together for good, for the glory of God, for those who trust Him and believe in Him. Not for everybody. And that doesn't mean that we're all going to have all of our prayers answered the way we want them to.

Now, on this end of it, and immediately following that, my human brain, finite brain, cannot imagine or fathom how the bright light that Robby Bellamy was and all the things that he did and all the missions he did, how him not being here on earth, how him not being my husband and how him not being my kids' father, how can that work for the best? How can that work for the good? I have no idea. But I only see right now. God sees before now and time eternity. So, I don't know. I know so many people through those prayers and through my walk through the grief of it all. I use my words a lot and I process through words. And so, I did that on Facebook. I let people see where I was spiritually and emotionally and all of it. There were so many people that were brought to a belief and a faith in Jesus through that, and Robby would've been the first one to say it's worth it.

I said this on one of the posts, and it's true. Robby would've been the first one to say, "It was worth it. It was worth it." That was one of the things, that holding on to knowing that it's for the good. I have no idea what that good is. I don't know what it's going to look like, but it's for the good. The other thing was the Bible tells us our days are numbered. Our days are determined before we are even born, before we're even conceived, our days are determined. They are numbered. Robby was going to die on January 13th. That was his day. It was going to be COVID, or it was going to be a heart attack, or it was going to be a random gunman, or it was going to be a car accident. Robby's day was January 13th. That's when he was going to go to Jesus, no matter how that looked. And holding on to knowing that brings peace.

DJJ:
COVID-19 did not discriminate based on race, gender, religious or political affiliation, or even socioeconomic status. It touched all our lives at some point and in some way. I think we were all afraid and anxious of the unknown.
What were your thoughts on COVID-19 and all the communication received from the government, CDC, radio/television, and so forth?

Shannon:
That's an interesting question. I am very skeptical of news media and the government. I do not believe that government, as an entity, has a concern for the individual person. I teach American government, right? Government as a being is not for the people. Government is for government. It just is. It's part of it. So, I did not trust them to have my personal well-being in mind. They have the whole society in mind. And so, I took the information they gave me, I did my own research in various ways . . . And that's if you were liberal or conservative. I think there was good information on both sides, but you had to delve into it, and you had to weed through so much. And the general populace doesn't have the time or the understanding or the desire to do that. They needed it narrowed down, and they needed to know that they personally were cared for. But that's not what government does. That's not what it's designed

to do. It wasn't going to do that. Too many people trusted that government was going to be their personal caregiver. That's not what government is.

So, for me and my family, the information that we were given, we were taking that, we were taking it from various different sources, and we were discerning on our own what was best for our personal selves. What the government was asking us to do was sometimes against what our personal convictions were. And sometimes what the government was asking us to do was 100 percent in line with what we felt was best for ourselves and the community. So, we wanted to help the community and we wanted to help ourselves. But trying to find that balance of what do we believe, what do we understand, discerning all of that was very difficult. It was overwhelmingly difficult, I think, for us. And my husband and I are both researchers and very intelligent. We were blessed in that, because I think there was a lot of others that didn't have that to be able to fall back on. Did that answer the question?

DJJ:
What were your thoughts on the vaccine when it first came out, and what are your thoughts now?

Shannon:
I have to give you a little background.
Okay. So, when I grew up as a missionary's kid, my parents were home missionaries at the Tennessee Baptist Children's Home here in Tennessee. They were house parents. My grandparents were house parents at one cottage, and my parents were house parents at another. So, I grew up with about 200 different girls coming in and out of our house as foster sisters. There was another family that lived with us, and that was from the time I was 13 to the time I was 22. There was another family that was house parents in another cottage that had a child. She received

the vaccines and had an adverse reaction to them, and that is very uncommon. Very, very not normal. But she started having seizures, hundreds of seizures a day from the vaccines. That is not a common thing; it's not typical. But it's in the back of my head, right?

So, fast-forward, I get married. I have my first baby. She gets all of her vaccines—she does great. I am not an anti-vaxxer. My son, on the other hand, when he was born, four days after his first set of vaccinations, started having seizures. And then we did not give him any more at that time, and he did not have that problem.

So, I got talked into a second set of shots when he was two, because the vaccinations are good, they're not . . . It's a good thing for your individual self and for society. And so, we tried again when he was two. Within three days he was having seizures again. So, he has diagnosed audio processing delay and he has mild Tourette's. The worst part of his Tourette's—most of them are not a big deal. His tics, he'll tic here and there. He does not do the cussing thing. He has mild . . . But he'll whistle, which sounds super no big deal, but it is a huge deal when he, it's a tic. He doesn't know he is doing it, and he does it over and over and over again and he won't stop. It's incredibly, ugh, not a good thing for lots of things, but he's fine now.

We have not done any more immunizations at all for him. He obviously cannot handle those. My third daughter, I was incredibly nervous giving her first round of shots, but we did, and she is fine. She is fully vaccinated with all of that, with all of the normal technical things. With that being said, when my oldest daughter was born, the chicken pox vaccination had just come out. Well, chicken pox, most people do not die of chicken pox, and so I chose not to give her that until we knew a little bit more about it. It was brand-new. So, I'm one of those that does a lot of research because I have this background of seeing this baby take vaccinations and have a hundred seizures a day, and I wanted to make sure that whatever I was putting in my children's body was the best for them.

So, if it was something that could be treated otherwise, let's do that, and let's only give them the things that are life-altering and/or not treatable otherwise. And so, we were just a little more cautious on our approach, not that we are anti-vax, but we didn't do all the big shots all at once, that Americans do. We did a more European approach, so we did half doses, and we only did two at a time. Which cost us more money because we had to go to the doctor more and we had to pay more copays. But for me, it was better for my children, and it was more comforting to me, just a little different approach. So not anti-vax, but this vaccination came out. None of us, I was the only one who had any comorbidities really at all. I am a huge vitamin crazy girl. We're the elderberry syrup before elderberry syrup was a big deal, right?

They call me "hoo-hoo" mom because I do all the "hoo" stuff. And so, we were already doing the zinc and all the things, and we were all healthy and we were all, I mean, my son who hasn't had vaccinations, when he went to the doctor recently for his foot was hurting him, we realized that he had not been to the doctor in seven years. I know that's bad. I didn't realize it. He's not been sick. So, we just, whoops. So, when the vaccination came out, there was not enough research. We didn't have comorbidities, we didn't have any of that, and we were isolating here. We were homeschooled. We weren't really out in the public. Robby was working from home at that time. He wasn't in the public. The churches were still closed down. We just didn't see that that very first shot coming out was something we were going to run and go do at that point. We were going to just wait, watch, and see. And make decisions and be very discerning when and if that was something we were going to utilize, and if we felt like that that was a good tool or not.

So, people ask me often—I think it is incredibly rude, honestly—they ask me if Robby was vaccinated. Like that would've made a . . . difference. I mean, he died. Does it matter really? But my answer honestly is at that time with that particular strand, 50 percent of the people were fully vaccinated, and 50 percent weren't. Whether Robby was part of one group, or the other doesn't matter.

DJJ:
I won't ask how your life has been impacted or changed by COVID-19 because that's obvious. But many say we're looking at COVID-19 through the rearview mirror.
Are you looking in the rearview mirror or looking clearly through the windshield in front of you and embracing the future?

Shannon:
That's a great question. I just had a conversation at dinner tonight before you came over about this very thing. A lot of people, a lot of widows—I am considered a widow—embrace that and embrace their widowhood and embrace a victim mentality of that. I choose not to do that. I choose to seek joy. I choose to seek life. Am I sad? Sometimes. Do I miss Robby? Almost all the time, but I choose to move forward. I choose to look through that windshield, and what's next? For the good, right? God has for the good for my life and my kids' life for the good. So, what is that good? If I'm looking in the rearview mirror, sad about what just happened, and overwhelmed about what just happened, and COVID and is it going to catch up to me? When you're looking in the rearview mirror, what you're looking at is, what's coming behind me and is it safe? Is it going to hit me? Is it going to come into my lane? Is it going to impact me in some way again? Because it already has once, right? If you're looking in the windshield, you're looking at what's coming up. I'm not

worried about what happened, I'm not worried about COVID and it overtaking my life again. I'm looking at what's next for the good.

Mrs. Shannon Bellamy

Families in every city in America had to contend with their worst nightmare—the death of a loved one. The initial shock leaves family members and friends experiencing a range of emotions as they search for answers and rationale for the tragedy. This is a solemn, grief-filled time when friends and family try to persevere as funeral arrangements are planned for the deceased person's last chapter.

Chapter 17

LIFE'S LAST CHAPTER: THE BELL TOLLS

At the end of life, we will not be judged by how many diplomas we have received, how much money we have made, how many great things we have done. We will be judged by "I was hungry, and you gave me something to eat, I was naked, and you clothed me. I was homeless, and you took me in."

—Mother Teresa

The COVID-19 virus ravaged the respiratory systems of many patients as they and medical personnel struggled to stave off death. There were heroic efforts and attempts to utilize every procedure and medicine to save lives. Intensive care units across the country and world were filled with dedicated professionals working around the clock in losing battles. In the final analysis, individuals passed away and families were faced with grieving and making funeral arrangements. These families were in for unexpected challenges as the funeral industry had to completely change how it operated. The funeral industry was experiencing unprecedented volumes, and the danger of COVID-19 was of paramount concern. This overwhelmed industry had to implement radical changes to protect staff and clients while providing services in a never-before-seen chaotic environment. Even now, the long-lasting ramifications of COVID-19 on the funeral service industry are not fully understood. Data from the last two years is just coming in and starting to be evaluated. According to the National Funeral Directors Association (NFDA), COVID-19 had a significant impact based on the statistics it has released:

- 74.4 percent of funeral homes reported the number of families served increased.
- More than 50 percent of NFDA-member funeral homes have begun offering live stream services since the pandemic.
- 40 percent of NFDA funeral homes now offer online cremation arrangements.
- The cremation rate across the nation is expected to exceed 50 percent by 2035.[65]

I had the opportunity to spend some time with Mrs. Melanie Burroughs Cole, President, and LFD—R. S. Lewis & Sons Funeral Homes, to discuss her business and what types of things she saw affecting it and the overall funeral service industry.

DJJ:
Tell me a little about you and R. S. Lewis & Sons.

Melanie:
Well, let me first start with R. S. Lewis & Sons. We were founded in 1917 by the Lewis family. Robert S. Lewis and his wife founded it, passed it on to their two sons, Clarence and Robert Jr., and then subsequently passed it on to their children. It was in their family for multiple generations. In 2011 Mr. Lewis passed away. His wife and a friend of my dad's, actually, were really good friends and so wanted to make sure that it stayed in the African American community, wanted it to be in good hands and kind of put some pieces together. Subsequently, my family ended up purchasing it in 2012. So, the Burroughs

65 Association, N. F. D. (2022, August 2). Data shows covid-19 impact on funeral service is significant. PR Newswire: press release distribution, targeting, monitoring, and marketing. Retrieved April 14, 2023, from https://www.prnewswire.com/news-releases/data-shows-covid-19-impact-on-funeral-service-is-significant-301597255.html

family has owned and operated R. S. Lewis & Sons since then. We then acquired the Patterson, J. O. Patterson funeral home and kind of married what we call the COGIC, Church of God in Christ, families together. It has been a labor of love. We are opening up our third location off of Austin Peay soon.

So, R. S. Lewis & Sons has just been an amazing beacon in the Mid-South community. We are the funeral home that prepared the remains of Dr. Martin Luther King before he was transported to Atlanta. We've done a number of different families and serviced families all over this community. And unfortunately, we do what we do, but we love what we do, and so we have been excited to make sure that we continue the work in this community because it's actually really needed.

DJJ:
As a little background, funeral directors often immerse themselves into the family situation and even make it harder on their own emotions. The constant exposure to death and unfortunate circumstances tend to numb your feelings. Sometimes there's depersonalization, and it can even lead to a lack of empathy sometimes. What is the most difficult part of being a funeral director?

Melanie:
Personally, the most difficult part is children. It's hard to see anyone pass away, no matter what their age is. But someone who's young and hasn't quite seen the world, hadn't had the opportunity . . . Burying children is probably one of the hardest things I've ever had to do.

Another hard thing is just burying people that you really know that you've grown up with, that you have loved your entire life, watching them go through that process and then having to be the last one to give them service. So those things have been the hardest for me personally as a funeral director.

Now, every funeral director is different, so everything might be different for them, but for me it's children and the people that I really, really have been close to, and kind of walking them through that process is really hard.

DJJ:

During the COVID-19 pandemic, how did funeral homes and families adjust by coming up with imaginative and innovative ideas to remember someone who has died?

Melanie:

Well, now it's probably not as innovative because we're in 2022 and everybody's using Zoom and all the different live stream mechanisms that weren't really that popular in 2019. Hardly anybody, a number of churches didn't even live stream. Subsequently, with the pandemic, people couldn't come. People couldn't travel. You couldn't get on a plane. People were having to drive really far. People didn't know whether or not they were going to get sick. Nobody wanted to pass it on. Nobody wanted to be the reason. So, people got creative because they live streamed. They used technology in order to connect . . . They did more videos. They did more pictures.

If you can think of it and imagine it, that's kind of what they did. They came up with different mechanisms to send to their loved ones because maybe mother couldn't come, grandma couldn't come. So, what were you going to do in order to make sure that grandma was able to actually celebrate that person? And so, we would've sent her things, or we would have to videoconference. Like, we were doing all kinds of mechanisms. Some families were just coming up with creative things that maybe I wouldn't have thought about, but everybody was putting their brains together at that point because we were all in the same boat, that we didn't know what we were doing. So, I would say it got a little interesting. But how people celebrate lives is just, even today, every life is just very different, and how they decide to celebrate that is really up to the family.

DJJ:
How have you seen funerals or memorials change in the time of COVID-19?

Melanie:
They really did. Especially, I would say, here in our chapel because churches closed down. But we kept our chapel here open. We were every other pew, three people to a pew in the very beginning. We weren't allowing as many people in the building because the health department even stated that, "Hey, it should be at this percent capacity." The capacity kept changing over months as people learned what was transpiring and what could be done. So, we kind of stuck to the early stages of what they were suggesting in terms of we were only doing pews, every other pew. If you came in here, you had to be masked up. If you needed to be double masked, you can be double masked. But there was a mask required. We had it everywhere. You could not miss that you had to have on a mask to be in our building.

So, it changed in that aspect because people . . . We came up with a phrase, "wink and wave." You were no longer hugging and kissing on your loved one to show them the compassion and the love. You now had to wink and wave and show that compassion completely different, number one, through your eyes because you couldn't show it through your mouth because you had a mask on, and you couldn't hug.

We weren't really encouraging hugging, which is really odd. That's the time when you really want to hug somebody. You want to show that compassion. But we didn't know what was going on. We didn't want people to get sick. We didn't want people to be in our place of business for those reasons. So, we didn't want to be the cause of it. So, every other pew, three to a pew, which meant that few people could come to a funeral service, which meant that we started live streaming and telling people where they could go to visit the website so that they could see it. They were going to have to pay their respects, not in person but online now, and figure out a way to be as compassionate as you could possibly be but also be safe. I wanted people to stay safe. The most important thing was that my staff and that the families we service stayed safe and didn't catch anything.

We kept the live stream up, so you can go back to the live stream as often as you want to. We had some families that asked us to take it down because it just made family members sad . . . One daughter said she just kept watching it over and over and over again and so kind of made her sad. So she asked us to take it down. We hid it. We didn't delete it. We just hid it in the event that she might want it again. She didn't want us to download and give it to her. She said, "Just take it down." We would give it to you if you wanted. We would download it. But we still have them all. We did videos for people up on our chapel screens, and then we would give them their video at the end of the service.

DJJ:

In the beginning, were there people who wanted to push back their services hoping to wait out the coronavirus, because they wanted more loved ones to attend the service in person?

Melanie:

In the very beginning, we did. Nobody knew, right? Nobody had any inkling that it would go on for so long. We thought maybe it might be the flu. And the schools were doing it. Schools were only week by week. Schools were week by week. The health department was week by week. Nobody knew what was going on. So, we thought maybe . . . they thought . . . Everybody thought and they said, "Well, we'll just push it back a week and we'll see how it's going." Then if you kept watching CNN, the numbers were just growing and growing and growing and growing and growing, and it was sad. And finally, they said, "Nope." People decided that we had to go ahead and have the service.

Unfortunately, it wasn't just that families wanted to wait. We had to start waiting because of cemeteries and scheduling and peoples' workers were catching COVID, which meant that they didn't have anybody to work, or it was spreading through their business. So, cemeteries cut back drastically on the number of services they would do, which means if they're cutting back, if you can imagine there might be, let's say, 10 cemeteries in Memphis. To their 10 cemeteries, there's probably 30 funeral homes. We're all going to the same place. People are dying at a much higher rate. Cemeteries are now saying, "Hey, I'm only burying four a day, maybe five." Everybody wants a Saturday service. Saturday services were going like . . . It was just going so fast. So, people were pushing out and pushing out.

We would come in and the West Tennessee Veterans Cemetery, they might be three weeks out before they could get a date. It was . . . I mean, when I say so sad, it was so sad that someone had to literally wait for weeks . . . They may have their service but then subsequently have to wait to bury their loved one for weeks because there just wasn't an opening. It wasn't anything to do with us. It was more or less that the cemeteries just didn't have . . . They didn't have the people. They didn't have the staffing. It was just going so fast.

So, it started to slow down probably in the last couple of months, I would say, as things have a little bit relaxed, the vaccine came out. Some people were eager to get the vaccine. At first, they were saying just first responders. We kept on the health department to say, "Yeah, but we might be the last responder, but we need to be in that same category." So, we started to be able to get it. Getting vaccinated was very important for us to make sure that we stayed as healthy for ourselves and for our children and just the people we were going home to.

At the time, I had a one-and-a-half-year-old, and I was coming to work every day, and nobody knew what COVID was doing to kids. Vaccines weren't even created for us, let alone children. I would never compare myself to a doctor, but I was going home, and I was de-dressing before I walked in the house because when you don't know, you just take it all off and you figure out . . . shower, and then I see my kid. So, it just was different. And we were all doing it. We all have families here.

My first priority, especially as an owner, is to make sure that my team stays safe. So, we were all doing the same exact thing. You de-dress before you go inside. We pretty much stayed COVID-free for a good little while. We had one person to get COVID really bad early on. He didn't get it from here or at a funeral, but he did get it. And it was hard. It's hard when somebody from your team goes out, like when you're one team member down, but your caseload is much higher than it used to be. Everybody was feeling it around here. Everybody was picking up slack wherever somebody else couldn't pick up.

Then we had spouses. Maybe they had to go to work, so they might be catching it. So, we were trying to make sure that we didn't catch it from our spouses and things like that. COVID-19 was a hell of a virus, let me say that. It was a big deal.

DJJ:
How did your role in providing comfort to the decedent's loved ones change?

Melanie:
I wouldn't say it changed, the way we provided the service. But I will say that the comfort level was we no longer hugged and

embraced. When you came into an arrangement room with one of us, now you can't bring six or seven people with you. You need to only bring the person, the next of kin, the person who might be helping you get through this and maybe one other person. And that's it. You couldn't bring your siblings. Everybody couldn't come and help pick out and help figure out how to celebrate their family member. That's their loved one too. They get to have a say. Normally, they would get to have a say, but this time they didn't get to. And so, it was different. It was different in that aspect. It also was very different because when you went to the hospital with COVID, people couldn't come visit you. Your wife couldn't come. She could have gone weeks looking at you over an iPhone.

So how do you comfort somebody who literally didn't get a chance to what they would deem, and what I would deem as well, as properly saying goodbye? They didn't get to hug them. They didn't get to kiss them. They didn't get to love on them to make sure that they knew that they weren't alone. So, comforting someone like that without giving them a hug is a little bit different.

But if they were Christian, and we knew that, we had different verses. A couple of our staff members are preachers, deacons, and they gave us tools to kind of help us to say, "Maybe this particular Scripture," or "Hey, this is who you should bring in with you so that they can hug and love on you, but we can't because you don't know where I've been. So, we don't want you to catch what I know I don't have." But at that time, there were no swabbing and getting checked, so it was different. So, we came up with different ways and different tools, but I don't think there's a right or a wrong way to be able to comfort somebody. Honestly, we were kind of going by it at the fly making sure that we didn't contribute to the spread because we hadn't experienced it. So, everything was new. Some of it was just really off of the top of our heads and the learning as we go. Yeah.

DJJ:
How has COVID transformed the death care industry for last responders?

Melanie:
I would say it's transformed us in a way . . . I think we were already kind of using precautionary term measures, but now it's kind of super more in the forefront, whether that's the outfits that you put on in terms of when you're walking around in the morgue or being masked up or winking and waving now. It's really changed in that aspect because we aren't as social anymore. The death care industry used to be, after someone passed, it was a place for you to come and celebrate life, and you were hugging people and in conversation. But yet now, it's not as much of that. You don't find as many repasses. People aren't lingering. Some people, baby boomers and even older than that, might tend not to come to your funeral. Now they're a little bit more cautious because they're in a protected class. Even if they take all the boosters they get, you don't know what kind of conditions they have, and so they don't want to be around a lot of people.

Young people are a little bit more, millennials, Gen Z, like Gen Alpha, they don't mind. We take a few more risk, but baby boomers and older than that, they're saying, "Eh, I'm going to come to the funeral, but I might stand in the back. I might not get to say bye. But I'm going to sign the book, and I'm going to leave and I'm going to call. I'll come see you at the house when it's just you. But I don't want to be around a bunch of people." And understandably.

DJJ:
How was the Memphis/Mid-South area impacted?

Melanie:
I think we were probably impacted just like any other area. If you think about scheduling, cemeteries being overwhelmed, overworked, I mean, a lot of industries were filling in. The first responders were feeling overwhelmed, overworked, but so was the back end. So, it really affected quality of life. You're tired; you're catching up. We're catching up on . . . I want to say catching up on rest, but we're catching up on remembering what is really important, and it's family and making sure you spend time with people, and work even looks different, just Zooming. You would think that this was not supposed to be a Zoom kind of industry. And yet we will Zoom. We have to Zoom now.

So, it's really affected, and I think even still now, cemeteries have still stuck to their new way of how many people they bury in a day. It's a little bit different because the death rate has gone down. However, they realize that the quality of life, their quality of life was extremely important, and trying to get in as many as possible just to accommodate funeral homes was no longer going to be something that they were willing to do. So now, scheduling just looks different for us in particular, not just us but funeral homes. So scheduling, how many funerals you can do in a day. Everything is different.

How many people we still allow into conference rooms. If we have the space to accommodate having larger families, then we will. But what if I don't have that? So, I don't like to make that kind of a habit because our families talk to each other, and unfortunately, word-of-mouth is how we get business. So, I have not wanted to start something that I can't give another family. I don't want to give you a different service than I give another family member that comes in here because they're going to say, "Well, you let such and such bring in 15 people." "Well, I don't have the space now because I've got something going on that you can't bring in 15 people in." I would feel the same way. It's been different. We're making it. We're making it.

DJJ:
Roughly how many deaths are funeral homes, crematoria, and cemeteries in the state (or Mid-South area) set up to handle? And how did this change with the pandemic?

Melanie:
I don't think that's even a . . . Not even sure you can quantify that. I think that funeral homes don't build to capacity. And during COVID-19, everybody, whether you were small or large, were at capacity. You were doing as many as you possibly could because peoples' loved ones were passing away. They had to come to you. So, in terms of numbers, it would vary because, especially over across the state of Tennessee, as the death rate was going up, all the funeral homes were feeling it, and we were all at capacity. We were all over capacity but trying to make sure that we give the best service and make sure that we celebrate somebody's loved one, whether we had one person in here or we had two or we had 10 or we had 12, it didn't matter. We still had to provide top-tier service, yet everybody was at capacity.

So, we were all doing the same thing. Every funeral home was. Mine, it was no exception to the rule. We were all doing it. Everybody's building was at capacity. So, if your building said you could have 225 people in this building, and it was 225 people if you could have 225 people. But of course, the health department was giving you kind of ramifications about what you could do. But that's kind of an open-ended question because we were all at capacity. So, the numbers, whatever that death rate was at that time, was exactly what every funeral home was facing.

DJJ:
Why was it taking so long to get funeral scheduled?

Melanie:
Oh, everybody was being extended. People who would've normally died from probably natural causes caught COVID. You're immunocompromised, but everybody's service was being affected. So, no matter if you died from a car crash or you died from natural causes, how we serviced you was going to take longer. How the medical examiner's office was going to service you was taking longer. They were overwhelmed. People also needed to be able to take care of their business. Like, you need a death certificate in order to take care of your business. Subsequently, the state went Zoom. They went to working from home. They had less people. Death rate is higher. People weren't getting death certificates for months. Months. Which means you can't take care of your business, which means you can't get your money. We feel bad, and we're the people who get you a death certificate. We put the information in. The state is the ones who certify it. But doctors were backed up. They didn't have time to sign because they were so busy. So, they were trying to sign as fast as they could, but even their fast wasn't fast enough.

So, stuff was just being pushed back. Things that used to take 2–3 weeks were now taking 8–10 weeks. The health department was telling us, "You need to tell people 8–10 weeks before they could get a death certificate." That's a long time. It's an extremely long time, whether you're having banking, or you just want that death certificate; that's yours to have. And so, you shouldn't have to wait three months. That means you don't have all your missing pieces in order to grieve properly.

There are five stages of grieving. Now, you stuck in like stage four, and you just cannot get that fifth piece because in four and five months you might get that last piece. And so now you're able to grieve. Nobody wants to start the grieving process six months down the road. They want to start it now because they want to get to the space where they're kind of okay, right? You're never okay, but you're kind of okay. You can function better. You can remember and have memories and the memories don't make you as sad. But when you're missing pieces, it just makes your life harder. It's already going to be hard. You're missing a person.

DJJ:
Have you seen the numbers start to stabilize and gradually return to pre-pandemic levels?

Melanie:
Yeah. They're stabilizing. You're still getting a little bit of COVID-19, natural causes, same thing. I wouldn't say they're going back to pre-pandemic, but they're stabilizing in a much more manageable level . . . The death rate has come down over the last two years, which is really good. You can also tell people are taking the vaccine. People aren't getting COVID as much now. Now we are in a tridemic with COVID-19, the flu, and RSV hitting our communities, but it's not as bad as it was, or it doesn't feel as bad as it was prior to. But I think we've been equipped with a lot more information now. We know a lot more, kind of like the NBC commercial: the more knowledge you have, the better off you are. So, we're a little bit more knowledgeable now, and so you can make better decisions when you have more knowledge.

DJJ:
Do you believe accurate information and data were shared at the onset of the pandemic, allowing you to operate effectively and respond to families seeking funeral services?

Melanie:
I think they gave us as much information as they possibly could. I don't think they knew, and so because they didn't know, they

didn't know what to tell us. So, we were all operating in the dark. It just so happened that my operating in the dark looks a lot different than somebody behind the desk operating in the dark. I think they did the best they could. I'm not going to fault anybody. Or could we have had more information? I think we could have. But would it have been accurate? Nobody knows. And even at the time, they just didn't know. This was just so new. So new.

DJJ:
R. S. Lewis' operating procedures and processes were changed. Were they changed forever?

Melanie:
Absolutely. We don't allow people to ride in the front seat with our driver anymore. No more. So, my limo that used to seat seven now only seats six. That's going to forever be it because I don't want that much of a close proximity to—and maybe not forever, but until I believe that we have a better grasp and a better handle on all these different viruses going on, my first priority is to make sure that my staff is well protected to the best that I can do. I have to do, based on the information that I receive, do the best I can to keep them safe.

We're already going to be amongst a lot of people. We're still wearing masks at funerals. Now it's not required by most churches. A lot of places are not requiring masks anymore. We have kind of been lenient about it here as well for the people coming in. However, the staff during funerals and when we have multiple people in the building for visitation or first viewing, things like that, we do ask . . . Our staff wears a mask. It's precautionary. A couple of us have young kids. None of us want to take anything home. So, if putting on a mask is going to be just a tad bit more helpful, we are going to take that precautionary step.

But yeah, our procedures have changed. Besides just the limousine, when we enter in peoples' homes to pick up loved ones, what that looks like, we would go in and embrace people and take information in a kind of paper format. It's all technology now. We're masked up. They're not to deviate from going exactly where they were supposed to go into incoming, straight back out, no sitting around. We don't do that anymore, unfortunately. So, we have to do a lot of comforting on the outside and then when you get here.

DJJ:
Melanie, while some funeral homes and morticians were working overtime to manage the flood of COVID patients, many families were not having traditional funerals anymore. Cremations were the preferred option for some families, and others are skipping the burial and most expensive pieces altogether while social distancing. "Some death care industry businesses are busier than ever, but also struggling to get the profit that they would bring in during an average year. In the past, cremation has only accounted for 10% of death care industry revenue, and they cost approximately 5–10% of what traditional funeral services with a casket and burial and memorial cost."[66]
How has that affected R. S. Lewis & Sons?

Melanie:
Our cremation rate has gone up. It's probably gone up for every funeral home, but in particular for R. S. Lewis and probably any African American funeral home in the state. So, in the Deep South, the statistics are there that African American families are more in tune with having traditional services, that we are slowly getting into cremation.

---

66 Mks&h. (2021, January 21). How the pandemic has impacted the Death Care Industry: MKS&H. MKSH. Retrieved April 14, 2023, from https://mksh.com/how-the-pandemic-has-impacted-the-death-care-industry/

But you have to think about cremation is really after . . . You may have celebrated your loved one. You've done everything that a traditional service has done except for you didn't go to an actual cemetery and be buried in a ground or in a mausoleum, but they have columbariums. People are doing the same exact thing. We have found that people still want to celebrate with their loved ones present and then have the cremation afterwards, and then they go into a columbarium or into an urn that they take home, or they go and scatter the ashes, the cremains.

So, we have seen some differences in how people are now choosing cremation versus burial. However, the traditional part of it, in terms of the demographic that we serve, has really kind of been the same. We've had a few here and there that have not been. But really and truly, people really want to follow the traditional . . . We haven't gotten there, I would say, in the Deep South. Now, if you go over on the West Coast and in the Northeast and in the Midwest, they're a little bit more progressive, where here in the Deep South, we're a little bit more traditional. We haven't quite gotten there yet.

DJJ:
COVID-19 changed our world. It seems that it has changed your industry. What do you see going forward?

Melanie:
What I see going forward is the funeral industry, it's changed, but I have to say it's changed for the better. We have now been able to reach more family members that couldn't come to funeral services that nobody thought to live stream years ago. So now, more people are being able to participate in different manners in celebrating their loved ones. We're more precautionary now. You have to take a little bit more precautionary measures than you ever did before because you never know what's going to happen in the future, what new epidemic or pandemic we may

encounter. So, while things did change, I think that some of it changed for the better. We are now a lot more adaptable; we're more flexible.

I think the socialization has changed. I think that's the part that I'm a little bit sad about in terms of what has gone away and is probably not coming back, has slowly kind of gotten to a space where it's kind of like in the middle, but people aren't really gathering like that anymore. People aren't having a bunch of people at their homes, which is what, after a funeral service, you went to the house, and you ate dinner and you sat there for hours. And no longer is that the case unless you are very immediate family. So that's changed. That's the sad part about it.

But the good things that have come out of the pandemic are more people are able to celebrate because we can live stream or we now can help somebody through Zoom, where something happens to the loved one here, but they're somewhere else, that you can actually still see them. It's different when it was on a phone call, but now you can see people, and so it's changed, not all of it for the best. But some things were really good things, and some things, they probably needed to change at some point. So yeah.

Melanie Burroughs Cole, President, and LFD – R.S. Lewis & Sons Funeral Homes

The COVID-19 pandemic had stinging effects on everyone as the virus raced across the country and the world. But in most cases, the contraction of the disease and the destruction it left behind were witnessed from afar. News reports and online stories recounted the daily devastation experienced by others. However, the reality became more up close and personal when the virus reached out and touched you personally.

Chapter 18

IT TOUCHED ME

Life is what happens while you are busy making other plans.
—John Lennon

After an intense two-year struggle to combat a deadly virus strain that claimed the lives of hundreds of thousands and wreaked havoc on businesses, the global economy, and our daily lives, COVID-19 now hit close to home. During this time, a massive collaborative effort known as Operation Warp Speed was launched, involving the United States government, pharmaceutical companies, and private firms, all working together to develop a safe and effective vaccine. The ambitious goal was to deliver 300 million vaccine doses by January 2021, offering a glimmer of hope for a return to normalcy.

However, the battle against COVID-19 continues to be a dynamic one. SARS-CoV-2, the virus responsible for COVID-19, constantly undergoes change, leading to the emergence of several significant variants, including alpha, beta, delta, and omicron.[67] These variants pose new challenges and underscore the importance of ongoing vigilance in our efforts to protect public health.

Finally, just as the world began to believe that COVID-19 was receding and a return to normalcy was on the horizon, a harsh awakening arrived in late 2020 with the emergence of the treacherous delta variant, first identified in India. It swiftly

---

67 Katella, K. (2023, February 3). Omicron, Delta, Alpha, and more: What to know about the coronavirus variants. Yale Medicine. Retrieved April 14, 2023, from https://www.yalemedicine.org/news/covid-19-variants-of-concern-omicron

ravaged not only that country but also Europe before making its way to the United States, where it unleashed a surge of cases. The impact was devastating, claiming countless lives, overwhelming hospitals, and pushing our health care system to the brink of collapse once more. This deadly variant proved to be a stern reminder to those who had previously underestimated the severity of the COVID-19 virus.

But the challenges didn't end there. Following the delta variant, the omicron variant was detected in South Africa. Though medical experts noted that omicron appeared to be less deadly than delta, it brought new concern due to its hyper-contagious nature. On December 1, 2021, the first case of omicron was reported in the United States, leading to a renewed state of uncertainty. Mask mandates, social distancing, and hesitancy to gather in crowds for usual activities like sporting events, restaurants, and movie theaters resurfaced.

The world found itself in a perpetual dance with these ever-evolving variants, reinforcing the importance of remaining vigilant and adaptive in the face of this ongoing global health crisis.

I had taken all the precautions—wearing masks, maintaining social distance, and getting vaccinated, including the booster shot. However, in January 2022 I began to experience symptoms that concerned me. A runny nose, sneezing, low-grade fever, and body aches persisted for several days, prompting me to get a COVID-19 test. The testing center was inundated with citizens seeking to determine whether they had the highly contagious omicron variant.

After a long wait, I finally underwent the test. The test itself was uncomfortable, with a medical professional inserting a swab deep into each nostril. The anxious wait for the test results led to thoughts of the potential implications of a positive diagnosis. My fears were confirmed—I tested positive. The email notification marked "POSITIVE" filled me with anxiety.

I worried about the strain of the virus I had and the stories I'd heard about how symptoms could worsen rapidly. My thoughts turned to a team member who was hospitalized with pneumonia from COVID-19, whose prognosis was grim. The uncertainty and fear of the unknown consumed me.

The local health department sent me instructions for isolation and requested details of my recent movements to notify those who may have been in close contact. My mental state oscillated between hope and fear as I prayed that my condition wouldn't deteriorate like others I had heard about.

Questions swirled in my mind—how did I contract the virus despite being cautious? I retraced my steps, wondering whether it was at the gym, the supermarket, or a simple exchange at the gas station. The positive diagnosis forced me to confront the reality of dealing with COVID-19 personally.

It was a stark reminder that, despite the various opinions and information available, facing the consequences of contracting the virus was a challenging and humbling experience. The journey of navigating the virus was one that no amount of preparation or caution could fully shield me from.

LONG-HAULERS

A long-hauler who was not able to participate in this project due to COVID complications said, "COVID-19 did a lot more than just kill people." Many people are suffering from varying degrees of long-term, debilitating illnesses and side effects associated with having contracted COVID-19. Some can no longer work or function as they have previously done. The lasting effects have taken on different forms. "People call Post-COVID Conditions by many names, including Long COVID, long-haul COVID, post-acute COVID-19, post-acute sequelae of SARS-CoV-2 infection (PASC), long-term effects of COVID, and chronic COVID."[68]

"Individuals with long COVID, or long haulers are COVID-19 survivors that have symptoms which persist. This includes headaches, shortness of breath, fatigue, palpitations and in some cases mental fog and cognitive issues."[69] Individuals with long-hauler symptoms are navigating an uncertain future as their bodies continue to struggle with the effects of the virus that continues to deceptively wreak havoc on their bodies. Researchers have shown that long COVID symptoms have impacted nearly every organ in the human body. A study in January 2023 by the Kaiser Family Foundation found long COVID may affect 10 to 33 million working-age adults in America. Scientists and doctors continue to study the disease, but there are many unknowns related to the prevalence and longevity of the illness, hence the wide range estimation of those affected in the United States.[70] The study also shows, "Fewer than Half of Working Age Adults with Long COVID Who Worked Prior to Infection Work Full-Time After Infection."[71]

Long-haulers perceive the world is turning the corner and placing COVID-19 in the rearview mirror—leaving them behind. But for them the ordeal and anguish continue, and they don't see a foreseeable end to the misery they've experienced

---

68 Centers for Disease Control and Prevention. (n.d.). Long Covid or post-covid conditions. Centers for Disease Control and Prevention. Retrieved April 14, 2023, from https://www.cdc.gov/coronavirus/2019-ncov/long-term-effects/index.html

69 Long covid: Long-term effects of COVID-19. Long COVID: Long-Term Effects of COVID-19 | Johns Hopkins Medicine. (2022, November 1). Retrieved April 14, 2023, from https://www.hopkinsmedicine.org/health/conditions-and-diseases/coronavirus/covid-long-haulers-long-term-effects-of-covid19

70 What are the implications of Long Covid for employment and health coverage? KFF. (2022, August 10). Retrieved April 14, 2023, from https://www.kff.org/policy-watch/what-are-the-implications-of-long-covid-for-employment-and-health-coverage/

71 What are the implications of Long Covid for employment and health coverage? KFF. (2022, August 10). Retrieved April 14, 2023, from https://www.kff.org/policy-watch/what-are-the-implications-of-long-covid-for-employment-and-health-coverage/

since contracting COVID-19. Challenges with obtaining disability insurance and other forms of health insurance are problematic, which introduces tremendous hardships when you can't physically work.

Although long-haulers are an issue that is directly visible and related to the havoc of the virus, there have been additional, more subterranean impacts on our thinking and way of life.

Chapter 19

UNMASKING DIVIDES—EMBRACING UNITY

This pandemic has magnified every existing inequality in our society—like systemic racism, gender inequality, and poverty.
—Melinda Gates

Despite all of the factions, partisanship, and politicization of this virus, we found ourselves in the same boat with an indiscriminate killer—COVID-19. It killed rich, poor, Black, White, Republican, Democrat, Independent, and all the like. It didn't matter how much money you had, your culture, religion, or where you lived.

Your fame, fortune, or status proved powerless against the insidious airborne killer we face today—hence, the solemn words "For Whom the Virus Tolls." It's disheartening to witness a significant portion of society becoming numb and defiant toward science, clinging to harmful thoughts, rhetoric, and vindictive obstructionism. History serves as a guide, reminding us of the dire consequences that arise from internal erosion and division.

In a society where polarization runs rampant, finding common ground seems nearly impossible. Biblical Scripture cautions, "Every kingdom divided against itself is brought to desolation; and every city or house divided against itself shall not stand" (Matthew 12:25, King James Version). Such polarization manifests even in matters supported by scientific methodologies and research, like COVID-19 findings. Despite well-established facts, misguided information and political affiliations led some to contest the validity of the pandemic's science.

Imagine this: scientists have proven that water freezes at 32 degrees Fahrenheit and boils at 212 degrees Fahrenheit, a truth upheld by the laws of thermodynamics. Yet in this polarized environment, one could argue fervently over the freezing point, depending on their political alignment. This example, though absurd, mirrors the state of many national conversations today.

To confront this growing menace, we must bridge divides and embrace reason over rhetoric. Concrete examples, not just ideologies, should govern our decisions. Only through collective understanding and shared purpose can we face the challenges that confront us all.

For Whom the Virus Tolls serves as a stark reminder that in the face of a pandemic, unity is our greatest strength. We must rise above polarization, respect science, and acknowledge the greater good that binds us together as a society.

COVID-19 has left an indelible mark on our world, exposing deep divisions and darker aspects lurking beneath the surface. What was once perceived as a seemingly perfect society has been revealed to be riddled with fissures and cracks in its foundation. The pandemic has had a profound effect on our society, raising concerns about the erosion of democratic principles.

One troubling consequence of COVID-19 has been the distortion of facts and truth and the erosion of trust in science. Throughout the pandemic, established scientific principles and medical facts were ridiculed and dismissed, replaced by spurious and unfounded information propagated by individuals with questionable motives. This has cast doubt on the very essence of the scientific community and its integrity.

Moreover, the pandemic severely damaged belief and trust in our government. False and misleading information has led a significant number of citizens to question the government's credibility, giving rise to conspiracy theories and propaganda. The constant gaslighting of the American people only exacerbated the crisis, as the virus continued to spread, and lives were lost.

COVID-19 has also demonstrated the interconnectedness of the world. It revealed how swiftly and significantly an event in one part of the world can affect people in distant corners. With the ease of air travel, any malady can reach Main Street, America, from the farthest reaches of the globe.

In light of the pandemic's repercussions, it is crucial to reassess the resilience of our democratic institutions. While the challenges have been immense, they also provide an opportunity to strengthen and reinforce the foundations of our democracy. Addressing the issues of misinformation, distrust, and division will be crucial to restoring faith in our institutions and healing the wounds inflicted by this global crisis.

The vast possibilities of our great future will become realities only if we make ourselves responsible for that future.

—Gifford Pinchot

We are undeniably stronger when united, recognizing our collective greatness and embracing our shared values over our differences. This unity becomes even more apparent during times of natural disasters or national emergencies, when we witness the heroic efforts of health care professionals and the entire community working together to combat a common foe. These moments serve as powerful reminders of our potential when we stand united. It's crucial to internalize these lessons and resist the temptation to revert to factions and tribalism when normalcy returns. Failing to do so jeopardizes our existence and the well-being of future generations.

What will we say when they look back and ask, *"Why didn't you seek the truth, uncover the facts, and hold everyone accountable?"*

What will we say when they look back and ask, *"Why didn't you work together and treat everyone with respect, dignity, and kindness?"*

In this chapter we explored the indiscriminate nature of COVID-19 as a deadly force affecting people across all walks of life, irrespective of wealth, status, or political affiliation. The pandemic highlights the consequences of a deeply polarized society in which science has become entangled with partisan ideologies. Drawing from historical and biblical references, we emphasized the importance of bridging divides and embracing collective understanding to confront this global menace. We examined how the pandemic has revealed the erosion of trust in scientific principles and democratic institutions, while urging for a concerted effort to restore faith in our society's foundations and unite for a resilient future.

Chapter 20

A SONG OF RESILIENCE AND REFLECTION

You cannot hope to build a better world without improving the individuals. To that end, each of us must work for his own improvement and, at the same time, share a general responsibility for all humanity, our particular duty being to aid those to whom we think we can be most useful.

—Marie Curie

As the pandemic swept across the world, it brought forth a defining moment in history. Our hearts overflow with gratitude for the men and women in the medical field who became beacons of hope amid the darkness. They answered the call to action, facing a once-in-a-lifetime challenge with unwavering bravery. In the most hostile and warlike conditions, they exhibited heroic effort, making unimaginable sacrifices and displaying unparalleled service.

The toll inflicted upon them was unfathomable, both mentally and physically. The weight of this burden pushed them to the brink, testing their physical resilience, challenging their psyches, and wearing down their emotional faculties to the point of sheer collapse and despair. Tragically, some of these dedicated heroes found themselves unable to cope with the overwhelming carnage they witnessed, leading them to take their own lives. We must also remember the many who laid down their lives in the pursuit of serving others, ultimately succumbing to the virus they fought so valiantly against. Their sacrifice should never be forgotten.

We must recognize the Herculean efforts of these health care professionals on a grand scale, acknowledging the depth of their commitment and selflessness. Though many of them humbly stated they were just doing their jobs, their actions spoke louder than any words. They exemplified what it truly means to help and care for others, setting an inspiring example for all.

While the medical community grappled with the pandemic's front lines, businesses faced their own battles. With unwavering determination, many fought tooth and nail to survive. They owe their resilience to the loyalty of employees and customers, as well as to adaptive leadership that navigated the treacherous waters of uncertainty. Despite facing skepticism, imperfect information, confusion, fear, anger, financial ruin, sickness, and death, they pressed on. Yet we cannot ignore the many businesses that succumbed to the overwhelming pressures of COVID-19, leaving behind a trail of heartache.

Amid the death and devastation, this pandemic has also served as a stark wake-up call for humanity. It forced us to confront our vulnerabilities and revealed both the best and worst in us. As we emerge from the darkest days, we must strive for a higher level of excellence and thoughtfulness in how we live our lives.

Let us embrace the lessons learned from this global disaster and carry them forward in our songs in the key of life. May we cherish the importance of unity and compassion, recognizing that we are all interconnected, regardless of borders or differences. Our resilience, both as individuals and as a collective, is a testament to the strength of the human spirit. As we rebuild, let empathy and kindness be our guiding principles, mending the wounds left behind.

This chapter is not just a reflection on the challenges faced but also a tribute to those who stood tall amid the chaos. It is a reminder of the power of the human spirit to triumph over adversity, to rise from the ashes and build a brighter future. We will remember the fallen, celebrate the survivors, and honor the sacrifices made.

In the echoes of history, may this chapter serve as a testament to the strength and resilience of humanity and a beacon of hope for generations to come. For it is in the face of adversity that we discover the true measure of our character, and it is through unity and compassion that we shall prevail. Together, let us create a world that cherishes life, values humanity, and stands prepared to face whatever the future may bring.

Chapter 21

Conclusion: A Psychological Awakening Amid the Pandemic

In every crisis, doubt, or confusion, take the higher path—the path of compassion, courage, understanding and love.
—Amit Ray

As we reflect on the outbreak of COVID-19, it becomes evident that there are hundreds, if not thousands, of stories out there that capture the myriad of emotions and challenges people endured during these trying times. While I can only offer a glimpse into some lives affected, I believe it's imperative to capture these intimate stories of disruption caused by the pandemic that held us captive for almost three years, leaving an indelible mark on our country and the world.

In the years to come, health care professionals, scientists, epidemiologists, and anthropologists will study and analyze the devastating impact of COVID-19. Beyond the physical toll, it's crucial to consider the damage inflicted on the psyches and consciences of individuals and our collective global society. Amid the pandemic, a dichotomy of emotions arose across the world. On one hand, fear, horror, tragedy, uncertainty, and loss of life reached unimaginable levels, shattering everyone. On the other hand, some saw the pandemic as a pressure relief valve for their hectic lives, where they had found themselves frantically maintaining an unsustainable pace. During my interviews, many described their pre-pandemic world as a chaotic and overwhelming place. Juggling the demands of family, career, education, and personal life had become an unforgiving hamster wheel that drained the life out of people mentally and physically, who would then wake up and do it all again the next day. It started to feel like a thankless effort. Many were on the brink of a nervous breakdown, spiraling into depression, or worse. The pandemic laid bare the insurmountable pressures faced by individuals in their job environments—filled with performance expectations, office politics, mundane tasks, and in some cases, toxicity. Individuals balanced precariously between the demands of work and caring for their families. Juggling responsibilities became suffocating, dampening any glimmers of happiness and joy. The pandemic, as catastrophic as it was, offered some an unexpected opportunity to pause and reevaluate their lives.

Surprisingly, many who shifted to remote work during the pandemic discovered a new effectiveness and improved mental and physical health. Relationships with family deepened, and a sense of purpose beyond work began to take precedence. It brought people closer to their families, improved relationships, and allowed them to live with more meaning and purpose. The sudden loss of loved ones to the virus served as a wake-up call, reminding people of life's fragility and the need to recalibrate their priorities. No one was immune from this disease, and many began to realize how precious life is and that it could be gone in a minute. In speaking with my mother, I recall her saying that "In spite of the negative aspects of COVID-19, it may have been the only thing to make the world pause and allow individuals to stop, reflect, and re-gather themselves—mentally, spiritually, and physically."

The pandemic sparked a psychological awakening, causing people to reevaluate their priorities and the essence of life itself. The "Great Resignation" emerged as countless individuals decided to quit their jobs, change careers, or retire, seeking to reclaim their sanity and embrace a more fulfilling life. The pandemic made it clear that life is short and fragile, and one should not allow any person, thing, or job to deprive them of happiness. Many refused to go back to places where their worth and value weren't appreciated, and more importantly, that were injurious to their health. People wanted to be able to live their lives on their own terms with more fulfilling pursuits. "About 50.5 million people quit their jobs in 2022, besting the prior record set in 2021, according to the federal JOLTS report. The pandemic-era trend of elevated voluntary departures came to be known as the Great Resignation. Most people quit to take new jobs, not to leave the workforce altogether. Ample job prospects, higher wages and remote work helped fuel the trend."[72]

However, not everyone felt the same way. Some longed to return to their fast-paced, high-stress jobs in big industries. The debate between working from home and returning to the office continues, with valid arguments on both sides. Leaders must listen to their employees, understand their needs, and find a balance that supports productivity, well-being, and collaboration. I would ask that leaders seek to truly understand the reasoning of employees and weigh all the factors transparently along with profits, losses, tradition, and leadership preferences.

In conclusion, the pandemic brought about a psychological awakening that forever changed the way we view work, life, and ourselves. It taught us to love and cherish ourselves, our families, and our friends, to embrace life's fleeting moments, and to prioritize our mental and physical well-being above all else. As we moved forward, we carried with us the lessons learned from this unprecedented time, forever shaped by the resilience and strength that emerged from the darkness.

72 Iacurci, G. (2023, February 1). 2022 was the 'real year of the great resignation,' says economist. CNBC. Retrieved April 18, 2023, from https://www.cnbc.com/2023/02/01/why-2022-was-the-real-year-of-the-great-resignation.html#:~:text=About%2050.5%20million%20people%20quit,known%20as%20the%20Great%20Resignation.

Somebody should tell us, right at the start of our lives, that we are dying. Then we might live life to the limit, every minute of every day. Do it! I say. Whatever you want to do, do it now! There are only so many tomorrows.

—Pope Paul VI

PHOTO GALLERY

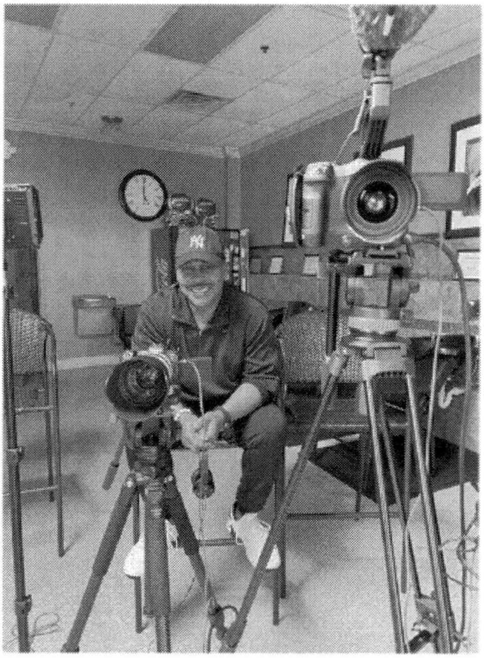

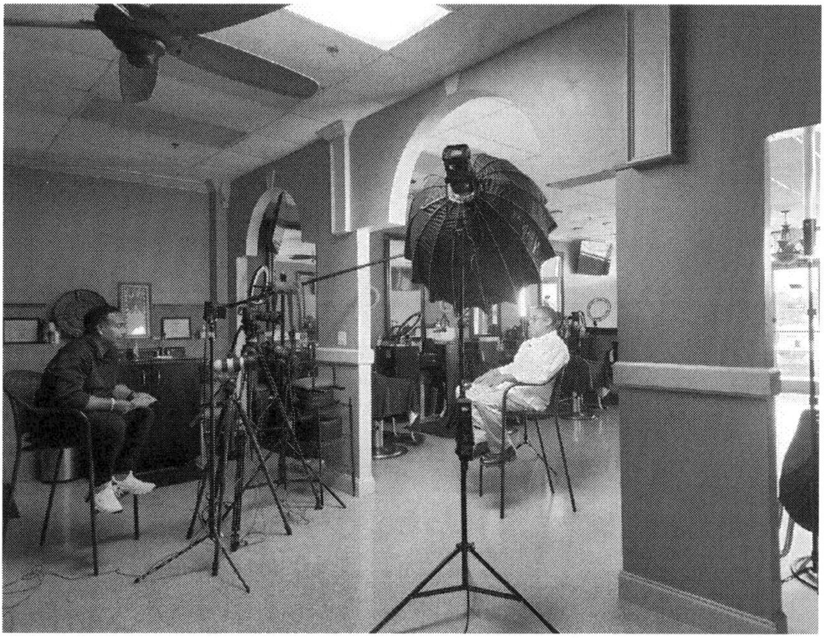

HOME

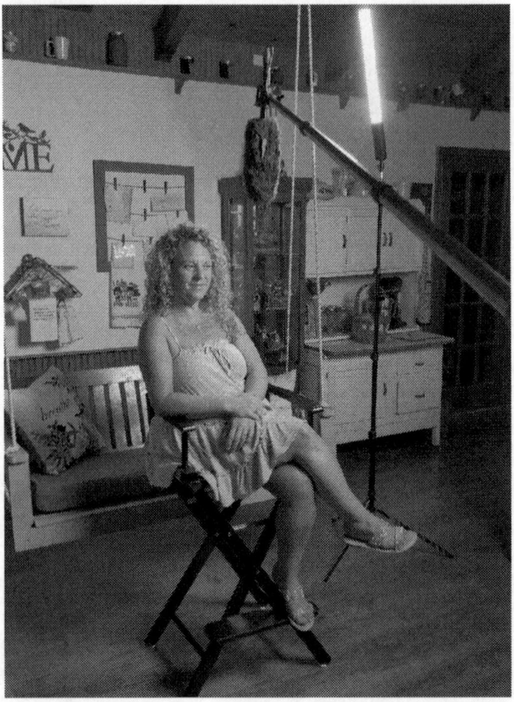

GRIND CENTRAL

ACKNOWLEDGMENTS

Dr. Ashish Joshi, MD, PhD, University of Memphis; City University New York (CUNY)
Dr. Bartholomew Orr, Senior Pastor—Brown Missionary Baptist Church
Dr. Stephen C. Threlkeld, MD, Threlkeld Infectious Disease, Baptist Memorial Health Care
Mr. Al Harris, Owner—The Barbershop Lounge
Mr. Ben Smith, Owner/Chef—Tsunami Restaurant
Mr. Brian "Breeze" Cayolle, Musician
Mr. David Williams, Blood Bank Regional Director
Mr. John Hamilton—JP Filmz
Mr. Kelcey Johnson, Executive Director—Hospitality Hub
Mr. Nate Vanderburg, Owner—Grind City Fitness
Mrs. Kathryn Wiggs, Administrative Director of Nursing—Methodist Le Bonheur Healthcare
Mrs. Melanie Burroughs Cole, President/LFD, R. S. Lewis & Sons Funeral Home
Mrs. Shannon Bellamy
Ms. Ranae Dubaj—Researcher
Ms. Sarah Farley, Communications, Methodist Le Bonheur Healthcare
Ms. Stephanie Norwood, Owner—StudioNorwood - Photography
Ms. Tomi Beckemeyer, Owner—SkinBody (Memphis & Nashville)
Circle Music Store
Jupiter Saxophone Company
Wilo & Company - Graphic Design
5J Entertainment

TESTIMONIALS

D. John Jackson brilliantly connects the dots to share intimate human stories against the backdrop of a global pandemic in his book, **Sangeeta Bhatnagar, Principal, SB Global Human Capital Solutions**

For Whom the Virus Tolls does an artful storytelling job weaving historical facts together with current day COVID challenges and intimate interviews with those that persevered through COVID-19, **Carrie Lazorchak, Chief Revenue Officer, GTM Strategist, Advisor & Mentor**

D. John Jackson takes a refreshing approach to show his passion for gathering insights about unheard experiences of individuals in a transparent and objective way, **Reggie Crenshaw, President & Chief Executive Officer (CEO), Nonprofit Leader**

ABOUT THE AUTHOR

D. John Jackson emerges as a distinguished global leader and accomplished Fortune 50 Executive, possessing an extensive background in strategic planning, engineering management, artificial intelligence, data science, and design thinking. Beyond these achievements, he holds the mantle of a best-selling author with his renowned book "What About Me," alongside his pivotal role as co-creator and executive producer of the captivating documentary film "What About Me," now available for streaming on Amazon Prime Video. He's both the creator and executive producer of a new documentary film titled "For Whom The Virus Tolls," aligning with his recently published book of the same name, and they are set to be released in tandem.

With an innate flair for creativity and visionary insight, D. John Jackson occupies the role of a film executive producer, strategist, futurist thinker, and a globally sought-after speaker. His expertise spans an eclectic array of subjects ranging from leadership and world history to STEM education, Diversity, Equity, and Inclusion (DEI), emerging technologies, artificial intelligence, economics, and the dynamics of global competition.

At the helm of his brainchild, 5J Entertainment, he stands as the driving force and CEO. This enterprise is unequivocally committed to the empowerment and enlightenment of audiences through diverse media forms. 5J Entertainment serves as a profound storytelling conduit, unearthing the latent and riveting human interest narratives, while shedding light on the unexplored and crucial stories that resonate with our world's fabric. In an era where such stories might remain untold, D. John Jackson's commitment to education, information dissemination, and the proliferation of positive imagery stands as a testament to his visionary leadership and unwavering dedication.

REFERENCES

(ASH), A. S. for H. (2022, August 4). HHS announces new campaign to increase U.S. blood and plasma donations. HHS.gov. Retrieved April 14, 2023, from https://www.hhs.gov/about/news/2022/08/04/hhs-announces-new-campaign-increase-us-blood-plasma-donations.html

Ashley Kirzinger. Follow @AshleyKirzinger on Twitter, A. K. F. @audrey__kearney on T., & 2020, A. (2020, April 20). KFF Health Tracking Poll – early april 2020: The impact of coronavirus on life in America. KFF. Retrieved April 14, 2023, from https://www.kff.org/coronavirus-COVID-19/report/kff-health-tracking-poll-early-april-2020/

Association, N. F. D. (2022, August 2). Data shows COVID-19 impact on funeral service is significant. PR Newswire: press release distribution, targeting, monitoring, and marketing. Retrieved April 14, 2023, from https://www.prnewswire.com/news-releases/data-shows-COVID-19-impact-on-funeral-service-is-significant-301597255.html

Barrett, D., & Heale, R. (2021, October 1). Covid-19: Reflections on its impact on nursing. Evidence-Based Nursing. https://ebn.bmj.com/content/24/4/112

Berlin, G., Lapointe, M., Murphy, M., & Viscardi, M. (2021, May 11). Nursing in 2021: Retaining the healthcare workforce when we need it most. McKinsey & Company. Retrieved April 10, 2023, from https://www.mckinsey.com/industries/healthcare/our-insights/nursing-in-2021-retaining-the-healthcare-workforce-when-we-need-it-most?cid=eml-web

Blunden, A. (n.d.). The collapse of Eastern Europe. Retrieved April 14, 2023, from https://www.marxists.org/subject/stalinism/origins-future/ch4-1.htm

Branswell, H. (2021, September 20). Covid-19 overtakes 1918 Spanish flu as deadliest disease in American history. STAT. https://www.statnews.com/2021/09/20/covid-19-set-to-overtake-1918-spanish-flu-as-deadliest-disease-in-american-history/

Business, T.-B. (2022, January 26). Fitness Industry Analysis Post-coronavirus: 3 surprising takeaways. Two. Retrieved April 14, 2023, from https://twobrainbusiness.com/fitness-industry-analysis/

Centers for Disease Control and Prevention. (2018, March 21). History of 1918 flu pandemic. Centers for Disease Control and Prevention. Retrieved March 31, 2023, from https://www.cdc.gov/flu/pandemic-resources/1918-commemoration/1918-pandemic-history.htm

Centers for Disease Control and Prevention. (n.d.). Long Covid or post-covid conditions. Centers for Disease Control and Prevention. Retrieved April 14, 2023, from https://www.cdc.gov/coronavirus/2019-ncov/long-term-effects/index.html

Covid-19 and health disparities: Insights from key informant interviews. (n.d.). https://www.healthaffairs.org/content/forefront/covid-19-and-health-disparities-insights-key-informant-interviews

COVID-19 working paper: The impact of COVID-19 pandemic on food-away ... (n.d.). Retrieved April 15, 2023, from https://www.ers.usda.gov/webdocs/publications/103455/ap-100.pdf?v=350

COVID-19's impact, from the perspective of restaurant owners. QSR magazine. (n.d.). Retrieved April 14, 2023, from https://www.qsrmagazine.com/consumer-trends/COVID-19s-impact-perspective-restaurant-owners

Croft, J. (2022, September 15). 'end is in sight' for COVID-19 pandemic, who chief says. WebMD. Retrieved April 14, 2023, from https://www.webmd.com/covid/news/20220915/end-in-sight-for-COVID-19-says-who

Desmon, S. (2022, January 12). More than 8 in 10 unvaccinated Americans don't want a COVID vaccine - Johns Hopkins Center for Communication Programs. Johns Hopkins Center for Communication Programs - Inspiring Healthy Behavior Worldwide. Retrieved April 14, 2023, from https://ccp.jhu.edu/2021/10/25/vaccines-covid-behaviors-dashboard-united-states-data/

Don't like how you look on zoom? more people are asking plastic ... (n.d.). Retrieved March 31, 2023, from https://www.gmtoday.com/health/don-t-like-how-you-look-on-zoom-more-people-are-asking-plastic-surgeons-to/article_9162f4b2-ee34-11ea-8364-7f4306673587.html

Era Mae Ferron, P. D. (2021, December 13). The top 5 minimally-invasive cosmetic procedures. The Writing Era Inc. Retrieved March 31, 2023, from https://www.thewritingera.com/blog/the-top-5-minimally-invasive-cosmetic-procedures

Exercise & Fitness. Harvard Health. (n.d.). Retrieved April 10, 2023, from https://www.health.harvard.edu/topics/exercise-and-fitness

H1N1 influenza (nursing) - statpearls - NCBI bookshelf. (n.d.). Retrieved March 28, 2023, from https://www.ncbi.nlm.nih.gov/books/NBK568734/

Haas, S., Kuehl, E., Moran, J. R., & Venkataraman, K. (2020, May 19). How restaurants can thrive in the next normal. McKinsey & Company. Retrieved April 14, 2023, from https://www.mckinsey.com/industries/retail/our-insights/how-restaurants-can-thrive-in-the-next-normal

Hellmann, D. M., Dorrough, A. R., & Glöckner, A. (2021, September 21). Prosocial behavior during the COVID-19 pandemic in Germany. the role of responsibility and vulnerability. Heliyon. Retrieved April 14, 2023, from https://www.ncbi.nlm.nih.gov/pmc/articles/PMC8482435/

How covid-19 exposed music industry fault lines and what can be done. UNCTAD. (2021, September 28). https://unctad.org/news/how-covid-19-exposed-music-industry-fault-lines-and-what-can-be-done

Iacurci, G. (2023, February 1). 2022 was the 'real year of the great resignation,' says economist. CNBC. Retrieved April 18, 2023, from https://www.cnbc.com/2023/02/01/why-2022-was-the-real-year-of-the-great-resignation.html#:~:text=About%2050.5%20million%20people%20quit,known%20as%20the%20Great%20Resignation

Impact of COVID-19 pandemic on Public Health. Monroe College. (n.d.). Retrieved April 14, 2023, from https://www.monroecollege.edu/news/impact-COVID-19-pandemic-public-health#:~:text=The%20Role%20of%20Public%20Health%20During%20Pandemics&text=Since%20pandemics%20are%20often%20considered,risk%20of%20catching%20these%20diseases.

Jayson Lusk. (2016, June 27). The evolution of American Agriculture. Jayson Lusk. Retrieved March 31, 2023, from http://jaysonlusk.com/blog/2016/6/26/the-evolution-of-american-agriculture

Jones, J. M. (2023, May 31). U.S. church membership falls below majority for first time. Gallup.com. https://news.gallup.com/poll/341963/church-membership-falls-below-majority-first-time.aspx

Katella, K. (2023, February 3). Omicron, Delta, Alpha, and more: What to know about the coronavirus variants. Yale Medicine. Retrieved April 14, 2023, from https://www.yalemedicine.org/news/COVID-19-variants-of-concern-omicron

Kaur, H., Singh, T., Arya, Y. K., & Mittal, S. (2020, October 29). Physical Fitness and exercise during the COVID-19 pandemic: A qualitative enquiry. Frontiers in psychology. Retrieved April 14, 2023, from https://www.ncbi.nlm.nih.gov/pmc/articles/PMC7673425/

Knight, K. R., Duke, M. R., Carey, C. A., Pruss, G., Garcia, C. M., Lightfoot, M., Imbert, E., & Kushel, M. (2022, March). COVID-19 testing and vaccine acceptability among homeless-experienced adults: Qualitative data from two samples. Journal of general internal medicine. Retrieved April 10, 2023, from https://www.ncbi.nlm.nih.gov/pmc/articles/PMC8547296/

Liang, S. T., Liang, L. T., & Rosen, J. M. (2021, May). Covid-19: A comparison to the 1918 influenza and how we can defeat it. Postgraduate medical journal. https://www.ncbi.nlm.nih.gov/pmc/articles/PMC8108277/#:~:text=Victims%20of%20the%201918%20influenza,response%20resulting%20in%20organ%20failure.

Long covid: Long-term effects of COVID-19. Long COVID: Long-Term Effects of COVID-19 | Johns Hopkins Medicine. (2022, November 1). Retrieved April 14, 2023, from https://www.hopkinsmedicine.org/health/conditions-and-diseases/coronavirus/covid-long-haulers-long-term-effects-of-covid19

Mask resistance during a pandemic isn't new – in 1918 many Americans were 'slackers'. [Home]. (n.d.). Retrieved March 31, 2023, from https://www.michiganmedicine.org/health-lab/mask-resistance-during-pandemic-isnt-new-1918-many-americans-were-slackers

Matta, S., Arora, V. K., & Chopra, K. K. (2020, December). Lessons to be learnt from 100 year old 1918 influenza pandemic viz a viz 2019 Corona pandemic with an eye on NTEP. The Indian journal of tuberculosis. Retrieved

March 31, 2023, from https://www.ncbi.nlm.nih.gov/pmc/articles/PMC7543972/

M;, V. B. S. S. (n.d.). The impact of covid-19 on blood donations. PloS one. https://pubmed.ncbi.nlm.nih.gov/35324952/

McFarling, U. L. (2021, March 10). The uncounted: People who are homeless are invisible victims of COVID-19. STAT. Retrieved March 31, 2023, from https://www.statnews.com/2021/03/11/the-uncounted-people-who-are-homeless-are-invisible-victims-of-COVID-19/

Mks&h. (2021, January 21). How the pandemic has impacted the Death Care Industry: MKS&H. MKSH. Retrieved April 14, 2023, from https://mksh.com/how-the-pandemic-has-impacted-the-death-care-industry/

New York State Association of County Health Officials. (n.d.). New York State Local Health Department Preparedness For and ... : Journal of Public Health Management and Practice. LWW. Retrieved April 14, 2023, from https://journals.lww.com/jphmp/Fulltext/2021/05000/New_York_State_Local_Health_Department.6.aspx

Number 2 in 2022: The decline in church attendance in Covid America. Institute for Family Studies. (n.d.). Retrieved March 31, 2023, from https://ifstudies.org/blog/number-2-in-2022-the-decline-in-church-attendance-in-covid-america

Ojin homepage. OJIN. (n.d.). Retrieved April 14, 2023, from https://ojin.nursingworld.org/table-of-contents/volume-26-2021/number-2-may-2021/the-impact-of-COVID-19-on-the-nursing-workforce/

Performing artists in the age of COVID-19: A moment of urgent action ... (n.d.). Retrieved April 14, 2023, from https://pure.qub.ac.uk/files/204727792/Performing_Artists_in_the_age_of_COVID_19.pdf

Perri, M., Dosani, N., & Hwang, S. W. (2020, June 29). COVID-19 and people experiencing homelessness:

Challenges and mitigation strategies. CMAJ. Retrieved April 14, 2023, from https://www.cmaj.ca/content/192/26/E716

Raghuwanshi, B., Behera, P., Singh, P., Khan, R., Munshi, R., Patil, A., & Chouhan, S. (2022, June). Blood Supply Management amid COVID 19 pandemic: Challenges and strategies. Journal of family medicine and primary care. Retrieved April 14, 2023, from https://www.ncbi.nlm.nih.gov/pmc/articles/PMC9480642/

Report: Pandemic leads to long-term industry changes. NRA. (n.d.). Retrieved April 10, 2023, from https://restaurant.org/education-and-resources/resource-library/new-2022-state-of-the-restaurant-industry-report-projects-trends/

Research: U-M Center for the history of medicine. U. (n.d.). Retrieved March 31, 2023, from http://chm.med.umich.edu/research/

Rizzo, N. (1970, August 6). Covid's impact on the fitness industry [35+ stats and facts]. Athletic shoe reviews. Retrieved April 14, 2023, from https://runrepeat.com/pandemics-impact-fitness-industry

Rodriguez, N. M., Lahey, A. M., MacNeill, J. J., Martinez, R. G., Teo, N. E., & Ruiz, Y. (2021, September 10). Homelessness during COVID-19: Challenges, responses, and lessons learned from homeless service providers in Tippecanoe County, Indiana - BMC Public Health. BioMed Central. Retrieved April 14, 2023, from https://bmcpublichealth.biomedcentral.com/articles/10.1186/s12889-021-11687-8

Rodriguez, N. M., Lahey, A. M., MacNeill, J. J., Martinez, R. G., Teo, N. E., & Ruiz, Y. (2021, September 10). Homelessness during COVID-19: Challenges, responses, and lessons learned from homeless service providers in Tippecanoe County, Indiana. BMC public health. Retrieved

March 31, 2023, from https://www.ncbi.nlm.nih.gov/pmc/articles/PMC8432956/

RT;, V. D. S. P. S. (n.d.). COVID-19: Impact on the musician and returning to singing; a literature review. Journal of voice : official journal of the Voice Foundation. Retrieved April 14, 2023, from https://pubmed.ncbi.nlm.nih.gov/33583675/

Six causes of World War I. Norwich University Online. (n.d.). Retrieved March 31, 2023, from https://online.norwich.edu/academic-programs/resources/six-causes-of-world-war-i

Smith, G. A. (2021, December 14). About three-in-ten U.S. adults are now religiously unaffiliated. Pew Research Center's Religion & Public Life Project. https://www.pewresearch.org/religion/2021/12/14/about-three-in-ten-u-s-adults-are-now-religiously-unaffiliated/

Staff, C. I. (2021, August 10). 22 percent of gyms have closed, $29.2 billion revenue lost since COVID-19 hit. Club Industry. Retrieved April 10, 2023, from https://www.clubindustry.com/industry-news/22-percent-gyms-have-closed-292-billion-revenue-lost-COVID-19-hit

Taylor, N. K., Faulks, M., Brown-Johnson, C. G., Rosas, L. G., Shaw, J. G., Saliba-Gustafsson, E. A., & Asch, S. M. (2022, November 22). Pandemic through the lens of Black Barbershops: COVID-19's impact and barbers' potential role as public health extenders. Journal of immigrant and minority health. Retrieved March 31, 2023, from https://www.ncbi.nlm.nih.gov/pmc/articles/PMC9684895/

The COVID-19 effect: World's nurses facing mass trauma, an immediate danger to the profession and future of our Health Systems. ICN. (n.d.). Retrieved April 10, 2023, from https://www.icn.ch/news/COVID-19-effect-worlds-nurses-facing-mass-trauma-immediate-danger-profession-and-future-our

The effect of COVID-19 on homelessness in the US: United way. United Way NCA. (2023, March 22). Retrieved April 10, 2023, from https://unitedwaynca.org/blog/the-impact-of-the-COVID-19-pandemic-on-homelessness-in-the-united-states/

The importance of midwives in achieving Universal Health Coverage. Wilson Center. (n.d.). https://www.wilsoncenter.org/event/importance-midwives-achieving-universal-health-coverage#:~:text=However%2C%20the%20world%20will%20need,legislated%20and%20regulated%2C%20said%20Knutsson.

The precarious state of msmes: Understanding the impact of COVID-19 and opportunities to support their recovery. Center for Financial Inclusion. (n.d.). Retrieved March 31, 2023, from https://www.centerforfinancialinclusion.org/the-precarious-state-of-msmes-understanding-the-impact-of-COVID-19-and-opportunities-to-support-their-recovery

The territorial impact of COVID-19: Managing the crisis across levels ... (n.d.). Retrieved April 15, 2023, from https://www.oecd.org/coronavirus/policy-responses/the-territorial-impact-of-COVID-19-managing-the-crisis-across-levels-of-government-d3e314e1/

Vennare, A., LinkedIn, & Twitter. (2022, October 5). The numbers behind the Boutique Fitness Boom. Fitt Insider. Retrieved April 10, 2023, from https://insider.fitt.co/boutique-fitness-boom-numbers-statistics/

What are the implications of Long Covid for employment and health coverage? KFF. (2022, August 10). Retrieved April 14, 2023, from https://www.kff.org/policy-watch/what-are-the-implications-of-long-covid-for-employment-and-health-coverage/

World Health Organization. (n.d.). Coronavirus. World Health Organization. Retrieved March 31, 2023, from https://www.who.int/health-topics/coronavirus

World Health Organization. (n.d.). Who coronavirus (COVID-19) dashboard. World Health Organization. Retrieved April 10, 2023, from https://covid19.who.int/

Made in the USA
Columbia, SC
23 April 2024

8dc8b27e-719b-455e-bcee-150daf42a3d9R01